Oracle Application Express for Mobile Web Applications

Roel Hartman
Christian Rokitta
David Peake

Apress

President and Publisher: Paul Manning
Lead Editor: Jonathan Gennick
Technical Reviewer: Scott Wesley
Editorial Board: Steve Anglin, Ewan Buckingham, Gary Cornell, Louise Corrigan, Morgan Ertel, Jonathan Gennick, Jonathan Hassell, Robert Hutchinson, Michelle Lowman, James Markham, Matthew Moodie, Jeff Olson, Jeffrey Pepper, Douglas Pundick, Ben Renow-Clarke, Dominic Shakeshaft, Gwenan Spearing, Matt Wade, Tom Welsh
Coordinating Editors: Brigid Duffy and Kevin Shea
Copy Editor: Kimberly Burton-Weisman
Compositor: SPi Global
Indexer: SPi Global
Artist: SPi Global
Cover Designer: Anna Ishchenko

Distributed to the book trade worldwide by Springer Science+Business Media New York, 233 Spring Street, 6th Floor, New York, NY 10013. Phone 1-800-SPRINGER, fax (201) 348-4505, e-mail orders-ny@springer-sbm.com, or visit www.springeronline.com.

For information on translations, please e-mail rights@apress.com, or visit www.apress.com.

Apress and friends of ED books may be purchased in bulk for academic, corporate, or promotional use. eBook versions and licenses are also available for most titles. For more information, reference our Special Bulk Sales–eBook Licensing web page at www.apress.com/bulk-sales.

Any source code or other supplementary materials referenced by the author in this text is available to readers at www.apress.com. For detailed information about how to locate your book's source code, go to www.apress.com/source-code.

Contents at a Glance

Contents

Foreword

When I was first introduced to a predecessor of Oracle Application Express (APEX) in 2001, building web applications for mobile devices wasn't something that many businesses were actively pursuing or even considering. At best, there were some efforts under way to make information available on mobile devices through protocols like WAP (Wireless Access Protocol) using languages like WML (Wireless Markup Language). And for most companies, even the idea of running their business applications using a desktop web browser was still fairly new. Companies that did make the jump to browser-based applications had to contend with different browsers and a general lack of support for web standards. With Internet Explorer 6 introduced that same year, and peaking at 95% market share the following year, most business then simply started building for that platform.

Twelve years on, things have gotten much more complex, yet also much easier in many respects. On the desktop side, there are now several popular browsers that need to be supported by businesses, with Chrome, Internet Explorer, and Firefox each slightly above or below a third of the overall usage share. And on the mobile side, there is an ever-growing variety of supported browsers, screen sizes, and supported features to contend with. Thankfully, most users now have modern web browsers installed on their desktops as well as mobile devices, which handle web standards quite well, thus freeing up time for front-end developers to focus their attention on user experience and optimizing page layout for different screen sizes and overall performance. And thanks to popular JavaScript libraries like Modernizr and Selectivizr, and concepts like "progressive enhancement," even users of older browsers are no longer left out in the dark and will be able to use modern web apps, albeit with reduced visual fidelity in some cases.

From our early beginnings in the development of Oracle Application Express, one of our guiding principles has always been to shield our customers as best possible from the user interface–related challenges and considerations outlined above. Starting with the introduction of user interface themes in 2004, the ongoing adoption of ever-evolving web standards, the transition to a tableless web layout in APEX 4.0, and the introduction of HTML5 and CSS3 features in APEX 4.2, customers are able to create great-looking web applications in a very short time, without ever having to write a single line of HTML or JavaScript code. Thanks to a wide variety of user interface themes, customers can choose a look that meets their needs and they don't have to concern themselves with questions related to page layout, cross-browser support, or accessibility.

When the iPhone came out in 2007 and the first Android devices followed a year later, web sites and applications that had been primarily designed for desktop use suddenly became usable for an ever-larger user base on mobile devices. Of course, initially using the mostly desktop-centric web apps on these devices wasn't very practical. Business addressed these deficiencies in a number of ways. Some built dedicated mobile versions of their web sites, others released native, platform-specific apps for mobile devices, and increasingly, businesses are adopting responsive web design principles to have their web sites and content scale to the space that's available.

For us on the Oracle Application Express development team, it became clear that our customers would also want to run their APEX applications on a variety of devices in the future and no longer be tied to their desktops. Adding support for mobile development thus became imperative, and with Oracle Application Express 4.2, we introduced full support for mobile web application development alongside our existing desktop-focused features. The choice of jQuery Mobile as the underlying framework for our mobile features was driven by the same desire to shield our developers from having to deal with the complexities of UI development that has guided us along. Using the same easy wizards that our developers have been using for years, it is now possible to create fully-functional mobile web apps with APEX in a very short amount of time and instantly deploy them to users worldwide, as all that is required to run these apps on mobile devices is a web browser, the URL of the app, and user credentials.

As senior development manager on the Oracle Application Express development team, I feel very fortunate that we have a very active and engaged user community that guides our efforts, provides ongoing feedback on our newest features, and spreads the word about APEX at various industry events around the globe. Having had the pleasure of seeing the authors of this book deliver presentations on APEX in general and our new mobile features in particular, I know that you will learn a great deal about the development of mobile web applications with APEX. I trust you will enjoy reading the book and will find it a great help on your way to getting started with and expanding your knowledge of mobile development with Oracle Application Express.

—Marc Sewtz
Senior Software Development Manager
Oracle America, Inc.

About the Authors

Roel Hartman is an experienced Oracle software architect. About 20 years ago, he started using Oracle RDBMS 5, Oracle Forms 2.3, RPT/RPF, and Oracle*Case 4.5. For the past few years, he has focused on Oracle Application Express.

Roel has been a speaker at UK Oracle User Group (UKOUG), Oracle OpenWorld, COLLABORATE, Oracle Development Tools User Group (ODTUG) Kscope, and a number of local Oracle user groups. He is an active participant in the Oracle APEX forum and keeps an (APEX-related) blog at http://roelhartman.blogspot.com. In June 2009, he received an Oracle ACE award, and in August 2010, he was appointed an Oracle ACE Director. He is a coauthor of *Expert Oracle Application Express* (Apress, 2011).

Roel is a director at APEX Evangelists in the Netherlands.

Christian Rokitta is an independent developer who has used Oracle tools and technology since 1992. After using the Oracle Web Toolkit and mod_plsql for many years, he switched to APEX in 2006.

Christian, born and raised in Germany, began his career as a programmer in the research department of a pharmaceutical company in Frankfurt am Main, where he got in touch with the Oracle database and emerging web technologies. In 1996, he immigrated to the Netherlands and worked for Oracle NL as a custom development consultant for three years, using Oracle Designer 1.3 and Developer 2000. After leaving Oracle, he worked for a small Dutch consulting company for ten years, where he developed a web-based reporting and content management tool built with mod_plsql. Using APEX as a development framework was a logical step for him to take.

In 2010, Christian began working as a freelance consultant, focusing on Oracle Application Express. Next to developing applications, he specialized in user interface design for APEX, offering his service under the brand name Themes4APEX (http://themes4apex.com).

Christian has been a speaker at several ODTUG Kscope conferences, Dutch OGh APEX Days (now called APEX World), and the Deutsche Oracle Anwendergruppe (DOAG) and Oracle Benelux User Group (OBUG) conferences. When time allows, he tries to publish on his blog, Oracle & Apex Geekery (http://rokitta.blogspot.com).

David Peake started his IT career in the banking industry in Melbourne, Australia. That is where he was introduced to Oracle Release 5 and Oracle Forms 2.3. Stints with other Oracle tools include Oracle Case, Oracle Designer, Pro*Cobol, Oracle RPT, Oracle Graphics, and even Oracle Glue, which was used to tie Visual Basic to an Oracle Database.

On June 6, 1993, David joined Oracle Consulting Services in Melbourne, Australia (the only reason he remembers the date is because it is also his mother's birthday and the year his first child was born). After stints in Brisbane and Sydney, he then transferred to Oracle New Zealand for an interesting long-term consulting project using Oracle Designer to generate a Tuxedo middle-tier and an Oracle Forms front-end. David then transferred to Oracle US to take a senior role on a similar consulting project in the United States. As that project was winding down, he faced a dilemma: Oracle Consulting was concentrating very heavily on Java, and his Oracle Forms/Designer and PL/SQL skills wouldn't help manage a team of Java developers. At the same time, a project in Chicago was looking for PL/SQL skills for a new tool called Project Marvel. In 2002, David jumped at the opportunity to work on the main beta site for what was later released as Oracle HTML DB, and then changed again to Oracle Application Express (Oracle APEX). To date, his IT career has concentrated primarily on large custom-development projects.

In 2006, David changed roles completely to take on the role of product manager for Oracle Application Express. This role encompasses many facets, including maintaining the collateral on the Oracle Technology Network (http://otn.oracle.com/apex), working closely with both the APEX development team and the APEX community, and discussing Application Express with customers.

One of David's passions is speaking engagements. Luckily, his role allows him to talk regularly at conferences around the world. David covers most of the major events, including Oracle OpenWorld, OTN Developer Days, UKOUG, Rocky Mountain Oracle Users Group (RMOUG), COLLABORATE, OGh APEX World, and, of course, the biggest Application Express conference—ODTUG Kaleidoscope (now Kscope). Whether at keynotes with 2,000 attendees, cameras, and so forth, or at small intimate rooms of 50 people—give David a projection device (preferably one that can also run demos off his iPhone with dongle) and a microphone (nice to have, but he can project his voice as necessary), and he is in his element.

About the Technical Reviewer

Scott Wesley has been working with Oracle products since the turn of the century. With experience spanning retail, government, finance, and construction sectors, Scott has actively researched and applied cutting-edge technologies from the Oracle product range.

As part of the Sage Computing Services team, Scott is a systems consultant and trainer specializing in Oracle Application Express, PL/SQL, Oracle Forms/Reports, and SQL, and supplementing with requirements analysis and design.

Occasionally, you'll find him in the OTN forums and on AskTom and PL/SQL Challenge, or presenting at Australian Oracle User Group (AUSOUG) events. In recent years, he has been the program chair for the AUSOUG Perth conference.

Look for him blogging at http://grassroots-oracle.com.

Acknowledgments

After writing just one chapter in *Expert Oracle Application Express* (Apress, 2011), I promised myself never to write a book. It is just an enormous effort. And I kept my promise until Dan McGhan asked me whether I was interested in coauthoring a book on mobile development with Oracle Application Express. And just after a few minutes, I was convinced it was a very good idea. Although Dan couldn't contribute to the book as he had planned to, specials thanks goes to him. Without Dan, this project wouldn't even have started.

Also, a special thanks to the Oracle Application Express development team. At the time of writing, APEX mobile functionality was brand-new, so we had to ask them a lot of questions. We even had to file a bug or two. Patrick Wolf spent quite some time solving our puzzles.

A big thank-you to Scott Wesley for reviewing the book.

Thanks to the Apress team that reviewed the chapters and tried to keep us on schedule. A special thank-you to Kimberly, who had a really tough job correcting all my Dutch-English.

And last but certainly not least, I would like to thank Linda, my wife, and my two daughters, Anna and Nina, for their support during the weekends and evenings that I worked on this book.

—Roel Hartman

I would like to thank Roel for asking me to participate in this book project. It has been a great experience. I want to also thank my wife and kids, not so much for the time I needed to work on this book, but for all those years they had to live with my Oracle "deviation." A special thanks goes to my oldest son, Moritz, for letting me borrow his Android phone to test the examples and create the screenshots.

—Christian Rokitta

Much like Roel, I had always avoided authoring a book. But when someone as nice and giving as Roel asks you to contribute, how can you possibly say no? I have to give kudos to the Application Express development team—they are a highly motivated, selfless, exceedingly professional group and an absolute pleasure to work with. Without their enormous talent, we wouldn't have the wonderful tool we have today. Special thanks to Anthony Rayner for his invaluable input. Last but not least, my family knows I love them and now that the book is behind me, it is time to take them out to hit the slopes.

—David Peake

Introduction

Welcome to *Oracle Application Express for Mobile Web Applications*. Writing this book was hard work, but good fun and a thorough learning experience. I hope you will learn as much from reading it as I did writing it. I also hope that you will really enjoy making all the cool samples on your favorite mobile device. Although mobile devices are already used more than desktop devices, this difference will grow exponentially over the next few years. So go mobile now and be ready for the future!

Who This Book Is For

The readers of this book are assumed to have a reasonably sound knowledge of Oracle Application Express. Throughout the book, the examples are based upon this knowledge, so there won't be a detailed explanation on how to build pages or how to implement certain features that aren't specific to mobile web development. When you need more background information about using Oracle Application Express, there are a few books that you might consider reading: *Beginning Oracle Application Express 4* (Apress, 2013), for the developer who is just starting with APEX; *Pro Application Express 4* (Apress, 2008) and *Oracle Application Express 4 Recipes* (Apress, 2011), for the more experienced developer who wants to scale up his or her knowledge; and *Expert Oracle Application Express 4* (Apress, 2011), if you want to know all the details about Application Express. For those that are just learning Oracle Application Express, there is a Getting Started page on the Oracle Technology Network (OTN) at `www.oracle.com/technetwork/developer-tools/apex/application-express/apex-getting-started-1863613.html`. This page has links to a number of different resources based on learning style.

The examples in this book are based upon version 4.2.1 of Oracle Application Express. So if you have a newer release of Application Express, there may be some differences.

How This Book Is Structured

The idea of this book is to introduce you to the art of building mobile web applications at a good pace. So we'll start with the basics: List Views, Forms, Charts, and so forth. Then we'll move on with enhancing the look and feel of the application with special attention to mobile-specific Dynamic Actions. And finally we'll dive into deploying an APEX application natively on a mobile device. The following is a brief description of each chapter in this book.

Chapter 1, "Introduction to APEX for Mobile Web Development," introduces and explains the need for web development for mobile devices.

Chapter 2, "Creating Mobile Web Pages," explains the necessary building blocks of mobile web pages.

Chapter 3, "Presenting Data Through List Views," walks you through the process of creating List Views for your data.

Chapter 4, "Accepting Input via Forms," covers building Forms for mobile web pages, including the use of grids and HTML4 input types.

Chapter 5, "Displaying Calendars and Charts," details the use of presenting data in the other formats APEX offers.

Chapter 6, "Implementing a Navigation Standard," covers the use of buttons, links, and other ways that users can find their way in an application.

Chapter 7, "Theming your Mobile Application," takes you a little outside of APEX and explains how to use ThemeRoller to give your application the custom look and feel you need.

Chapter 8, "Working with Dynamic Actions," details all the specific differences between Dynamic Actions for desktop and for mobile devices.

Chapter 9, "Deploying Applications Natively," offers a step-by-step description on how to use PhoneGap to leverage your APEX application by using native device capabilities like the camera.

Chapter 10, "Securing Your Mobile Applications," addresses mobile-specific security risks and describes ways to mitigate these risks.

Downloading the Code

The code for the examples shown in this book is available on the Apress web site (`www.apress.com`). A link is on the book's information page under the Source Code/Downloads tab. This tab is located underneath the Related Titles section of the page.

Contacting the Authors

Should you have any questions or comments—or even if you spot a mistake you think we should know about—you can contact the authors at `roel@apex-evangelists.com`.

CHAPTER 1

■ ■ ■

Introduction to APEX for Mobile Web Development

Why is there so much hype around building mobile applications? The short answer is that mobile applications are the next frontier. Business professionals face increasing time constraints and the need to increase productivity, but there is only ever going to be 24 hours in a day. The answer is the ability to work from almost anywhere at any time. The majority of professionals carry a smartphone that is connected to a strong, reliable network provider. Mobile applications can be instrumental in allowing the busy user community to be more productive.

What sort of mobile applications are required? The traditional need for applications that support employees in the field, including emergency workers and service and sales people, will continue to expand. It is no longer good enough to have a mobile application that simply provides address and other contact information; nowadays, field personnel want to be equipped with service or sales history, background information, and so on. What about those who manage these field staff? Recently, the district supervisors of an ambulance service were given mobile applications that allow them to see in real time where their personnel are located, where they are headed, their current status, and the number of patients who are waiting for service. These features allow the supervisors to leave their desks but still stay fully informed and be able to make decisions as required.

There is also a large range of new mobile applications being requested by the business community for less traditional use cases. Employees who generally sit at a desk in a corporate office are looking for applications that allow them to do administrative and human resources tasks from any location. By using mobile applications, consultants on customer sites could benefit from the ability to remotely enter their time and expenses. Managers should be able to approve vacation requests and check on vital performance indicators while sitting at the airport waiting for a flight, and without needing to open a laptop and find Internet service. What about the database administrators who are on call 24/7? Wouldn't mobile applications that allow them to review the health of a database and perform specific tasks while riding on the train be good for business?

Another class of mobile applications is those designed for customers. Banks, news services, fast-food companies, service providers, television companies, and more are all coming out with mobile solutions. Think about the tasks that you used to perform on your computer that you now perform on your smartphone. Providing that an application is useful and easy enough to use, it helps improve customer satisfaction. Obviously, customer-focused applications are markedly different from those built only for internal business use. Not only is it imperative that these applications are secure and only allow properly authenticated customers access to their data (but no one else's), it is also important that these applications are of the highest quality because they provide customers an entrance point to the business.

The Application Express development team sends a number of team members to Oracle OpenWorld, where each member handles many duties, including overseeing sessions, hands-on labs, demo grounds, and customer meetings. In past years, multiple copies of a spreadsheet were handed out to the team so that each member knew his or her responsibilities. In 2011, the spreadsheet was replaced with a mobile application, and each team member was simply given the URL for the application. The application itself was relatively simple and took less than two hours to build. The majority of time was spent entering and tweaking the data. Not only did this eliminate the need for multiple spreadsheets, last-minute changes could also easily be incorporated. Given the very low cost of development, the return on investment was very quick.

Look at your current business processes. You are sure to find many use cases where mobile applications can improve productivity or simply increase your users' satisfaction. Making these tasks easy to use and more accessible should meet both objectives.

Designing Mobile Applications

As the underlying technology for building applications changes, so too does the way developers need to design the applications. The first mainstream business applications were developed for the old green-screen mainframe applications and were character based. Users navigated around using the Tab key and various key combinations. Many airline reservation systems still use such systems. If you watch a person at the check-in desk or at the departure gate, you will notice that they never use a mouse but press a variety of different key combinations to quickly navigate around the system. Such applications are difficult to learn and nonintuitive, but are exceedingly efficient for a skilled operator.

Following mainframe applications, the next major advance was client-server and desktop applications. As personal computer usage boomed and nearly everyone had one on their desks, business applications were designed to run under Microsoft Windows. The design philosophy with these applications was to fit everything required onto a single screen. A specific screen size was normally specified in the application design. Developers were not allowed to build a screen that didn't fit the available real estate. As a result, developers generally designed input forms with multiple items on a single line and left very little white space. Navigation and specific operations primarily used function keys (F1–F12), tabs, and buttons, often with keyboard shortcuts. Another common attribute of such applications, especially when using Oracle Forms, is the multi-use screen. You navigate to a screen, press a function key to enter query criteria, press another function key to execute the query, and then scroll up and down through the records. Once you find the required record, you update it on the same screen before pressing another function key to save the changes. Client-server applications generally require end-user training and take time to master.

The Internet changed application design once again. Instead of just back-office applications, the Internet ushered in the explosion of self-service applications. Arguably, the most popular applications on the Internet are retail applications such as Amazon and other shopping sites that are aimed at customers instead of internal users. The most important design goal of such applications is that they are exceedingly easy to use and look good to customers. The same design philosophy has also been adopted with web-based business applications. It is now common to use vertical scrolling and layout input forms in a visually pleasing manner, rather than cramming as much as possible into a single screen. Given that web-based applications are run on a variety of devices, not just Microsoft Windows–based PCs, navigation and operability no longer rely on function keys or keyboard shortcuts, but rather simplified tabs, buttons, and links. The goal of business web-based applications is to concentrate on the business processes, rather than training users how to use the application.

Mobile applications present new challenges with respect to application design. Developers must take into account the very small screen compared to a desktop monitor, and instead of a mouse, users use their fingers. The way in which users navigate on mobile applications is significantly different from desktop applications. Mobile application navigational aids such as tabs are generally replaced by a list on the home page, as seen in the stark differences between Figure 1-1 and Figure 1-2.

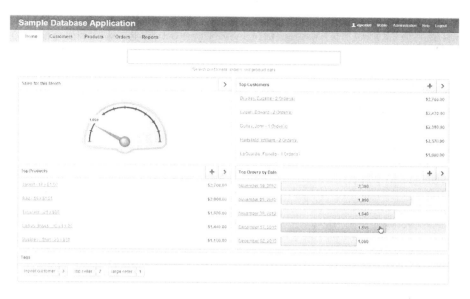

Figure 1-1. *Desktop home page*

Figure 1-2. *Mobile home page*

Given the limited real estate on the screen, constructs such as breadcrumbs are removed, and instead of having a Cancel button, users utilize the built-in Back key. It is important to include a Home button or icon on every page to allow users to readily get back to the first page of the application. There are also several events that are specific to mobile devices—such as swipe, tap, and orientation change—that can be utilized to improve the user experience.

Looking at the Sample Database Application that is included with Oracle Application Express (APEX) 4.2, you first notice that the one application includes both desktop and mobile user interfaces. Each page can only be associated with one user interface. If a user logs into the application with a mobile device, the mobile pages will be rendered; if a desktop is used, the desktop user interface is shown. From either user interface, controls are provided to switch to the other user interface. Both provide the same functionality but the user experience is significantly different with either user interface.

Common constructs in desktop web-based applications, such as a report linking to a form, are generally replaced by a list linking to a form in mobile applications. One of the reasons lists are so prevalent in mobile applications is that they are easy for users to select using touch, as opposed to a report where selecting the correct record can be difficult. Lists generally only display a few of the most important data elements and a user can press anywhere on a list entry to drill-down to the next level of detail. Simple reports can be included in a mobile application, but care must be taken to ensure the report displays well on mobile devices in both portrait and landscape orientations.

With respect to Application Express, other constructs such as interactive reports, tabular forms, and master-detail pages are not supported on mobile pages. If you need to present a parent-child relationship, one alternative is to use a form for the parent with a list for the child records. Instead of maintaining the children records in a table on the same page as the parent, you need to define an additional page. One key advantage of this design is that you are only updating one child record at a time, so it is easier to implement business rules. Again, using the Sample Database Application, the Orders pages show an example of this page design. The desktop user interface uses a master-detail form (see Figure 1-3) with validations to ensure that the quantity is between 1 and 10, and another validation to check that the product is only on each order once. The mobile user interface (see Figure 1-4) uses a separate page to maintain the order items, and instead of validations, there is a select list showing 1 to 10 for quantity, so there is no need for a validation. Similarly, the select list for product limits values returned to only those values that are not already on the order and the existing record, so a user can never select a duplicate.

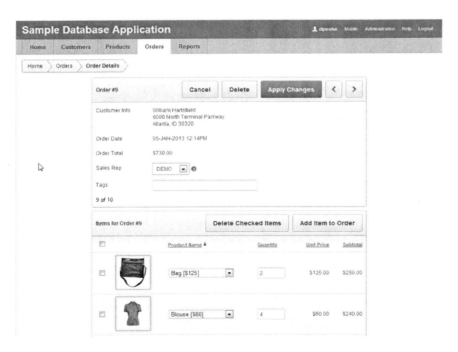

Figure 1-3. *Desktop master-detail page*

Figure 1-4. *Mobile master-list page (left) and detail page (right)*

The mobile theme and templates in Oracle Application Express are built using jQuery Mobile. This allows the Application Express engine to be able to invoke the majority of events on a mobile device, such as tap, swipe, and so on. When on a mobile page, you will see a number of these mobile-specific events available under Dynamic Action events. It has also allowed the inclusion of HTML5 attributes such as e-mail, URL, and phone number input selections. If you run the Sample Database Application on a modern mobile device that supports full HTML5 and then edit a customer, you should see that the input keyboard changes when you edit the e-mail, phone numbers, and URL items. Within the text item definition is a new attribute—subtype—that allows you to specify the onscreen keyboard. These features will allow you to develop a mobile application with rich user interactivity.

Web-Based vs. Native Mobile Applications

The two main types of mobile applications are web-based and on-device or native applications. Native mobile applications are those that are built for a specific mobile operating system, such as iOS, Android, Windows Mobile, or BlackBerry. Native mobile applications are written in the target operating system's application development language: Objective-C for iOS, Java for Android, and so forth. Mobile web-based applications, on the other hand, are written as web applications and are accessed using the mobile device's browser.

There are currently many advantages to creating native mobile applications. Native mobile applications can better access the various features of the mobile devices on which they run, including contacts, cameras, and more. Additionally, these applications are known to perform better than their web-based counterparts do. Applications can be built to run locally and incorporate a local data store, such as SQL Lite, so that they can continue to work when disconnected from the Internet. In order for native applications to integrate with the Oracle database, it is generally required to utilize Web Services. Native applications are downloaded onto the device and stored locally.

Mobile web-based applications have their own advantages. One of the biggest advantages is that a single codebase can generally be accessed from any mobile device, regardless of the mobile operating system. To access the application, you simply enter the relevant Uniform Resource Locator (URL) into the mobile browser. Another major advantage is that the code itself is not stored on the device but on the server delivering the application. Therefore, performing application updates is very simple and can be delivered to everyone simultaneously, simply by updating the server hosting the application. This is in stark contrast to native applications where the user is responsible for manually downloading the latest version of an application. Given that the developer can't guarantee that every user is running the latest version—because it is up to users to download the upgrade once they are aware of it—the developer of a native application may have to incorporate additional code to handle version discrepancies or raise an error when a user tries to use an older version of the application.

One of the largest disadvantages of mobile web-based applications is that they rely on an Internet connection in order to function. At the same time, emerging technologies such as HTML5's application cache and local storage are rapidly bridging the gap between what's possible between native and web-based mobile applications. To allow mobile web-based applications to interact with on-device components such as the camera or contact list, there are various programs, such as PhoneGap (covered in Chapter 9), which can be utilized to wrap the application. Such solutions still require the Internet access needed by the underlying web-based application.

When you review the business applications on your phone, they are predominantly native applications. There will probably be some web-based mobile applications as well. When you open your web browser on your mobile device, chances are it presents a site from your service provider, the phone maker, or most likely a search engine like Google. Remember that those same native applications are most likely "customer" applications, such as those provided by your bank to allow to you to do online banking. Here again, programs such as Phone Gap can be utilized to deliver a native application, but underneath, it is still a web-based application.

Oracle Application Express is designed to declaratively build web-based applications. Application Express 4.2 was specifically designed to allow developers to rapidly build web-based applications that can be run on the desktop, a mobile device, or both. The mobile user interface is a collection of templates that are based on the jQuery Mobile framework. Utilizing this framework enables mobile web-based applications to run seamlessly on any mobile device, old or new. The jQuery Mobile framework is designed to correct rendering anomalies or differences between operating systems, and for older devices that don't have full HTML5 capabilities to render functional controls. From an Application Express developer's perspective, you use the same application builder, the same SQL and PL/SQL, and the same method of building a mobile application that you are used to using when building a desktop application.

When deciding whether to build a native or web-based mobile application, it is important to understand the requirements of the application. If you determine that you have to build native mobile applications, you must realize that your development team will need to become proficient in multiple languages and that you will have several different code bases. This makes the development effort longer and more costly and the resulting applications harder to maintain. On the other hand, building web-based mobile applications with Oracle Application Express only requires SQL and PL/SQL skills and you can utilize a single code base.

Responsive Design

One of the recent user interface design principles being adopted is responsive design. *Responsive design* refers to a set of techniques that allow developers to create content that can dynamically adapt to fit various devices, from desktops to cell phones. On larger screens, the user gets the full experience. On smartphones and tablets, the layout adopts itself to the size of the device's screen. This is done by having certain elements shift position, resize, or become hidden entirely. This ability has been made possible by new capabilities and techniques in web design, such as media queries, fluid grids, and flexible images. The goal is to make all essential content available in a user-friendly and visually pleasing way on any device.

The concept of creating a web application using responsive design techniques is quite appealing because it allows developers to maintain a single set of application and business logic that is accessed from browsers that have anywhere from a few hundred pixels to several thousand. In order for this to work, the content for any given page must be able to adapt to the device on which it is being displayed. There are, however, some downsides to responsive web design. The upfront cost of designing a truly responsive page are much higher and require a much higher level of understanding grid layout, HTML, and CSS.

Oracle Application Express 4.2 introduces a responsive user interface theme: Theme 25. This theme provides the building blocks and templates for achieving a responsive layout. However, it is up to the developer to use those templates and to arrange the page content in such a way that the result is truly responsive. It is not just a matter of picking one set of templates vs. another set of templates.

Also note that converting an existing application to Theme 25 requires you to review the pages of the application to ensure that the appropriate template and layout are defined.

For examples of responsive applications, review the Sample Database Application that ships with Application Express 4.2 or the Oracle Cloud site (http://cloud.oracle.com). First, review the applications on your desktop in full-screen mode. Then, resize your browser, making it progressively narrower. You will notice as you resize that the regions automatically resize to fit the available screen width. At a certain threshold, the regions will realign from being next to each other (horizontal) to stacked vertically (see Figure 1-5). Similarly, if you are on a data entry form, such as Customers, the items will resize and then the labels will move from left of the items to above the items, and all the items will be the same width, as they are when you build mobile application pages.

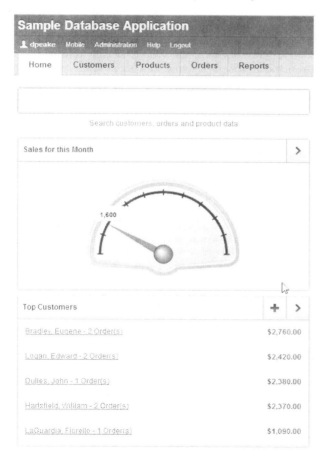

Figure 1-5. *A responsive application with stacked regions*

Choosing Responsive Design, Desktop, or Mobile

You can run almost any Application Express application on any device, providing it has a browser and an Internet connection. Desktop applications can be run on tablets and mobile devices, and mobile applications can be run on personal computers. That said, the user experience of running a desktop application on a mobile device, or a mobile application on a personal computer, is not ideal and in the former case, it can be difficult and very frustrating. Given the small screen size on mobile devices, you may have to scroll around the screen excessively, some components may not render or operate correctly, and you will often need to zoom-in to be able to use controls such as tabs, buttons, and links. This is why the extra investment required to develop a desktop application using responsive design can be beneficial. It provides a good user experience on desktops and a relatively good experience on tablets and mobile devices. One limitation is that responsive design cannot take advantage of mobile-specific events such as touch and orientation changes.

Mobile design focuses on creating content that is specifically targeted to mobile devices. It is typically done in addition to or instead of a desktop application. To facilitate this, mobile applications need to be built with extremely minimal, semantic HTML that is optimized for mobile connections. Desktop applications, on the other hand, are generally much heavier, with substantially more content on a page, including larger headers, tabs, breadcrumbs, rich page content, and so forth. However, page weight is not a major concern for a computer with a strong Internet connection. When you run a responsive design application on a mobile device, it is heavier than a purpose-built mobile application, so it will take noticeably longer to load and process pages if the device does not have a strong connection.

The decision to create a single responsive application or a targeted mobile application is one that must be made carefully. Consider when and where the end users will be using the application and the content that is being presented. The more time spent using the application on a mobile device, the more the user will benefit from an application targeted to that device. Informational sites such as marketing pages, catalogs, and libraries are well-suited to responsive design. Processing or productivity applications that require data entry and quick response times would be better suited to being built specifically for mobile devices, where you can benefit from utilizing the device's native controls and better performance.

If you already have a desktop application and you have decided to build a complimentary mobile solution or you have decided to build both a desktop application and a mobile application from scratch, you will need to decide whether you have them defined in a single application or in two distinct applications. The advantage of having two distinct applications is that you can manage them independently and release them separately. The advantage of having both user interfaces in a single application is that you can have a single URL and utilize the device autodetection to render the correct user interface, depending on the device used to log into the application. To provide this capability, it is important to define login pages, home pages, and global pages (formerly page 0) for each user interface. If you access the single application from a desktop, it will display the desktop login page, and then once logged in, it will show the desktop home page. Whereas if you access the same application from a mobile device, it will display the mobile home page once logged in.

Now that you understand the importance of designing for mobile devices, please continue through the book to learn how to build these applications with Oracle Application Express.

Wrap Up

Armed with knowing why mobile applications are becoming so popular, how to design them, the differences between native and web-based applications, and how to choose between building a mobile application or an application using responsive design, you should now get cracking on the next chapter and start developing your own mobile solutions. You should remember that building web-based applications with Oracle Application Express isn't always the best solution. There are a few use cases where pragmatic analysis of the various options may prove another tool to be better suited. In the time it takes others to argue the virtues of their preferred mobile application development tool, however, using Application Express, you can be half way through the development of your mobile solution.

CHAPTER 2

■ ■ ■

Creating Mobile Pages

APEX pages, aimed at mobile devices, are built using the jQuery Mobile framework. Therefore, to understand and influence the way APEX generates these pages, it is necessary to understand how the jQuery Mobile framework is built up and how the different parts of this framework are used in your APEX development environment.

In this chapter, you will learn the elements that are used to create a jQuery Mobile page and the different ways to show a page. This will be the start of our first mobile application!

How jQuery Mobile Pages Are Constructed

Basically, a jQuery Mobile page is very similar to any other HTML page. When you look at the HTML source, it contains an HTML header and an HTML body. The header references a specific jQuery Mobile CSS file and two jQuery files: a core jQuery file and a jQuery Mobile file. As jQuery Mobile is built upon a specific version of the jQuery core, you have to be sure to use a version of the jQuery core that is certified to work with your version of jQuery Mobile. So for instance, jQuery Mobile 1.1.1 requires either jQuery 1.6.4 or 1.7.1 and jQuery Mobile 1.2.0 requires jQuery version 1.7 or higher.

You can host the referenced files on your own domain, but when you use just the standard files, you could also let your users hammer other companies' huge hardware by using a content delivery network (CDN). The jQuery files, amongst others, are hosted by Google, Microsoft, and jQuery itself. As we are developing for mobile devices, which are usually not used exclusively within the network of your company, that should be no problem. To be clear, as CDNs only host standard files, you may need to host additional or modified files from your own domain.

■ **Tip**　Reference standard files from a CDN to reduce load on your own servers. There is even a setting within APEX to do that declaratively: navigate to Application Properties and then to User Interface, and you'll see the options shown in Figure 2-1.

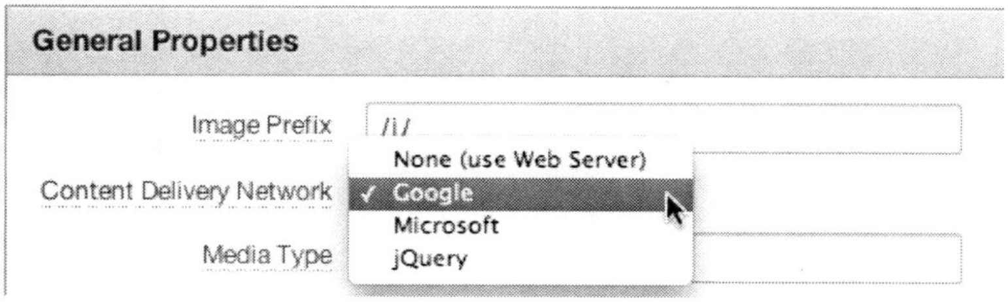

Figure 2-1. Choosing your content delivery network

The HTML body of a jQuery Mobile page, the part that makes the actual content, contains your actual page definition. And that page definition can be broken up into three parts: header, content, and footer.

The main difference in this HTML structure is the use of an additional "data-role" attribute within the already familiar HTML tags. The jQuery Mobile and CSS do the magic of transforming your HTML document to a good-looking application on a mobile device. In jQuery terminology, that is called *enhancing* or even *autoenhancing*.

So the most basic jQuery Mobile page would consist of only the HTML in Listing 2-1.

Listing 2-1. Your First Mobile Page

```html
<!DOCTYPE html>
<html>
 <head>
  <link rel="stylesheet" href="http://code.jquery.com/mobile/1.1.1/jquery.mobile-1.1.1.min.css" />
  <script src="http://code.jquery.com/jquery-1.7.1.min.js"></script>
  <script src="http://code.jquery.com/mobile/1.1.1/jquery.mobile-1.1.1.min.js"></script>
 </head>
 <body>
  <div data-role="page">
   <div data-role="header">The header on the top</div>
   <div data-role="content">The content in the middle</div>
   <div data-role="footer">The footer at the bottom</div>
  </div>
 </body>
</html>
```

Copy this HTML code in text editor, save it as a file with an .html extension. Then open the file in a browser on your mobile device, mobile simulator, or regular browser. You'll see a page like the one in Figure 2-2. Of course, for accessing the file from your mobile device, you have to put it in on a web server that is accessible by your device.

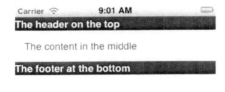

Figure 2-2. *Running a basic jQuery Mobile page*

Before we dig any deeper into the different page types that jQuery Mobile offers, we will create our first mobile application!

Your First Mobile APEX Application

Before you can start creating your application, you need to have access to a workspace in an APEX 4.2 (or higher) environment. The easiest way to get that access is to sign up for a workspace at http://apex.oracle.com, but of course you can host your own. In this book, we'll use a standard workspace at http://apex.oracle.com, with the Sample Database Application installed.

Start creating an application using the Application Creation wizard. In the second page of the wizard, you'll see the first reference to "Mobile" in the User Interface drop-down list (see Figure 2-3). Select the jQuery Mobile Smartphone interface and continue, accepting all default settings until you arrive at the User Interface Theme page of the wizard.

Figure 2-3. *Select the mobile user interface*

On the next-to-last page of the wizard, you can select a theme for your mobile application (see Figure 2-4). At the start of APEX 4.2, there is only one theme to choose from, but there might be more in the future. And you can add your own custom themes as well.

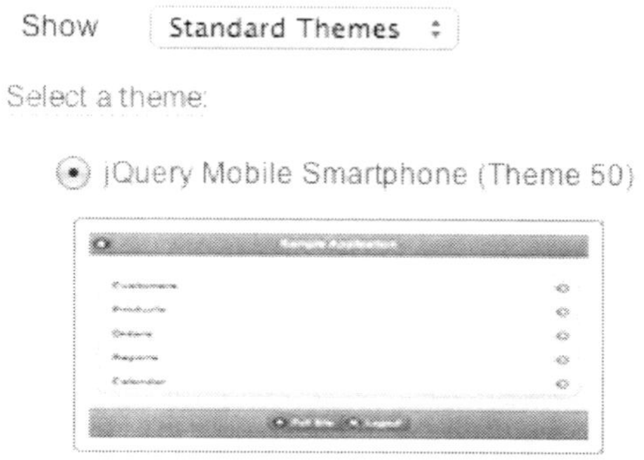

Figure 2-4. *Select a theme for your mobile application*

Now just finish the wizard and create your application. You'll end up with a mobile application with three pages, like the one shown in Figure 2-5.

Page▲	Name	Updated	Updated By	Page Type	User Interface	Group	Lock	Run
0	Global Page - jQuery Mobile Smartphone	23 minutes ago	-	Global Page	jQuery Mobile Smartphone	Unassigned	🔓	▶
1	Home	23 minutes ago	-	Home	jQuery Mobile Smartphone	Unassigned	🔓	▶
101	Login	23 minutes ago	-	Login	jQuery Mobile Smartphone	Unassigned	🔓	▶

1 - 3

Figure 2-5. Your first three-page mobile application

Now it is time to run this mobile application! Just open your application's home page URL in your mobile device browser, and you'll see the login screen that was just created for you (see Figure 2-6).

Figure 2-6. The login page of your mobile application

Notice the positioning of the prompts: on a mobile device with a smaller screen estate, the prompts are positioned above the fields. When you rotate the device, the prompts are automatically positioned before the fields (see Figure 2-7). Also, when you open the page on a mobile device with larger screen estate, like an iPad, the fields are positioned before the fields. All this, including the detection of the rotation, is done for you by jQuery Mobile!

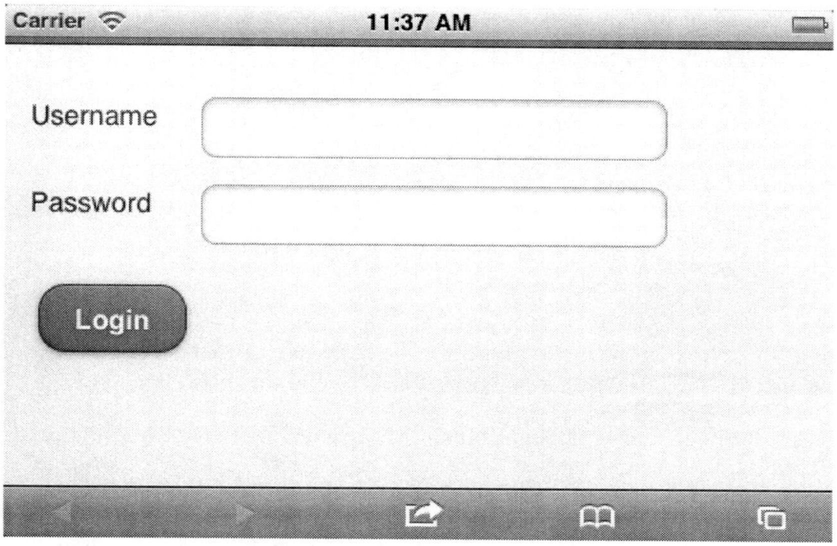

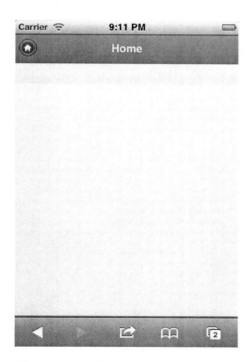

Figure 2-7. *The login page on a horizontal rotated device*

After logging in, you'll see an empty home page, as shown in Figure 2-8. The home page includes a nice Home icon that navigates to page 1, which is the Home screen.

Figure 2-8. *The home page of your mobile application*

When you inspect the definition of the home page in the APEX development environment, you won't find a reference to that Home icon anywhere. That's because the header (and footer) are defined on page 0, named Global Page - jQuery Mobile Smartphone. Remember the HTML layout of a jQuery Mobile page contained the following:

```
<body>
  <div data-role="page">
    <div data-role="header">The header on the top</div>
    <div data-role="content">The content in the middle</div>
    <div data-role="footer">The footer at the bottom</div>
  </div>
</body>
```

The "page" is defined in the page template; the "header" and "footer" are defined on the Global Page, as regions—with their own templates—on the top and the bottom positions on the page. The region(s) you define on a page make up the "content" of the HTML.

While you are on page 0, take a look at the definition of the Home button. The magic of that button is all defined by the button attributes: `data-icon="home"`, `data-iconpos="notext"`, and `data-direction="reverse"`. The image is defined by the `data-icon` attribute. Try changing that to `data-icon="grid"` and see what happens: the home icon is replaced by a grid icon. The names you can use for the icons and how they look are determined by the icon set and the theme you are using. You can also use your own icon set. More about that in Chapter 8. The icon position (`data-iconpos`) can be left (the default), right, top, or bottom. Just play around with it and see what happens. The attribute `data-direction="reverse"` will result in using the reverse version of the transition that was used to show the page. Transitions will be covered later in this chapter.

Now it is time to add more content to your application. Just for demo purposes, we create a page to select and edit records from the EMP table. So create a new page, pick a Form on the next page of the wizard, and then you'll see a page like Figure 2-9. There are a few differences compared to creating a form for a desktop application. At first, you see there is no Master-Detail or Tabular Form option, as these make no sense in the mobile world. And there is a new option: Form on a Table with List View. Let's pick that one.

Figure 2-9. *Create a new Form page: Form on a Table with List View*

Set the name of the List View page and region to "Employees" and look at the Region template options. There are quite a few—and all different from a regular desktop theme. For now, go for the "plain" one. On the Datasource page of the wizard, pick your EMP table, and on the third page of the wizard, specify the column you want to see in the list: ENAME. Just continue through the wizard and select all columns to be included in the Form page. Now run the page. You see pages like the ones shown in Figures 2-10 and 2-11. Notice the List View comes with an additional Search feature! Just play around with it and edit some data. And see what happens when you rotate your device. Now you can enhance the Form page by changing the labels, adding format masks, and so forth, as you would do in a regular desktop application.

Figure 2-10. *Employees List View*   **Figure 2-11.** *Employees Form View*

To navigate from the Home screen to the List View, you need to add an HTML region to page 1, with a Page Item button that redirects to page 2. Thanks to jQuery Mobile, all links in your application are loaded using Ajax. Therefore, the href attribute of the link is used. And you get the loading spinner for free. But the button you just created on page 1, doesn't contain an href attribute—it does a redirect! Luckily, the APEX development team changed the generated code to cover that. Prior to APEX 4.2, a button element like you just created contained an href attribute like

```
href="javascript:redirect('f?p=100:2');"
```

In the new version, that has been changed to

```
href="javascript:apex.navigation.redirect('f?p=100:2');"
```

15

This function takes care of the proper way of navigating with respect to the kind of browser and application you are running. So for a mobile page, it calls the jQuery Mobile method: `$.mobile.changePage(url)`. This is one of the many methods jQuery Mobile has to offer. In order to show how this works, change the action of the button you just created on page 1 from Redirect to Page in This Application to Defined by Dynamic Action. Then create a Dynamic Action, defined as "on click of this button, execute a piece of JavaScript." And here is the JavaScript to execute:

```
apex.jQuery.mobile.changePage('f?p=&APP_ID.:2:&SESSION.');.
```

See Figures 2-12 and 2-13 for the details. And you'll see exactly the same behavior as before, but now you know what happens behind the scenes!

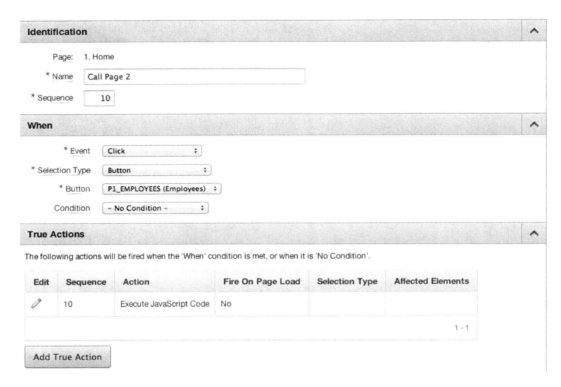

Figure 2-12. Dynamic Action definition for navigation button

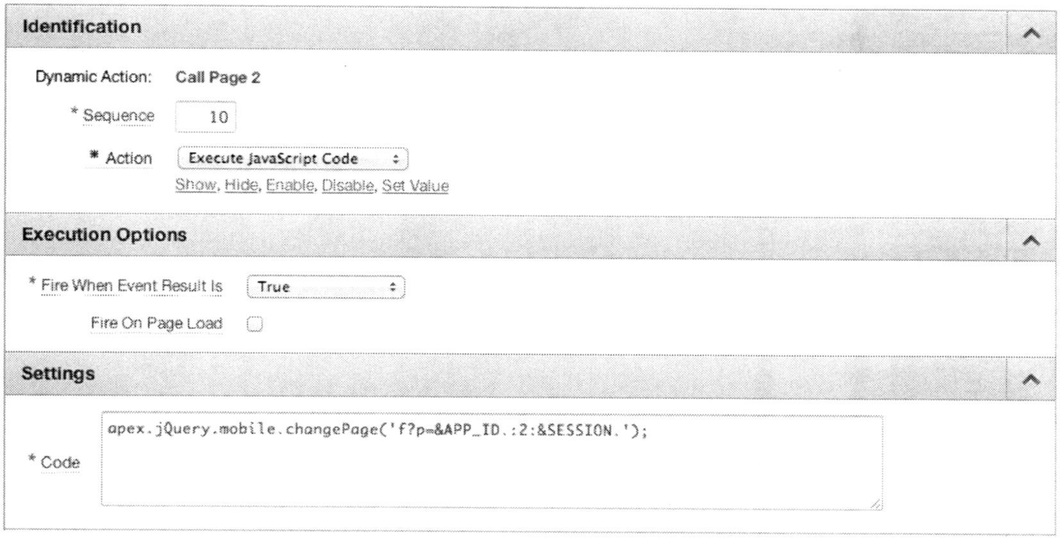

Figure 2-13. *Definition for navigation button*

Another way of linking pages is adding an anchor tag somewhere on the page. So go to the region on page 1 and set the Region Source to:

```
<a href="f?p=&APP_ID.:2:&SESSION.">Link to Employees</a>
```

You see a regular link when you run that page, but the mobile-style navigation is already there. When you add `data-role="button"` as an attribute, you'll end up with a handmade button that's very similar to the one you created earlier. So, as you just experienced, jQuery Mobile enhances all links with this `data-role="button"` attribute—all regular button type input fields and regular button elements are enhanced as well—so they all look and act as native as possible.

Dialogs

The pages you've created until now are regular pages. But there is another type of page: a modal dialog. You can turn any page into a dialog by adding a `data-rel="dialog"` to the anchor that links to that page. The called page is automatically enhanced with rounded corners, extra margins, and a dark background, so it looks like the dialog is on top of another page.

As an example, change the anchor you created in the Region Source on page 1 to:

```
<a href="f?p=&APP_ID.:2:&SESSION." data-role="button" data-rel="dialog">Link to Employees</a>
```

As a result, you see the Employee list appearing as a dialog (see Figure 2-14). Notice the difference from Figure 2-10: no header, no footer, and a small change in layout. In order to clearly distinguish a dialog from a regular page, you could apply another template to the page. To get a clearer distinction, change the default Page template setting in page 2 from "Use Theme Default" to "Popup", as shown in Figure 2-15.

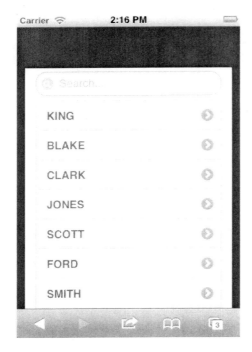

Figure 2-14. *Employee List View as a dialog using a Page template*

Figure 2-15. *Employee List View as a dialog using a Popup template*

In APEX 4.2, it isn't possible to call a dialog page declaratively. So adding `data-role="dialog"` to the attributes of a button that does a redirect—like the first one you created on page 1—doesn't do anything, as these settings aren't propagated to the call of `apex.navigation.redirect('f?p=100:2');`. But, as in many cases, Dynamic Actions come to the rescue! With adding a role option to our previously created Dynamic Action JavaScript call, you can make it work. So change the line of code to

```
apex.jQuery.mobile.changePage('f?p=&APP_ID.:2:&SESSION.',{role:"dialog"});,
```

Then examine the result!

As this popup for a list of employees isn't very functional in this case, you should change page 2's Page template setting back to the default value. But that now we know how to do it, let's create a better example: a tiny dialog for quickly adding an employee directly from the list.

Start with creating the Form:

1. Run the Create Page wizard and create a new page (4) with a Form on a Table EMP that just shows the ENAME and only the Create and Cancel buttons. Let the Form branch back to page 2 on Cancel and Submit.

2. Change the Page template to Popup.

3. Change both Button templates to 100% Button.

Now that we've got the Form, we need to add an icon on top of the List View to navigate to the Form:

1. Create a button with a name like **Quick Create EMP** on page 0 (because that is the location of the definition of the page header), as shown in Figure 2-16. Notice the `data-icon="plus"` setting and the condition to render the button only on page 2.

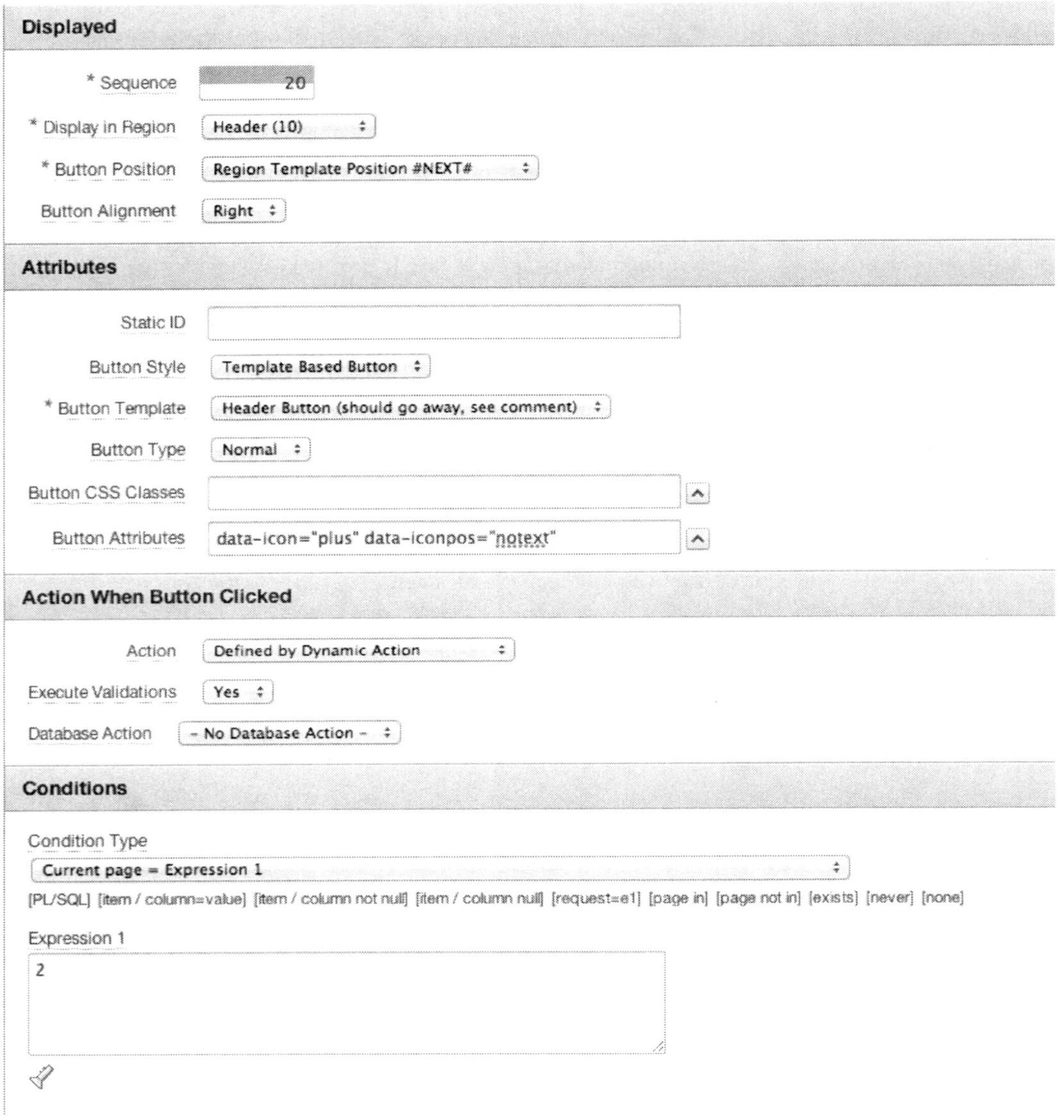

Displayed

* Sequence   `20`

* Display in Region   `Header (10)  ⇕`

* Button Position   `Region Template Position #NEXT#  ⇕`

Button Alignment   `Right  ⇕`

Attributes

Static ID   `[                              ]`

Button Style   `Template Based Button  ⇕`

* Button Template   `Header Button (should go away, see comment)  ⇕`

Button Type   `Normal  ⇕`

Button CSS Classes   `[                          ]  ⌃`

Button Attributes   `data-icon="plus" data-iconpos="notext"  ⌃`

Action When Button Clicked

Action   `Defined by Dynamic Action  ⇕`

Execute Validations   `Yes  ⇕`

Database Action   `- No Database Action -  ⇕`

Conditions

Condition Type

`Current page = Expression 1                                              ⇕`

[PL/SQL] [item / column=value] [item / column not null] [item / column null] [request=e1] [page in] [page not in] [exists] [never] [none]

Expression 1

```
2
```

Figure 2-16. Button definition of the "quick create" icon

2. Create a Dynamic Action on click of that button, with the piece of JavaScript you used earlier (with the `{role:"dialog"}` addition), but of course you need to change the page number from 2 to 4. To prevent the popup from showing up when the page is loaded, you might want to switch the default Fire On Page Load setting.

Run the application and then click the plus icon in the List View. You'll see a small dialog pop up. You can enter a name for a new employee (see Figure 2-17). When you enter a name and press the Create button, you are redirected to the List View and can find the newly entered coworker there. This example assumes that the primary key, empno, is autopopulated in a trigger.

Figure 2-17. *Dialog for quickly entering a new employee*

Transitions

While you tested the navigation of your application, switching from Home screen to List View to Form Page, you probably noticed the neat page transitions. This is one of the features that don't apply in a regular desktop application. On a mobile device, these transitions provide a very native look and feel to web applications.

The Page Transition Defaults are defined on the Theme level. Navigate to Edit Theme, and you'll see a region where you can set the defaults for a page and a popup (see Figure 2-18).

Transition Defaults

Page Transition	Slide ⇕
Popup Transition	Pop ⇕

Figure 2-18. *Specifying the Transition Defaults on Theme level*

Just change these values and examine your application. Did you notice any difference? If you did, you restarted your application or did a complete page refresh. If not, you probably expected the new settings to be applied when you move to another page—or at least when you move to a third page. So, why didn't it work?

This behavior is caused by a small piece of JavaScript that is generated into your page by the APEX engine (see Listing 2-2). In this piece of code, the properties defaultPageTransition and defaultDialogTramsition are set, but the code will only run on the "mobileinit" event. And that event doesn't run when you move from page to page using the standard Ajax style page loading. It will only run when the page is completely reloaded!

It might be worthwhile to notice that the definition of this mobileinit function should always be located before the reference to the jQuery Mobile JavaScript files, because it contains a default setting for jQuery Mobile.

Listing 2-2. The mobileinit Function

```
<script type="text/javascript"
apex.jQuery(document).on("mobileinit", function() {
  apex.jQuery.mobile.defaultPageTransition = "slide";
  apex.jQuery.mobile.defaultDialogTransition = "pop";
});
</script>
```

Due to the required location of this mobileinit function, it is rather impossible to make some changes to this code, other than changing the setting of these values in the APEX Builder. In a later version, the APEX development team might offer us a hook—as an application level attribute—where we can add some JavaScript code that will be generated into this mobileinit function. We've seen how to specify the default transition, but can we change that on a Page level as well? On some pages, you want the show sliding in from the left and others popping up. As you can see in Figure 2-19, you can override the template default setting on Page level. But as you try this, you might see nothing happens. Due to a bug (#14605541) in APEX 4.2, the engine doesn't use these settings at all. This is fixed in the first patch set. Be aware: the transition you specify here is the one applied when you move out of the page.

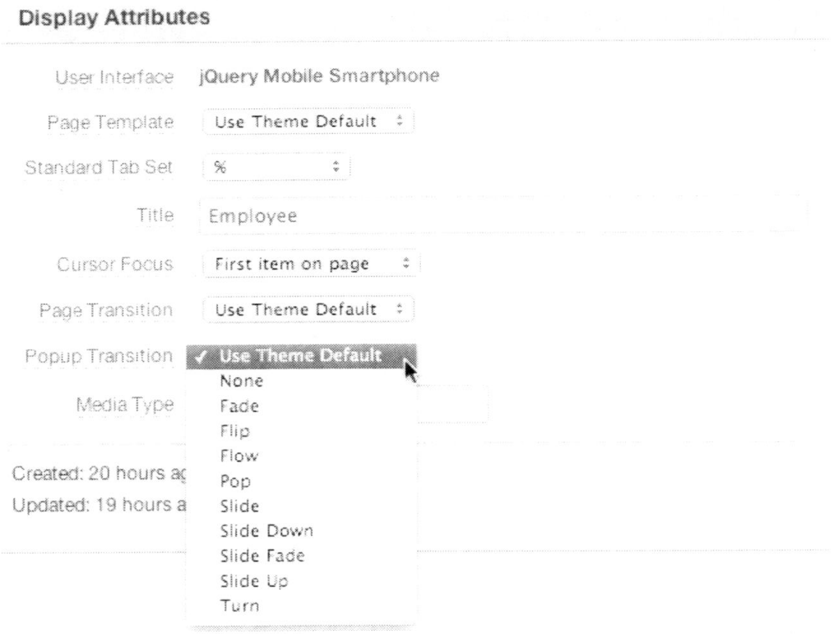

Figure 2-19. *Transition settings on Page level*

When you don't have access to APEX 4.2.1 and are limited to 4.2, are you stuck? Can't you define or change transitions on Page level at all? Luckily, we do have full control over the two ways of linking pages manually, as we did before. We can add a data-transition attribute to the anchor tag we created earlier on Page 1. So you get something like

```
<a href="f?p=&APP_ID.:2:&SESSION." data-role="button" data-rel="dialog"
data-transition="turn">Link to Employees</a>.
```

Valid values for data-transition are: "fade", "flip", "flow", "pop", "slide", "slidedown", "slidefade", "slideup", "turn", and "none".

The JavaScript code in the Dynamic Action can be changed in similar fashion:

```
apex.jQuery.mobile.changePage('f?p=&APP_ID.:2:&SESSION.',{role:"dialog", transition:"fade" });.
```

Another aspect of page transitions is the "loading indicator" that shows up between every page. The look and feel of this indicator can (in theory) be changed to your own likings and standards. But that requires access to the mobileinit function, and like we've just seen, that's not natively available in version 4.2 of APEX.

Popups

The first shipped version of APEX 4.2 contains jQuery Mobile 1.1.1. But things change fast in this new world, so a new version, 1.2, ships with APEX 4.2.1. One of the many new features in jQuery Mobile 1.2 is the popup widget. Because a popup might look very similar to a dialog, there are some huge differences:

- A dialog takes over the page, whereas a popup shows on top of a page.

- Any page can be turned into a dialog by adding a data-rel="dialog" attribute to the link. However, a popup is an element that already exists in the page.

Popups are probably more suited for tooltips, menus, and small messages. Even the small page that you created earlier for quickly entering an employee might be a good use case for a popup. Creating a popup is very similar to creating a dialog: add the data-role="popup" as an attribute to a div that contains the popup contents. To open the popup, you have to use an anchor tag that links to the div using the id and has a data-rel="popup" attribute.

Just like in older versions of APEX, you can replace the substitution strings in the header of your Page template with references to newer versions of jQuery and jQuery Mobile, but then there is no guarantee that the standard APEX components will continue to work as before. And because jQuery Mobile doesn't support multiple versions of jQuery Mobile on the same page (unlike jQuery), you can't just add a newer version onto an existing template.

Note Be aware of the different use of the words "popup" and "dialog" in APEX and jQuery Mobile. "Dialog" is not used in APEX, but a jQuery dialog is termed an APEX popup. And a jQuery popup is not natively used in APEX yet.

Loading Widgets

When a new page is loaded, you see a standard loading widget that looks like a spinning wheel. When you have a requirement to change that into something else, you might find yourself stuck, as this widget is usually defined in the mobileinit function. And as we've seen previously, you can't add or change any code in that generated piece of JavaScript. But again, Dynamic Actions is your friend here!

Create a Dynamic Action on page 0, the Global Page, that fires on Page Load and executes the snippet of JavaScript that you see in Listing 2-3.

Listing 2-3. Tweaking the Loading Widget

```
apex.jQuery.mobile.loadingMessageTextVisible=true;
apex.jQuery.mobile.loadingMessage="APEX is processing...";
apex.jQuery.mobile.loadingMessageTheme="e";
```

When you refresh your page and navigate to another page, you see a different loading indicator, like the one shown in Figure 2-20.

Figure 2-20. *A different loading widget*

Templates

As with regular desktop applications, all pages, regions, labels, and so forth are structured using templates. One of the things that is different is the integration with the jQuery Mobile theming framework. The framework contains multiple color "swatches;" the default ones are named "a" through "e". You can apply a swatch to any rendered HTML element—like pages, headers, buttons, and so forth—simply by adding the data-theme="d" attribute. A combination of elements with either the same or different data-theme settings make up your specific template. And the choice isn't limited to just these five swatches. You can make up 21 more if you like!

So for instance, changing the data-theme in the body of the Popup template to "a" results in a totally different looking dialog (see Figure 2-21).

Figure 2-21. *Dialog after applying a different data-theme*

Mixed Applications

The application we have until now is a "mobile only" application. You can run it on a regular desktop browser, but it doesn't look that good, mainly because our screen estate on the desktop is so much bigger. If you need to develop an application for desktop and mobile use, you have two options: develop two different ones as very different APEX applications or create one APEX application for two different targets. The advantage of the latter is that it is easier to share building blocks of code—so you only have to develop, test, and deploy it once and use it twice.

To add a desktop user interface type to our application, go to Edit Application Properties, select the User Interface tab, and click the Add New User Interface at the bottom. Just create one, picking the theme that you like—Theme 25 as an example—and you get another three pages generated for you: Global Page - Desktop, Login, and Home. Set the Auto Detect switch to Yes for both user interface types. When you try to access your application from a desktop browser without specifying a page number (like http://apex.oracle.com/pls/apex/f?p=13716), you will see a login screen different from what's seen on a mobile device. You might have noticed you get a Global Page for every user interface, so you can define global coding and behavior, depending on your user interface, without using a lot of conditional rendering.

Wrap Up

In this introductory chapter on jQuery Mobile and APEX, we covered quite a lot of subjects:

- The constructs of a jQuery Mobile page.

- How to navigate from one page to another using three different techniques: the declarative APEX, an HTML anchor element, and Dynamic Actions.

- How to show a page as a jQuery dialog.

- Transitions and how to change them—and what works and what doesn't.
- The upcoming Popups feature.
- Modifying templates to change the look of the application.
- Mixing mobile and desktop applications.

This was all the basic stuff you need to know before moving to the next chapters, which will cover every aspect in a lot more detail.

CHAPTER 3

Presenting Data Through List Views

One of the main differences between an APEX desktop application and a mobile application is the presence of the List View region type in the mobile world. Often, a List View is one of the first things you see when you open up an APEX mobile application. Even in the previous chapter, a List View was one of the first pages we created!

In this chapter, you will learn how to create a List View and how to use the all-powerful built-in options. And if that's not enough, we will also add some cool features using jQuery Mobile plug-ins.

Create a Basic List

In this chapter, we will base our list examples upon the DEMO_PRODUCT_INFO table. So let's start with creating a new report page with a List View region, as shown in Figure 3-1.

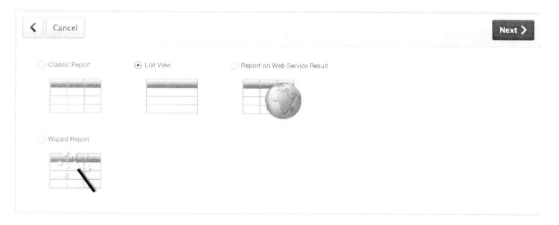

Figure 3-1. *Creating a page with a List View region*

Note that there is no interactive report–type available for a mobile theme because these kinds of reports are hard to use on a small mobile device. On the next page of the wizard, keep the suggested page number, and set both the page name and the region name to Products. Then you have to enter the Region Source, which is the SQL query that we will use for our Products List. We will start with the smallest query, so you can enter

```
select product_name from demo_product_info
```

The next page in the wizard shows a number of interesting features: keep them all unchecked for now because we will cover those later in this chapter. Note the Text Column property is set to PRODUCT_NAME because that is our only column. Then finish the wizard and run the page. You will see what's shown in Figure 3-2.

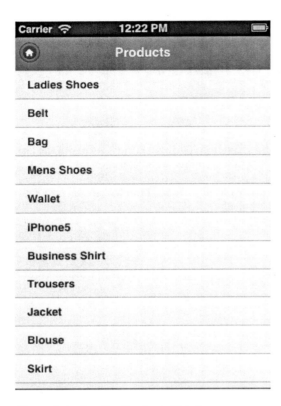

Figure 3-2. *Our first Products List view*

In the next section, you will learn how to style this list by adding pictures, dividers, links, and other features.

Style Your List

Edit the Products List region and open the Region Attributes tab. There you see the same settings we stepped through in the wizard (see Figure 3-3). The next few subsections discuss these settings in detail. We won't discuss them in the order listed in the wizard. Instead, we'll discuss them in the order we find most useful.

Settings		^

	☐ Advanced Formatting
	☐ Show Image
	☐ Show List Divider
Features	☐ Has Split Button
	☐ Enable Search
	☐ Is Nested List View
	☑ Inset List
Text Column	PRODUCT_NAME ⇕
Supplemental Information Column	– select – ⇕
Counter Column	– select – ⇕
Link Target	

Figure 3-3. The List View settings

The Inset List Feature

The first setting we will examine is the Inset List. This setting is often used when a list is not the only item on a page, but when it is embedded in a page with other types of content. An Inset List has some margins around the content area and rounded corners. Compare the Inset List in Figure 3-4 to the same list rendered in Figure 3-2. Can you spot the differences?

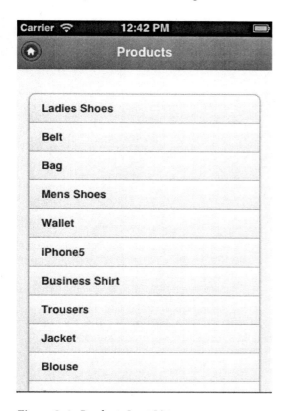

Figure 3-4. Products Inset List

The Enable Search Feature

Go to the Region Attributes, uncheck the Inset List feature, and check the Enable Search feature. Three new search options appear: Search Type, Search Column, and Search Box Placeholder (see Figure 3-5).

Search Type	Client Side
Search Column	– select –
Search Box Placeholder	Search for a Product…

Figure 3-5. *List View search options*

The Search Type has five options: one for client-side search and four for server-side search. Server-side search can be either exact or like and either case sensitive or insensitive. When you use server-side search, you always have to hit the Search button on the virtual keyboard. Client-side search, however, has an immediate effect: searching is performed on every keystroke. This setting is far more user-friendly and intuitive, but can have one disadvantage: all records will be loaded into the browser, regardless of the Number of Fetched Rows setting at the bottom of the Region Attributes page. So it works great, but it's dependent on the record set size and your bandwidth.

Tip   From an end-user perspective, client-side search is the preferred option, as long as the record set size (in your production environment) and your bandwidth guarantee an adequate performance.

Using the Search Column property, you can define how the search should be performed against a column other than the one defined as Text Column. To see that feature on action, add the PRODUCT_DESCRIPTION column to the Region Source query and use that column as the Search Column. When you now run the page and search for "simple", the Ladies Shoes are returned— obviously because that word is contained in the product description. But, as you experienced, this is only useful (from an end-user point of view) when that column is shown one way or another. And we'll take care of that later on.

In the Search Box Placeholder, you can define the HTML5 placeholder attribute: the light-gray text in an input field that disappears when you enter text (see Figure 3-6). This feature is often used instead of the old-fashioned, more intrusive tool tip.

Figure 3-6. *The Search Box Placeholder set to Search for a Product. . .*

The standard value of the placeholder is Search. . . . You can change the default value of that placeholder for all search boxes in all List Views by defining a Text Message with APEX.REGION.JQM_LIST_VIEW.SEARCH as the name, and defining the text as whatever you want to show as the placeholder. You can find the Text Messages in the Globalization region of the Shared Components page (see Figure 3-7). Of course, this change will only have an effect if you didn't override the default on the Region level by defining your own placeholder text.

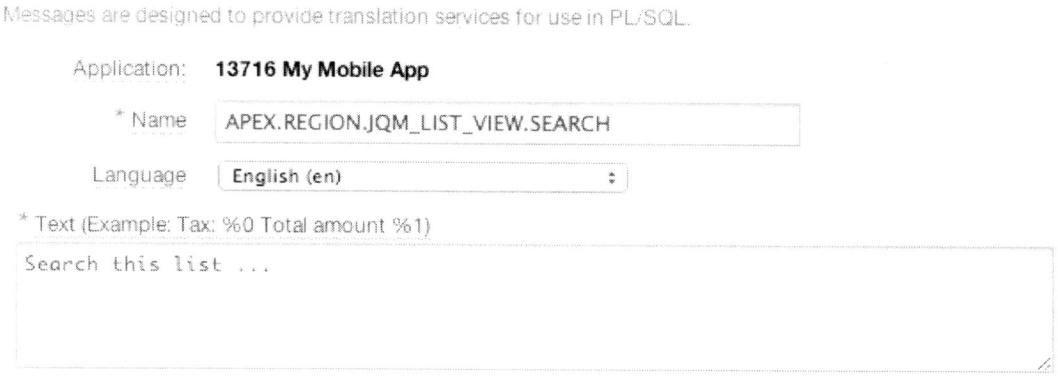

Messages are designed to provide translation services for use in PL/SQL.

Application: **13716 My Mobile App**

* Name   APEX.REGION.JQM_LIST_VIEW.SEARCH

Language   English (en)

* Text (Example: Tax: %0 Total amount %1)

Search this list ...

Figure 3-7. *Change the default value of the Search Placeholder in List Views*

The Show List Divider Feature

The next thing we will explore is the Show List Divider feature. First, add the CATEGORY column to the Region Source query. Then tick the Show List Divider option and select CATEGORY as the List Divider Column (see Figure 3-8). When you run the page, you see nice dividers between the actual Product records. Just as a reminder, the colors are defined by the theme you pick for your application.

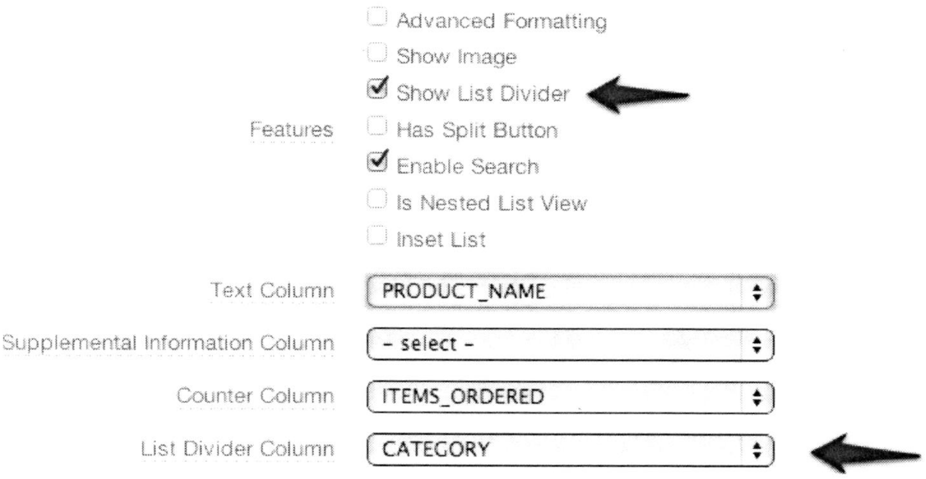

Features

☐ Advanced Formatting
☐ Show Image
☑ Show List Divider ⬅
☐ Has Split Button
☑ Enable Search
☐ Is Nested List View
☐ Inset List

Text Column   PRODUCT_NAME

Supplemental Information Column   – select –

Counter Column   ITEMS_ORDERED

List Divider Column   CATEGORY ⬅

Figure 3-8. *Defining the List Divider*

To show the difference between the dividers and the actual records, we need to define a Link Target. Later, we will define a more useful Link Target, but for now just entering **'javascipt:void(0);'** will do. The result will be similar to Figure 3-9. From the output, you see we should have added an ORDER BY clause to the query as well.

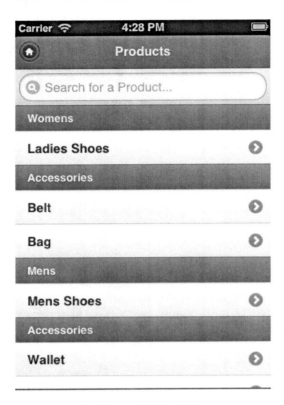

Figure 3-9. *List View with List Dividers*

The Counter Column Feature

For the Counter Column feature, we need to add another column to the Region Source. Add the following subquery as a new column to your query. You might also need to add "p" as the table alias for the DEMO_PRODUCT_INFO table.

```
( select count(1) from demo_order_items i where i.product_id = p.product_id ) as items_ordered
```

Next, pick your new column as the Counter Column, as shown in Figure 3-10.

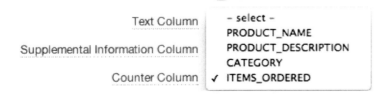

Figure 3-10. *Define the Counter Column*

You get the very cool-looking counter indicators shown in Figure 3-11.

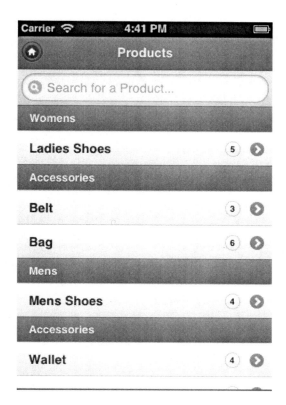

Figure 3-11. *List View with Counter Column*

The Show Image Feature

The next feature to explore is Show Image. Before we can use this feature, we have to add an image to display. There's an image contained in the PRODUCT_IMAGE column, which you should add to the select statement. Then navigate to the Region Attributes of our list and switch on the Show Image indicator. Another four properties appear in the Settings region, as shown in Figure 3-12.

Image Type	Image stored in BLOB ⬍
Image BLOB Column	PRODUCT_IMAGE ⬍
Image Primary Key Column 1	ROWID ⬍
Image Primary Key Column 2	– select – ⬍

Figure 3-12. *Additional image settings*

Apart from showing an image or an icon contained in the record itself, you can also show an image or icon referred to by a URL that is a column in the record. That ability might be useful when you store the images on your web server.

The size of the image is defined by the jQuery Mobile CSS. An image created this way in a List View gets the ui-li-thumb class. In the CSS file, the max-width and max-height of items in this class is set to 80 pixels. If you think that the images are too big for a small device, you can add the CSS snippet in Listing 3-1 to the Inline CSS region of the page.

Listing 3-1. CSS to Reduce the Image Size

```
/* Reduce size thumbnail */
.ui-li-thumb
{
  width  : 50px;
  height : 50px;
}

/* Reduce li height with thumb */
.ui-li-has-thumb
{
  height : 52px;
}

/* Reposition counter and icon */
.ui-li-has-count .ui-li-count,
.ui-btn-icon-right > .ui-btn-inner > .ui-icon
{
  top : 33%;
}
```

When you add the snippet from Listing 3-1 and rerun the page, you'll get something similar to what's shown in Figure 3-13. So although it was quite cumbersome in previous releases of APEX to show images in reports, in this version it is simply a breeze!

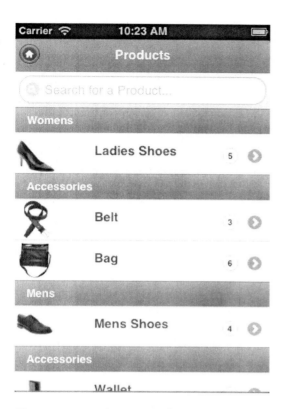

Figure 3-13. *Products List with images*

Tip Be careful when showing large-sized images in your report. Although they might show up tiny, the full image is loaded. And that might result in a page size of several megabytes. So when you need to show both full-size and thumbnail images, you have to store both, either in your database or on your web server.

The Link Target Feature

In order to use the Link Target feature, we need to create a form to manage the product information. To quickly create a new Form page on the DEMO_PRODUCT_INFO table, select the PRODUCT_ID as the Primary Key, accept all defaults on the next pages, and set the branching to our Products List page.

Back to the definition of the Products List page, add the PRODUCT_ID column to the select statement. Replace the dummy "javascript:void(0);" code we added earlier, with

```
f?p=&APP_ID.:22:&APP_SESSION.::&DEBUG.::P22_PRODUCT_ID:&PRODUCT_ID.
```

Of course, you need to replace the page numbers, 22 in this example, with the page number of the Product form page you've just created. The link is now actually working and navigates to our very rudimentary Product form page. But we will enhance the look and feel of that page in the next chapter.

The Has Split Button Feature

A list isn't restricted to only one page to link to. Without any wizardry, you can even have two! So let's assume we want to add another link to enter an Order for a selected Product.

Create another Form page, this time on the DEMO_ORDER_ITEMS table. Select ROWID as the Primary Key. Opt to make only the Create button because we don't need a Save or Delete. Then, branch back to our Products List page. This page doesn't look that impressive—and creating a record doesn't work due to the foreign key constraint to the Order table. But we'll fix all that in the next chapter. We only need the page for creating the additional link.

Navigate back to the Region Attributes of the Products List region and select the Has Split Button feature. Another property, Split Button Target, appears. Just copy the URL from the Link Target and paste it into the Split Button Target. Again, change the page numbers to the number of the newly created Order Item page. Running the Products List page now shows a splitter on every row, as shown in Figure 3-14. Clicking the first part of the row navigates to the Products page. Clicking the right arrow shows the Order Item page.

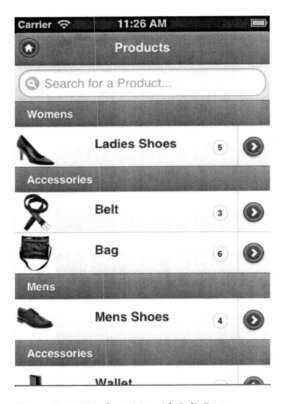

Figure 3-14. *Products List with Split Button*

The Is Nested List View Feature

The Is Nested List View feature isn't applicable in the Products List because it is designed for hierarchical queries. You can quickly try it out by creating a new List page with an SQL statement:

```
SELECT empno, ename, mgr, level
FROM emp
START WITH mgr is null
CONNECT BY PRIOR empno = mgr
```

In the Region Attributes, select ENAME as the Text Column, enable the Is Nested View List feature, and pick Level as the Nested List Column. When you run the page, you can walk through the hierarchy of the EMP table.

The Advanced Formatting Feature

Although we've already managed to style our list from a very basic text-only version to a version with images, counters, and two links—we've got even more options.

Add the column LIST_PRICE to the SQL query. Then, in Region Attributes, click Advanced Formatting. Another four options appear. Here we can style our list even further. Figure 3-15 shows an example.

The first option is used to style the list by overriding the standard list or divider theme. The List Entry Attributes can be set to pick an icon other than the standard right arrow. Text Formatting, the only required one (even when you just want to use another icon), gives you the opportunity to show more in the list than just the Product Name. In this

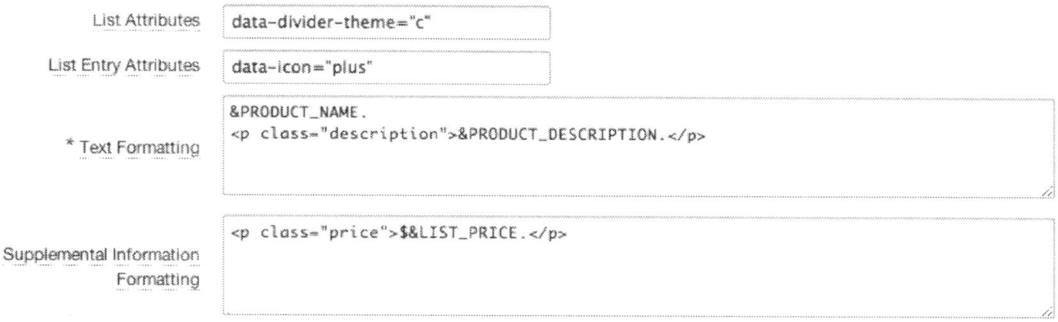

List Attributes	data-divider-theme="c"
List Entry Attributes	data-icon="plus"
* Text Formatting	&PRODUCT_NAME. <p class="description">&PRODUCT_DESCRIPTION.</p>
Supplemental Information Formatting	<p class="price">$&LIST_PRICE.</p>

Figure 3-15. Advanced Formatting example

example, we add the Product Description to the list. And when even that is not enough, we can add Supplemental Information. We'll use the Product Price for that. The Supplemental Information is usually a short piece of text that shows up on the right side of the list item, just before the counter. Please note the classes that are assigned to the paragraph tags of the additional elements. These are used in Listing 3-2 to get the exact look and feel we want.

Listing 3-2. Complete CSS for the Products List

```
/* Reduce size thumbnail*/
.ui-li-thumb
{
  width  : 50px;
  height : 50px;
}

/* Reduce li height with thumb */
.ui-li-has-thumb
{
  height : 52px;
}
```

```css
/* Reposition counter and icon */
.ui-li-has-alt.ui-li-has-count .ui-li-count,
.ui-btn-icon-right > .ui-btn-inner > .ui-icon
{
  top    : 20px;
  right  : 45px;
}

/* Move Text to left */
.ui-li-has-thumb .ui-btn-inner a.ui-link-inherit
{
  padding-left : 55px;
}

/* Style Price and Description */
.price
{
  position     : absolute;
  right        : 45px;
  top          : 37px;
  font-size    : 11px;
  color        : blue;
}

.description
{
  font-size    : 10px;
  margin       : 0px -1px;
}
```

Once we've put everything in place and rerun our page, we get a nice looking page with additional text, colored pricing information, another icon for adding an Order, and a new divider (see Figure 3-16).

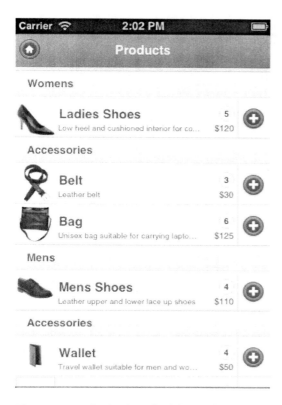

Figure 3-16. *The final result of the Products List*

Number of Fetched Rows

Without doubt, you are familiar with the Pagination options for a report in a regular desktop application. These kinds of paginations don't work very well on a mobile device. That's why a mobile application in APEX works slightly different in this area. In the Advanced region of the Products List's Region Attributes tab, you'll find the Number of Fetched Rows setting. The default value of this property is 15. Originally, the DEMO_PRODUCT_INFO table didn't contain that number of records, so for this example, change it to 5. When you run the page, you will see that changing this setting has no effect at all. That's because the Search Type setting is still set to Client Side, so all records are loaded anyway. Change that setting to one of the server-side settings. When you run the page again and scroll down, you see a Load more... option at the bottom of your list, as shown in Figure 3-17. Clicking it will load another five records.

Figure 3-17. *The new mobile Pagination style*

If you don't like the Load more . . . text, you can change it by defining a Text Message with APEX.REGION.JQM_LIST_VIEW.LOAD_MORE as the name, just as we did with the default Search field placeholder.

Add Swipe-to-Delete Functionality

In many iOS applications, you can delete data from a List View by swiping over the row, which brings up a Delete button to delete the data. See Figure 3-18 for an example of the Evernote application.

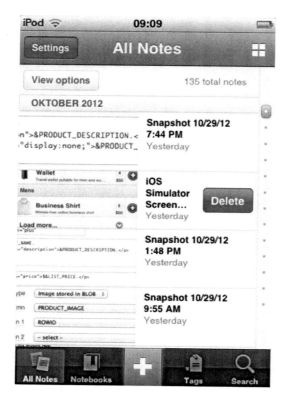

Figure 3-18. *Example of swipe-to-delete*

Wouldn't it be cool if we could implement this native application functionality in our apex mobile web application?

Implementing swipe-to-delete requires a number of steps:

1. We want to execute something when we do a swipe-right on one of the rows. Create a Dynamic Action on the Swipe-Right event. The Selection Type is a jQuery Selector that selects all list items that are not one of the dividers. Also excluded is the Load more... item at the bottom of the list. Here's the jQuery Selector:

   ```
   li[data-role!="list-divider"]:not(".apex-load-more")
   ```

2. We need to execute a JavaScript function that we will define later, so you can simply enter **swipe2Delete(this);**. Prevent this function from running immediately when the page is loaded by unchecking the Fire On Page Load property.

3. For the actual deletion of a record, you need to create a Hidden Item (like P13_PRODUCT_ID). Be sure to set the Value Protected property to No because we will assign a value to this item using JavaScript.

4. Create an "On Change" Dynamic Action on the field that will execute a piece of PL/SQL. Be sure to set Page Items To Submit to P13_PRODUCT_ID. For example:

```
DELETE FROM DEMO_PRODUCT_INFO
WHERE PRODUCT_ID = :P13_PRODUCT_ID;
```

5. Now we can add our swipe2Delete JavaScript function to the page in the Function and Global Variable Declaration section (see Listing 3-3).

Listing 3-3. The swipe2Delete JavaScript Function Declaration

```javascript
function swipe2Delete( pThis )
{
  var $li = $( pThis.triggeringElement );

  // This disables links on the page. If you click anywhere else, it removes the delete button
  $('li').bind('tap click', function(e){
      $('.deleteButton').slideUp();
      $('.deleteButton').remove();
      $('li').unbind('tap click');
      return false;
  });

  // Remove any existing Delete Button
  $('.deleteButton').slideUp();
  $('.deleteButton').remove();

  var deleteButton = $('<a>Delete</a>')
                      .attr( { 'class': 'deleteButton ui-btn-up-r'
                             ,  'id'   : $li.find('.id').text()
                             // this tells me which list item to delete
                             });
  // add the button to the list item and show it
  $li.prepend( deleteButton );
  $('.deleteButton').slideDown();

  // Have the delete button delete the item
  $('.deleteButton').bind('tap click', function () {
      event.preventDefault();
      var $del = $(this);
      $s('P13_PRODUCT_ID', $del.attr('id'));  // Fire my real deletion
      if ( $del.parent().prev().attr('data-role')=='list-divider' &&
           $del.parent().next().attr('data-role')=='list-divider'
         ){ // Delete List Divider as well
        $del.parent().prev().remove();
      }
      $del.parent().remove();                     // remove the row
  });

}
```

6. In the JavaScript function, you might have noticed the use of an "id" within the list item. This "id" is used to determine the PRODUCT_ID that is about to be deleted. We need to add that PRODUCT_ID to the HTML of the list item. This can be done by adding a line to the Text Formatting property, as shown in Figure 3-19.

```
&PRODUCT_NAME.
<p class="description">&PRODUCT_DESCRIPTION.</p>
* Text Formatting    <p class="id" style="display:none;">&PRODUCT_ID.</p>
```

Figure 3-19. *Adding the PRODUCT_ID to the HTML of the list item*

7. The only thing we need is (quite a lot of) CSS to mimic the native styling of the Delete button (see Listing 3-4).

Listing 3-4. CSS to Style the Delete Button

```
.deleteButton
{
  -moz-border-radius    : 5px;
  -webkit-border-radius : 5px;
  float       : right;
  height      : 15px;
  line-height : 15px;
  margin      : 8px 100px 0 0;
  padding     : 0.6em;
  position    : absolute;
  right       : 0;
  top         : 0;
  z-index     : 10;
  display     :none;
}

/* red color buttons */
.ui-btn-up-r
{
  border        : 1px solid #953403;
  background    : #2567ab;
  font-weight   : bold;
  color         : #fff;
  cursor        : pointer;
  text-shadow   : 0 -1px 1px #953403;
  text-decoration : none;
  background-image : -moz-linear-gradient(top, #ec4a0b, #ad390c);
  background-image : -webkit-gradient(linear,left top,left bottom,color-stop(0,
#ec4a0b),color-stop(1, #ad390c));
  -ms-filter: "progid:DXImageTransform.Microsoft.gradient(startColorStr='#ec4a0b',
EndColorStr='#ad390c')";
}
```

```css
.ui-btn-up-r a.ui-link-inherit
{
  color : #fff;
}
.ui-btn-hover-r
{
  border       : 1px solid #953403;
  background   : #f15c22;
  font-weight : bold;
  color        : #fff;
  text-shadow : 0 -1px 1px #014D68;
  background-image : -moz-linear-gradient(top, #f15c22, #f15c22);
  text-decoration   : none;
  background-image : -webkit-gradient(linear,left top,left bottom,color-stop(0, #f15c22),
color-stop(1, #f15c22));
  -ms-filter: "progid:DXImageTransform.Microsoft.gradient(startColorStr='#f15c22',
EndColorStr='#f15c22')";
}
.ui-btn-hover-r a.ui-link-inherit
{
  color : #fff;
}


.ui-btn-down-r
{
  border        : 1px solid #225377;
  background    : #79ae21;
  font-weight : bold;
  color         : #fff;
  text-shadow : 0 -1px 1px #225377;
  background-image : -moz-linear-gradient(top, #bc770f, #e6590c);
  background-image : -webkit-gradient(linear,left top,left bottom,color-stop(0, #bc770f),
color-stop(1, #e6590c));
  -ms-filter: "progid:DXImageTransform.Microsoft.gradient(startColorStr='#bc770f',
EndColorStr='#e6590c')";
}


.ui-btn-down-r a.ui-link-inherit
{
  color : #fff;
}


.ui-btn-up-r, .ui-btn-hover-r, .ui-btn-down-r
{
  font-family : Helvetica, Arial, sans-serif;
}
```

After all this work, it is finally time to see our work in action. Run your page in your mobile browser and try to swipe-right on a row. The Delete button appears, as shown in Figure 3-20. When you click the Delete button, the corresponding record is deleted from the database and from the list. Thanks to the definition of the foreign key, which is cascade on delete, the corresponding Order Items are deleted as well. And when you delete the last record of a category, the divider is removed!

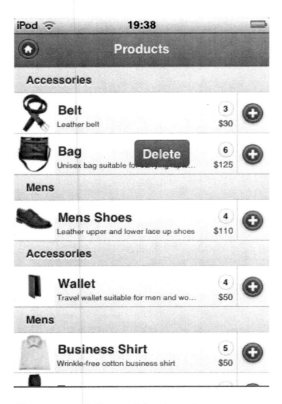

Figure 3-20. *Swipe-to-delete in action*

Add Automatic Push of Next Records

In the default setting, you have to click the Load more... link to load the next set of records. Although this feature is seen a lot in native applications, you may also see a feature where a list is automatically extended with the next set of records when the bottom of the list is reached. We will implement this feature.

First, we need to download and install an external jQuery plug-in called Waypoints. You can get that from http://imakewebthings.com/jquery-waypoints. Download the files and upload the minified JavaScript function as a static file for the current application. Next, reference that static file in the File URLs section of our page as #APP_IMAGES#waypoints.min.js. Create a Dynamic Action that fires on Page Load and executes the JavaScript code you see in Listing 3-5.

Listing 3-5. JavaScript for Automatic Pushing of Records

```
$('div[data-role="content"]').waypoint(function(event, direction)
{ if (direction=='down') {
    // Mimic a click to fire loading
    $('li.apex-load-more').hide();
    $('li.apex-load-more').trigger('vclick');
    // Recalculate waypoint position after 3 seconds - loading might take a while
    setTimeout(function(){$.waypoints('refresh');$('li.apex-load-more').show();},3000);
  }
},
```

```
{
  offset: 'bottom-in-view'   // bottom of the page
, onlyOnScroll : true
});
```

This code snippet attaches a Waypoint method on the div that holds the content of our list. When the bottom is in view, and we're scrolling down, it mimics a click on the list item that holds the Load more... text. The effect is that the next set of records is automatically loaded when the bottom of the list is in sight. The timeout is added because it might take a few seconds to load the data—depending on what you are loading, the number of records, and the speed of your internet connection. So you might tweak that setting of 3 seconds to something higher or lower.

List View Exercise

You've now been exposed to all the functionality that APEX provides relating to list views. To reinforce your learning, set yourself the goal of creating a similar List View on the DEMO_CUSTOMERS table. For links that both maintain the customer information and add new orders, you must create two plain forms on both tables. Your result should resemble what's shown in Figure 3-21.

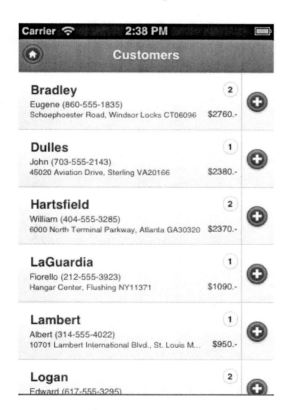

Figure 3-21. *List View of Customers*

As you can see, there are quite a number of fields shown on every list element. Wouldn't it be nice to offer your users the possibility to search on all the data elements, very similar to the interactive report-type of row search functionality? There is a simple and elegant way to accomplish that. Just add an additional field to the query, containing of a concatenation of all fields, as shown in Listing 3-6.

Listing 3-6. Full Query for the Customer's View

```
select c.customer_id
     ,       c.cust_last_name
     ,       c.cust_first_name
     ,       c.cust_street_address1
     ,       c.cust_city
     ,       c.cust_state
     ,       c.cust_postal_code
     ,       c.phone_number1
     ,       ( select count(*) from demo_orders o where o.customer_id = c.customer_id ) order_count
     ,       ( select sum(order_total) from demo_orders o where o.customer_id = c.customer_id )
order_value
     ,       c.cust_last_name        ||
             c.cust_first_name       ||
             c.cust_street_address1||
             c.cust_city             ||
             c.cust_state            ||
             c.cust_postal_code      ||
             c.phone_number1         as search_field
from demo_customers c
order by c.cust_last_name
```

Next, switch on the Enable Search option and select SEARCH_FIELD as the Search Column. To indicate the search on all columns, you may change the Search Box Placeholder value to something that points to that functionality (see Figure 3-22).

Search Type	Client Side
Search Column	SEARCH_FIELD
Search Box Placeholder	Search on all fields...

Figure 3-22. *Enable search on all fields*

When you now run your application and search for "Lo", you'll see that it immediately filters the results on the City, First Name, and Last Name, as shown in Figure 3-23. So with hardly any effort, you offer your users functionality that they will love!

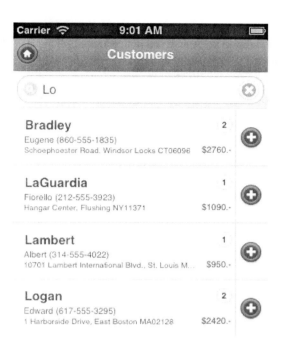

Figure 3-23. *Searching for "Lo" on all fields*

Implement Custom Sorting

The option to sort on different columns is one of the last things that we are missing when compared to a desktop version of a report. There are probably a number of ways to solve this, but in this paragraph, we will use another jQuery Mobile plug-in and add some JavaScript to do it.

The first step is to enable our query to support dynamic sorting. Therefore, add the code from Listing 3-7 to the SQL statement.

Listing 3-7. Enable Dynamic Sorting

```
order by  case :P27_ORDER_BY
          when '1' then c.cust_first_name
          when '2' then c.cust_last_name
          when '3' then c.cust_city
          else c.cust_last_name
          end
```

Next, add the P27_ORDER_BY field (where the number may vary, depending on your current page number) as Select List to your Reports region. Set the Page Action when Value Changed property to "Redirect and Set Value". We need to submit the page and we can't use a partial page refresh, because that is not supported for List Views. We need just a static list of values, so set the List of Values definition to "STATIC:1,2,3". When you run the page, you should be able to test this functionality. Because this takes up valuable screen estate, we want to hide this field. Set the Template property to No Label and create a hidden div around the Select list by setting the Pre Element Text to

47

`<div style="display:none;">` and the Post Element Text to `</div>`. The Select List should no longer show up on your page. We will create a more native and fancier way to offer this functionality to the user. If you notice a small gap where the Select List used to be, you can get rid of it by setting the Item Display Position region property to Below Content.

Find yourself a little (16 × 16 pixels) image that you like and load it up as an Application image. Then go to the Global Page - jQuery Mobile Smartphone, page 0. In the Header region of that page, define a new button using that image. Give it a Static ID, set the Action to Defined by Dynamic Action, and show it only on the Customer List View page (see Figure 3-24 for all the settings).

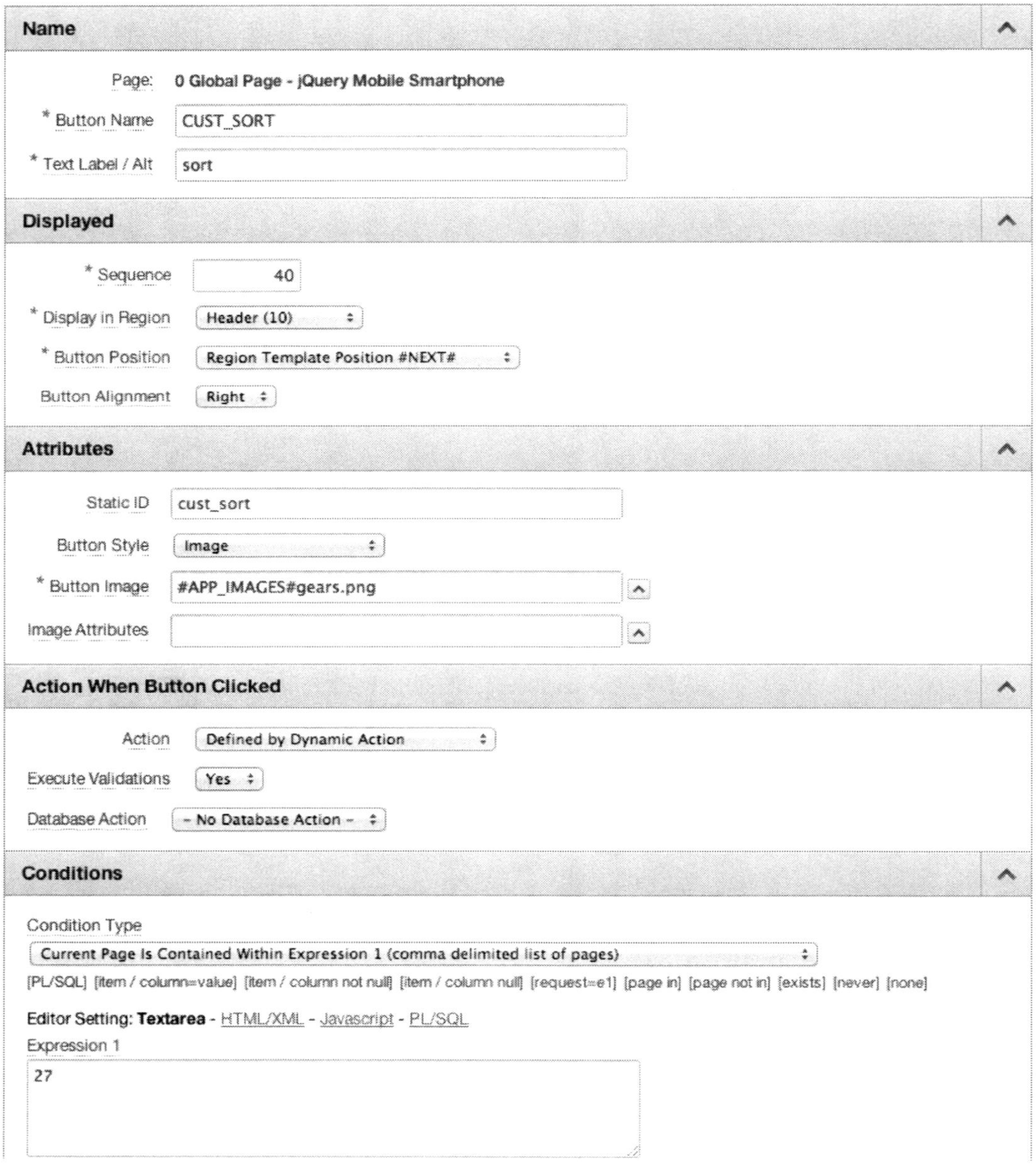

Name

Page:	0 Global Page - jQuery Mobile Smartphone
* Button Name	CUST_SORT
* Text Label / Alt	sort

Displayed

* Sequence	40
* Display in Region	Header (10)
* Button Position	Region Template Position #NEXT#
Button Alignment	Right

Attributes

Static ID	cust_sort
Button Style	Image
* Button Image	#APP_IMAGES#gears.png
Image Attributes	

Action When Button Clicked

Action	Defined by Dynamic Action
Execute Validations	Yes
Database Action	– No Database Action –

Conditions

Condition Type
Current Page Is Contained Within Expression 1 (comma delimited list of pages)

[PL/SQL] [item / column=value] [item / column not null] [item / column null] [request=e1] [page in] [page not in] [exists] [never] [none]

Editor Setting: **Textarea** - HTML/XML - Javascript - PL/SQL
Expression 1

27

Figure 3-24. Add button with a custom image to the header

48

Now it is time to download the necessary SimpleDialog2 jQuery Mobile plug-in from http://dev.jtsage.com/jQM-SimpleDialog/demos2. Upload the Cascading Style Sheet and JavaScript files to your application. Reference those in your page by setting the File URLs property in the JavaScript section of the Customer List View page to

```
#APP_IMAGES#jquery.mobile.simpledialog2.min.js
```

And the File URLs property in the CSS section to

```
#WORKSPACE_IMAGES#jquery.mobile.simpledialog.min.css
```

To show the SimpleDialog, create a Dynamic Action on your page that fires on the Click event of the button on page 0. We can define that by using a jQuery Selector on the ID: #cust_sort. The True Action is the execution of the JavaScript code, as shown in Listing 3-8.

Listing 3-8. Showing the SimpleDialog

```
$('<div>').simpledialog2({
    mode: 'blank',
    headerText: 'Sort on',
    headerClose: true,
    themeHeader:'c',
    themeInput:'c',
    blankContentAdopt :true,
    blankContent :
'<div data-role="fieldcontain">'+
'<fieldset id="RG_sorter" data-role="controlgroup" data-mini="true">'+
'<input type="radio" name="sorter" id="FirstName" value="FirstName" onchange="sortOn(1);"/>'+
'<label for="FirstName">First Name</label>'+
'<input type="radio" name="sorter" id="LastName" value="LastName" onchange="sortOn(2);"/>'+
'<label for="LastName">Last Name</label>'+
'<input type="radio" name="sorter" id="City" value="City" onchange="sortOn(3);"/>'+
'<label for="City">City</label>'+
'</fieldset>'+
'</div>'
  });
```

This code creates a SimpleDialog containing a radio group with three options: First Name, Last Name, or City. There are more options available for this plug-in—just check the documentation on the site from which you downloaded the code.

The only thing we are missing right now is the definition of the sortOn function that's called on the change of a radio group option. We need to define that in the Function and Global Variable Declaration property of the JavaScript section of the page. See Listing 3-9 for the definition.

Listing 3-9. Definition of the sortOn Function

```
function sortOn( pSelected ){
// 1=FirstName, 2=LastName, 3=City
// Set P27_ORDER_BY to the sort field and destroy the popup
$('#P27_ORDER_BY').val(pSelected);
apex.jQuery.mobile.sdCurrentDialog.close();
$('#P27_ORDER_BY').trigger('change');
}
```

This code sets the value (1, 2, or 3) of the selected option to our hidden Select List, destroys the SimpleDialog, and fires the Change event on the Select List—because this won't fire when we set the value using JavaScript.

Now we're done and ready to test our dynamic sorting functionality! Run the page and click the button in the upper-right corner. When everything works as expected, you'll see something like what is shown in Figure 3-25. Clicking one of the options will reload the page with the correct sorting applied!

Figure 3-25. *Dynamic sorting using the SimpleDialog plug-in*

Wrap Up

In this chapter, we learned everything about List Views. We covered all options and settings, and we know what effect they have on the user interface. We have even implemented some really cool features—swipe-to-delete, infinite scrolling, and custom sorting—by using external jQuery plug-ins. Now that you have learned how to use these plug-ins, you might search the Web to see what else they can do to enhance the look and feel of your application.

CHAPTER 4

Accepting Input via Forms

In the previous chapter, you saw how to create lists and generated some very basic forms. In this chapter, you will improve these forms so that they look exactly the way you want. You will learn about the available input types that are specially aimed at mobile devices. And you will add some features in order to mimic a native application-style as closely as possible.

Revisiting the Login Page

While testing the results of your effort in the previous chapters, you probably saw the login page more than just a couple of times. You might have noticed that although its functionality is fine, it doesn't look that good—and that's an understatement (see Figure 4-1).

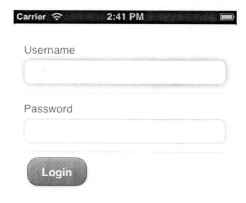

Figure 4-1. *The original login page*

When you look at some of the native applications on your mobile device, you should have noticed that the login screens of those applications look quite different—or better. Figure 4-2 shows four examples of login pages.

Figure 4-2. *The login pages of four native mobile applications*

So what are the main differences between these good-looking pages and our login page? First, their use of limited screen estate is efficient—placeholders, not prompts (or labels), are used before the input field. Second, the Login button is typically just as long as the input fields. Third, to reduce space, the input fields are placed closely together. And last but not least, they all use color or a picture in the background.

That's exactly what we will do to make our login page look as good as Facebook's, for example. Open the definition of our mobile login page, usually page 101, and make the following changes:

1. For both input fields, P101_USERNAME and P101_PASSWORD, set the Template property to "No Label" and set the value of the Placeholder property to what was previously the label value.

2. Change the Template property of the Login button to "100% Button."

3. Assign a Static ID of "login" to the Login region to easily address that region in our CSS.

4. Find a nice image (like the Directory.png in this example), load it up, and show it on the login page by specifying in the Region Source of the Login region:

```
<img src="#APP_IMAGES#Directory.png" id="logo"/>
<p class="logotext">i-orderbook</p>
```

5. Set the Item Display Position of the Login region to "Below Content" in order to show the input fields below the image.

6. Assign first-row and last-row classes to the input fields, as shown in Figure 4-3 (the definition of these classes is handled in the next step).

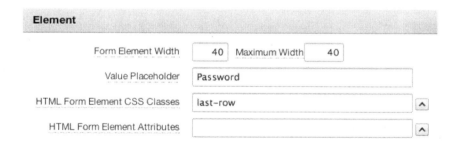

Figure 4-3. *Assigning the classes to the input fields*

7. Apply the CSS from Listing 4-1 to the CSS Inline region of the page.

Listing 4-1. CSS for the Login Page

```
/* Define the size of the Logo Image */
img#logo
{
  max-height : 20%;
}

/* Define (Uploaded) Font for the Logo Text */
@font-face
{
 font-family : facebook_font;
 src         : url('#APP_IMAGES#FACEBOLF.OTF');
}
```

```css
p.logotext
{
 color         : white;
 text-shadow   : none;
 font-family   : facebook_font;
 font-size     : 25px;
 margin-top    : 0.5em;
 margin-bottom : 0.5em;
}

/* Define the top side rounded corners for a first-row*/
input.first-row
{
 -webkit-border-radius : 0.4em 0.4em 0em 0em;
 border-radius :  0.4em 0.4em 0em 0em;
}

/* Define the down side rounded corners for the Password */
input.last-row
{
 -webkit-border-radius : 0em 0em 0.4em 0.4em;
 border-radius : 0em 0em 0.4em 0.4em;
}

/* Define the less-than-standard rounded corners for the button */
div.ui-btn-corner-all
{
 -webkit-border-radius: 0.4em;
 border-radius:  0.4em;
}

/* Place fields (Username / Password) close to each other */
div.ui-field-contain
{
 padding    : 0em;
 margin     : 0em 0em 0em 0em;
}

/* Remove the thin line between Username and Password */
div.ui-br
{
 border  : none;
}

/* Define (relative) positioning and sizing of the Login Region */
#login
{
 margin-left  : 10%;
 margin-right : 10%;
 text-align   : center;
}
```

```
/* Remove the background image and set color to blue */
.ui-page,
div.ui-content.ui-body-c
{
 background-color : #3B5998;
 background-image : none;
}
```

The result should look something like Figure 4-4, which is way better than the original! It looks particularly great on a smaller device, even when you rotate the device. For a larger device, you might want to add some specific settings to reduce the size of the input fields and buttons, but we will come back to that later.

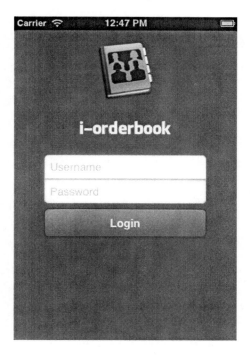

Figure 4-4. *The improved login page*

Tip Uploading a font file into the database and referencing it in CSS code just to create one little piece of text may not be the best solution from a performance perspective. In a production environment, you should create a tiny image with that font and use the image instead.

As one last enhancement, we need to change the loading message to something that indicates that the login process has started when the button is pressed. Create a Dynamic Action that fires Before Page Submit and executes this JavaScript code (switch off Fire On Page Load):

```
apex.jQuery.mobile.loadingMessageTextVisible=true;
apex.jQuery.mobile.loadingMessage="Login in progress...";
apex.jQuery.mobile.loadingMessageTheme="d";
```

When you log in again, you'll see that message pop up, especially when your connection is somewhat slower.

Grid Layout

A *grid layout* is used to achieve different layouts by dividing the space for blocks on a page. They look similar to HTML tables, so you can align elements into rows and columns; but a grid doesn't have a content structure, so it's far more flexible than tables. The combination of media queries and the CSS that controls a grid layout means that different layouts can be defined, depending on the screen size and the orientation of a device.

Using Grid Layout

Before proceeding to enhancing the other pages, you need to understand the way jQuery Mobile implements a grid layout. By using the grid layout, it is possible to build pages with two to five columns. Grids are not specified using special data attributes, but by simply using plain-old CSS classes. The base is a `ui-grid` class, which uses up all the space, so it is defined as 100% width, with no borders, margins, or padding. The `ui-grid` class has four swatches ("a" to "d"), each representing a two- to five-column layout.

So the class `ui-grid-a` results in two columns that are evenly spread. Similarly, `ui-grid-c` gives you four columns, each taking up 25% of the available space. Thus, the following code is the definition of a four-column layout:

```
<div class="ui-grid-c">
    Your four column content
</div>
```

The next step is to define what goes into which column. That can be done using the `ui-block` class. As with the `ui-grid` class, you can use the swatches to define the column. `ui-block-c` would be the third column.

```
<div class="ui-grid-c">
    <div class="ui-block-a">First column</div>
    <div class="ui-block-b">Second column</div>
    <div class="ui-block-c">Third column</div>
    <div class="ui-block-d">Fourth column</div>
</div>
```

Keep in mind that when working with a mobile phone's limited screen estate, four columns might be the maximum usable. But that also depends on the width and the height—and even the type—of the content of the columns.

A new row (speaking in table terminology) is defined by a new element with the `ui-block-a` class. So the code in Listing 4-2 will result in a page, as shown in Figure 4-5.

Listing 4-2. A Four-Column Grid Layout

```
<!DOCTYPE html>
<html>
 <head>
  <link rel="stylesheet"
        href="http://code.jquery.com/mobile/1.1.1/jquery.mobile-1.1.1.min.css" />
  <script src="http://code.jquery.com/jquery-1.7.1.min.js"></script>
  <script src="http://code.jquery.com/mobile/1.1.1/jquery.mobile-1.1.1.min.js"></script>
  <style>* { font-size: 50px }</style>
 </head>
```

```
<body>
  <div data-role="page">
    <div data-role="header" data-position="fixed">Grid Header</div>
    <div data-role="content">
      <div class="ui-grid-c">
        <div class="ui-block-a">Row1-Col1</div>
        <div class="ui-block-b">Row1-Col2</div>
        <div class="ui-block-c">Row1-Col3</div>
        <div class="ui-block-d">Row1-Col4</div>
        <div class="ui-block-a">Row2-Col1</div>
        <div class="ui-block-b">Row2-Col2</div>
        <div class="ui-block-a">Row3-Col1</div>
      </div>
    </div>
    <div data-role="footer" data-position="fixed">Grid Footer</div>
  </div>
</body>
</html>
```

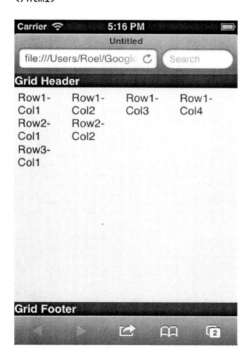

Figure 4-5. *A four-column grid layout*

Although grid classes are usually applied to div elements, you can apply it to any container element—such as a fieldset, for example.

When we contain the contents of all elements inside a div with two classes—ui-bar (to apply some default inside padding) and ui-bar-b (for the background gradient and font styling) and add an inline style for the height and the padding—you can clearly see how nicely the grid is laid out.

So replace this:

```
<div class="ui-block-a">Row1-Col1</div>
```

With this:

```
<div class="ui-block-a">
  <div class="ui-bar ui-bar-b" style="height:200px;margin:10px;">Row1-Col1</div>
</div>
```

Repeat that for the other content. The result will look like what's shown in Figure 4-6.

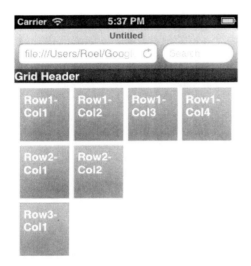

Figure 4-6. *A four-column grid layout with styling*

Finally, you are not limited to the standard, even distribution of the columns. You can specify a different width on each cell (see the example in Listing 4-3 and the result in Figure 4-7).

Listing 4-3. A Four-Column Grid with Uneven Distribution of the Cells

```
<div class="ui-grid-c">
 <div class="ui-block-a" style="width:20%;">
  <div class="ui-bar ui-bar-b" style="height:200px;margin:10px;">Row1-Col1</div>
 </div>
 <div class="ui-block-b" style="width:20%;">
  <div class="ui-bar ui-bar-b" style="height:200px;margin:10px;">Row1-Col2</div>
 </div>
```

```
<div class="ui-block-c" style="width:40%;">
  <div class="ui-bar ui-bar-b" style="height:200px;margin:10px;">Row1-Col3</div>
</div>
<div class="ui-block-d" style="width:20%;">
  <div class="ui-bar ui-bar-b" style="height:200px;margin:10px;">Row1-Col4</div>
</div>
<div class="ui-block-a" style="width:34%;">
  <div class="ui-bar ui-bar-b" style="height:200px;margin:10px;">Row2-Col1</div>
</div>
<div class="ui-block-b" style="width:66%;">
  <div class="ui-bar ui-bar-b" style="height:200px;margin:10px;">Row2-Col2</div>
</div>
<div class="ui-block-a" style="width:50%;">
  <div class="ui-bar ui-bar-b" style="height:200px;margin:10px;">Row3-Col1</div>
</div>
</div>
```

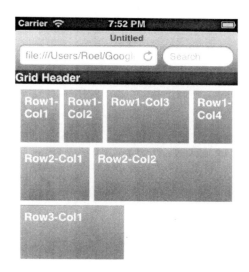

Figure 4-7. A four-column grid with uneven distribution of the cells

Using Grid Layout in APEX

In every region and item definition in APEX, you can find a Grid Layout region. These settings control the generation of the HTML that is doing the grid magic.

As long as you keep the default settings of Start New Row as "Yes" and Column as "Automatic", there is no grid layout generated, because it is not needed. Grid generation starts when you set either the Start New Row to "No" for an item and/or when you set the Column to a value higher than 1 (see Figure 4-8).

Figure 4-8. *The Grid Layout region*

Let's look at our Edit Customer form. When you change the setting of the CUST_LAST_NAME item to Start New Row = "No", Column = "Automatic", and New Column = "Yes" (the two last settings are the same as setting only Column to "2"), you'll notice that both CUST_FIRST_NAME and CUST_LAST_NAME are rendered next to each other (see Figure 4-9).

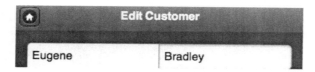

Figure 4-9. *Customer first and last name in a grid layout*

When you inspect the generated HTML, you'll see code like Listing 4-4, which should look familiar to you now.

Listing 4-4. *Grid Layout Generated by APEX*

```
<div class="ui-grid-a apex-grid-debug">
  <div class="ui-block-a">
    ..content..
  </div>
  <div class="ui-block-b">
     ..content..
  </div>
  .. more divs with class "ui-block-a"
</div>
```

You can probably figure out quite easily how to position three items—like City, State, and Postal Code—on the same row. But you need to start a new grid on the first item; otherwise, you'll end up with three columns for your whole page.

You might be wondering whether or not you can implement a more flexible grid layout. Because, in our example, the first and last names are evenly distributed: both get 50% of the available space. But, because a first name is usually shorter than a last name, how can you implement a 40% to 60%—or any other distribution?

In order to accomplish that, we need to make a tiny adjustment to the Page template. In the Grid Layout section of the Page template, there is a Column Template property. By default, this is set to

```
<div class="ui-block-#COLUMN_ALPHA#">#CONTENT#</div>
```

When you compare this HTML code to the code used in Listing 4-3, this is exact the spot that we need to add a `style="width:40%;"` setting. Therefore, you have to add the `#ATTRIBUTES#` substitution string to that HTML code. There are a lot more available substitution strings (see the available online help for the Column Property). So, the Column Property should be set to

```
<div class="ui-block-#COLUMN_ALPHA#" #ATTRIBUTES#>#CONTENT#</div>
```

At runtime, the `#ATTRIBUTES#` string will be replaced by anything you define as Column Attributes for your page item. To make the difference even clearer, let's define a 20%/80% distribution. Set the Column Attributes for the CUST_FIRST_NAME item to "20%" (see Figure 4-10) and the CUST_LAST_NAME item to "80%".

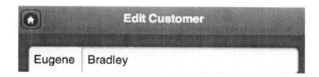

Figure 4-10. *Use Column Attributes to get a flexible grid layout*

You should now get an uneven distribution of both name fields, as seen in Figure 4-11. You can clearly spot the differences between it and Figure 4-9. And now you've got the tools to create every grid layout that you need!

Figure 4-11. *Customer first and last name in a flexible grid layout*

Collapsible Content

One way to optimize the use of the limited screen estate on mobile browsers is with *collapsible elements*, in which some information on the screen is hidden but it is present in the HTML, so it can be revealed without a roundtrip to the server.

Using Collapsible Content

With jQuery Mobile, using collapsible content is a breeze. By embedding the content in a container and adding the `data-role="collapsible"` attribute to the container, you'll get a collapsible header that expands when you click it. The necessary HTML is shown in Listing 4-5.

Listing 4-5. HTML Code for a Collapsible Element

```
<div data-role="collapsible" data-collapsed="true">
  ... collapsed content ...
</div>
```

It is also possible to group collapsible elements into a group, thus creating a collapsible set. This acts as an *accordion*-style element: expanding one automatically collapses any others. HTML-wise, this can be done by embedding a series of collapsible elements in another element with the data-role-"collapsible-set" attribute. Listing 4-6 shows some example code.

Listing 4-6. HTML Code for an Accordion-Style Collapsible Set

```
<div data-role="collapsible-set">
  <div data-role="collapsible" data-collapsed="true">
    ... collapsed content ...
  </div>
  <div data-role="collapsible" data-collapsed="true">
    ... more collapsed content ...
  </div>
  <div data-role="collapsible" data-collapsed="true">
    ... even more collapsed content ...
  </div>
</div>
```

Using Collapsible Content in APEX

APEX supports this jQuery Mobile feature very well. In your Edit Customer form, create three additional HTML regions: Address, Contact, and Other. Move the five address-related items to the Address region; the e-mail, URL, and phone items to the Contact region; and the tags item to the Other region. For all three regions, set the Parent region to the region containing the First and Last Name items (you might want to rename that one to "Customer") and the template to "Collapsible Normal (closed)". When you run the page, you'll get three collapsible blocks that you can open independently of each other. You can also embed a collapsible region into another collapsible region by setting the Parent region of a collapsible region to another region that is also collapsible.

To create a collapsible group, create another HTML region (name it something like "Collapsible Set"), and set the Parent template to the Customer region and the template to "Collapsible Set". Next, change the Parent region of the three collapsible regions from "Customer" to this "Collapsible Set". You get the nice-looking grouping with accordion functionality (see Figure 4-12).

Figure 4-12. *Collapsible set*

You can style the collapsible regions by specifying additional "data-" attributes in the Region Attributes property of the region:

- Using the data-iconpos attribute, you can position the icon on the top, right, or bottom of the region.

- With the data-theme attribute, you can set the header color of the collapsible region to one of the other swatch colors (by default, "a" to "e").

- The most interesting is the data-content-theme attribute. When you set that attribute (by setting the Region Attribute of the Collapsible Set region to data-content-theme="b"), the content of the expanded collapsible region looks as if it really belongs to the region header, as shown in Figure 4-13 (here, all prompts and used placeholders are removed, as we did for the login page).

Figure 4-13. Collapsible region with the data-content-theme attribute set

HTML5 Input Elements

HTML5 has several new input types for forms. These new features allow better input control and validation. When your cursor enters an input field on a mobile browser, it automatically pops up with a virtual keyboard. That is just fine for the regular text fields. But when you require a number field, a URL, or an e-mail address, you always have to switch to another keyboard using the lower-left key. An HTML5 browser can present the right keyboard for certain item types when you tell it what it is.

For the CUST_EMAIL item, go to the Settings region and select E-Mail as the Subtype (see Figure 4-14).

Figure 4-14. HTML5 element settings

When you run the page and navigate to the E-mail field, you'll see that the "space" key is replaced by a smaller "space" key, an @ key, and a dot key. This enables your users to input an e-mail address without having to switch the keyboard. Something similar happens when you set the Subtype for the URL item to "URL" and the Subtypes of both Phone Number items to "Phone Number".

Under the hood, the `type` attribute of the generated HTML is different: instead of the standard `type="text"`, APEX generates `type="email"`, `type="url"` or `type="tel"`. This setting is interpreted by your mobile browser to show a different keyboard (see Figure 4-15).

Figure 4-15. *Showing the virtual telephone keyboard for a Phone Number item*

You might have noticed that "Number" wasn't one of the subtypes in the select list. Let's assume CUST_POSTAL_CODE requires a numeric input; you would expect setting the Display As property of that item to "Number Field" would do the trick. But alas, that doesn't work. However, when you set the Format Mask property to "99999", you do get the numeric virtual keyboard! This "trick" only works for format masks that contain neither group nor decimal separators. Under the covers, the input field is still generated with the `type="text"` attribute, but now there is also a `pattern="[0-9]*"` attribute added, which tells the browser only the characters 0 to 9 are allowed.

Another way to accomplish this is by defining the item as a Number Field, but instead of using the format mask, execute this piece of JavaScript when the page is loaded:

```
$('.number_field').each(function(){this.type="number";})
```

This sets the `type` attribute of all fields with the `number_field` class (which it gets by defining it as a Number Field) to `"number"`. The effect is that, instead of a telephone number keyboard, a full-blown numeric keyboard is shown (see Figure 4-16).

Figure 4-16. *A numeric field showing the full-blown numeric keyboard*

■ **Tip** To execute this piece of JavaScript, it might be useful to create a Dynamic Action on page 0 that fires this piece of JavaScript on the Page Load event.

In Figure 4-16, you see that we aligned all fields closely together. This was done by adding a few additional classes, very similar to the input.first-row and input.last-row classes we already had. You also might notice that the last column of the third row doesn't completely match. That is solved by adding the following CSS snippet:

```
/* Fix the width of the third column in a three column grid so it adds up to a 100%
*/
div.ui-grid-b  div.ui-block-c
{
  width : 34%;
}
```

You could use the Column Attributes to set the width, but by using the CSS, it is automatically fixed for all three column rows.

Other Mobile Input Elements

Apart from the regular input elements, whether they are HTML5-specific or just regular HTML input elements, jQuery Mobile offers a few widgets to enhance the user experience.

Slider

Besides using a virtual keyboard to enter a number, you can also use a slider widget. The CREDIT_LIMIT item is an excellent candidate for a slider implementation. As you can imagine, Postal Code makes less sense (even when you're sure it is always numeric).

To use this in your application, navigate to the CREDIT_LIMIT item and set Display As to "Slider". Make sure to set Start New Grid to "Yes", otherwise the slider will be rendered within 50% of the screen width because of the definition of the 50%/50% columns for the First and Last Name. You should also check the settings of the slider to handle the values currently stored in the database. So the Minimum and Maximum value should be 0 and 10,000, respectively. Increasing and decreasing by steps of 100 should be fine. Highlight can be set to "Yes" for better visibility. And if you want, for a nicer effect you can set the HTML Form Element Attributes to `data-mini="true"`.

Select List

In our form, the CUST_STATE is still a regular input field. Let's change that to a Select List, using

```
select state_name, st from demo_states
```

as the SQL for the LOV definition. When you run the page, it doesn't look that good because the screen estate is way too small to render the full name of the state in the third column. Your first solution would probably be to Set Start New Row to "Yes." But that wouldn't help that much because the field will render within the first 50% column. So you need to specify to use a new grid for this item.

To keep your form easy on the eye, you should consider setting the HTML Form Element Attributes to `data-theme="c"` in order to replace the blue of the Select List with a nice-looking gray. You might even test whether you fancy the addition of `data-mini="true"` to that property to get a more subtle effect. And with an additional snippet of CSS (see Listing 4-7), the Select List will blend in nicely within the rest of the screen layout. Note the element ID is hard-coded, so you should change it to the ID that matches yours. It would have been better to use the HTML Form Element CSS `Classes` property, but the classes entered there are ignored during runtime (which is actually a bug in jQuery Mobile that might be fixed in version 1.4).

Listing 4-7. CSS to Style the Select List

```
/*
  Fix the Select List styling : Same rounded corners and border color
*/
#P28_CUST_STATE-button
{
 -webkit-border-radius : 0em 0em 0.4em 0.4em;
 border-radius         : 0em 0em 0.4em 0.4em;
 border-color          : #999;
}
```

This Select List is rendered as a popup page. By default, a smaller-sized Select List (10 entries or less) is rendered as a native Select List.

With that, our Edit Customer form is almost finished. We still need to enhance the look of the buttons at the bottom of the form. Enhancing the navigation items will be covered in depth in the next chapter. For now, set the Button template of the first button at the bottom of the form to "Button - First of ControlGroup" and likewise to the last one. The result should be similar to Figure 4-17.

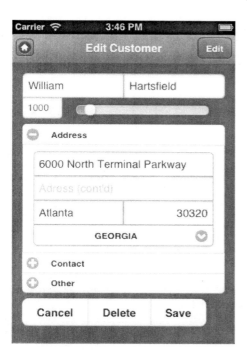

Figure 4-17. *The Edit Customer form with all its features*

Radio Group

Let's move to the Edit Product form. Because uploading images is not supported on all mobile devices, we will just show the product image on this page. So change the Display As property of the PRODUCT_IMAGE item from "File Browse" to "Display Image" and set the Filename Column and BLOB Last Updated Column in the Settings region to the correct values. Setting the Label to "No Label" isn't sufficient for this item type to remove the label from the output, so you have to clear the Label property. Also, hide the MIMETYPE, FILENAME, and IMAGE_LAST_UPDATE items.

The CATEGORY item is an excellent candidate to show as a Radio Group. The LOV for this item can be defined as either static or as an SQL query, as follows:

```
select distinct category d, category r from demo_product_info
```

Also, for optimal use of the limited screen estate, set the HTML Form Element Attributes property to data-mini="true". If you want a more consistent look and feel, you can add CSS to set the rounding on the top and bottom elements of the Radio Group to match the rounding on the other elements (see Listing 4-8).

Listing 4-8. Setting the Rounding on the Radio Group Element

```
/* Tweak Radio Group settings
*/
.ui-corner-bottom {
 -moz-border-radius-bottomleft        : .4em;
 -webkit-border-bottom-left-radius    : .4em;
 border-bottom-left-radius            : .4em;
 -moz-border-radius-bottomright       : .4em;
```

```
  -webkit-border-bottom-right-radius  : .4em;
  border-bottom-right-radius          : .4em;
}

.ui-corner-top
{
  -moz-border-radius-topleft          : .4em;
  -webkit-border-top-left-radius      : .4em;
  border-top-left-radius              : .4em;
  -moz-border-radius-topright         : .4em;
  -webkit-border-top-right-radius     : .4em;
  border-top-right-radius             : .4em;
}
```

Flip Toggle Switch

The Edit Product form contains a candidate for a Flip toggle switch. Change the Display As property of the PRODUCT_AVAIL item to "Yes/No." You can keep it like that and show it with a label, but you can also make it more user-friendly by changing the values of the toggle. In order to do so, change the Settings property in the Settings region from "Use Component Settings" to "Custom" and fill in the new fields as shown in Figure 4-18.

Figure 4-18. *Customize the toggle switch*

■ **Note**   Yes/No is a component. When you want to change the component settings for all instances of a component, navigate to Shared Components, select "Component Settings" in the User Interface region, and search for the component. You can change the values and the labels of your component for the whole application. You will particularly need this feature when you are building an application in another language or when you're using a different standard for Yes/No values (like 1/0)!

When you want to tweak the setting of the toggle, you can use the CSS from Listing 4-9 to blend it in nicely.

Listing 4-9. Tweaking the Toggle Switch

```
/* Tweak toggle settings
*/
select.yes_no + div.ui-slider-switch.ui-slider-mini
{
 width       : 100%;
 height      : 34px;
 top         : 0px;
 margin-left : 0px;
}

select.yes_no + div.ui-slider.ui-slider-switch.ui-btn-corner-all,
select.yes_no + div.ui-slider.ui-slider-switch.ui-btn-corner-all
  span.ui-slider-label.ui-btn-corner-all
{
  -moz-border-radius    : 0em;
  -webkit-border-radius : 0em;
  border-radius         : 0em;
}

select.yes_no + div.ui-slider.ui-slider-switch.ui-btn-corner-all
  a.ui-slider-handle
{
  -moz-border-radius    : 0.4em;
  -webkit-border-radius : 0.4em;
  border-radius         : 0.4em;
  width                 : 30px;
  height                : 30px;
  margin-left           : -19px;
}
```

With some rearranging of the items and using the grid settings to get a better result, you should be able to get a good-looking page, like the one shown in Figure 4-19.

Figure 4-19. *The Edit Product form*

Adding Swiped Navigation

When you want to navigate from one customer to another in the Edit Customer form, you have to get back to the list and pick another one. You might be familiar with the out-of-the-box Form Pagination feature APEX offers, and we will now implement that with a mobile twist.

First, create a dummy HTML region that will hold all the buttons and items that will be added using the Form Pagination. We'll use a separate region to make it easier to hide the region as a whole because we don't need to actually see the items and buttons that will be rendered.

Then, create a new Form Pagination process on the Edit Customer form and base it on the DEMO_CUSTOMER table. Select the dummy region you've just created as the Region To Include Navigation and CUST_LAST_NAME as the Row Navigation Order (see Figure 4-20).

Page:	28 - Edit Customer
Table Owner:	DEMO
Table Name:	DEMO_CUSTOMERS
* Region to Include Navigation	Dummy (80) ⬍
Row Navigation Order	CUST_LAST_NAME ⬍
Secondary Navigation Order	- Select Sort Column 2 - ⬍

Figure 4-20. *Defining the Form Pagination process*

When you now run the Edit Customer form, you'll see the (big) navigation buttons and a counter are added to the page. We will use these navigation buttons in a Dynamic Action. To make it easier to do so, add a Static ID that is equal to the Button Name to both button definitions, as shown in Figure 4-21.

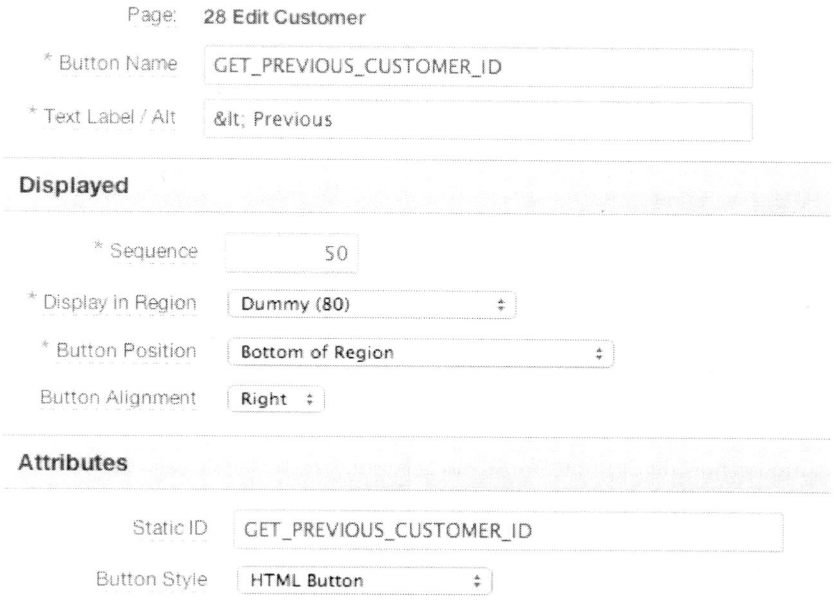

Page: 28 Edit Customer

* Button Name: GET_PREVIOUS_CUSTOMER_ID

* Text Label / Alt: < Previous

Displayed

* Sequence: 50

* Display in Region: Dummy (80)

* Button Position: Bottom of Region

Button Alignment: Right

Attributes

Static ID: GET_PREVIOUS_CUSTOMER_ID

Button Style: HTML Button

Figure 4-21. Set the Static ID of the navigation buttons

Now we only have to define two Dynamic Actions: one for swiping to the left to get the next customer and one for swiping to the right to get the previous customer. So define a Dynamic Action that fires on the Swipe-Left event on the Customer region (see Figure 4-22).

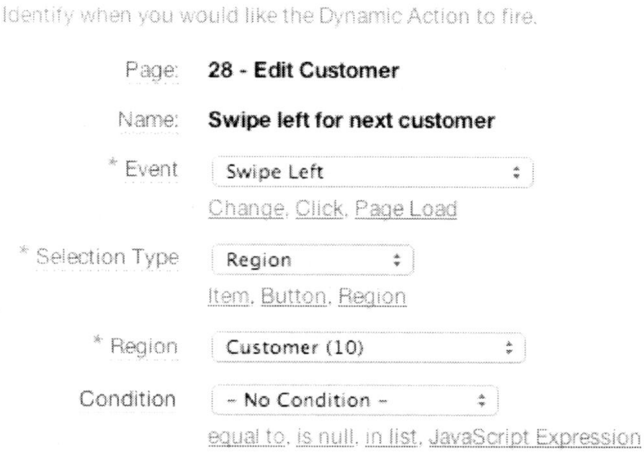

Identify when you would like the Dynamic Action to fire.

Page: 28 - Edit Customer

Name: Swipe left for next customer

* Event: Swipe Left
Change, Click, Page Load

* Selection Type: Region
Item, Button, Region

* Region: Customer (10)

Condition: - No Condition -
equal to, is null, in list, JavaScript Expression

Figure 4-22. Define Swipe-Left event on Customer region

The Action part of the Dynamic Action definition is the execution of a piece of JavaScript (uncheck Fire On Page Load; otherwise, you might get very unwanted behavior) in which we mimic a press on the Next button:

```
apex.event.trigger('#GET_NEXT_CUSTOMER_ID','click');
```

Repeat these steps for the Swipe-Right event and the Previous button. The only thing we need to do now is hide the dummy region. Because we still need the actual items and code from that region, we can't use a condition to hide it because it wouldn't render at all. So we need to add `style="display:none;"` to the Region Attributes of the dummy region. When that is not enough to hide the region, inspect the template used for the region, because in the standard setup the `#REGION_ATTRUBUTES#` substitution string is missing in the template. The template should start with something like this:

```
<div id="#REGION_STATIC_ID#" #REGION_ATTRIBUTES#>
```

Now you can navigate through your list of customers within the Edit Customer form using the more native Swipe-Left and Swipe-Right events.

Changing the Delete Confirmation Dialog

When you press the standard Delete button in the Edit Customer form, you get a confirmation dialog like the one shown in Figure 4-23.

Figure 4-23. *The standard delete confirmation dialog*

Apart from the fact that it is rather ugly, it is also very different from a more native delete confirmation. In a native application, clicking a Delete icon usually shows a confirmation dialog at the bottom of the screen. Figure 4-24 shows some examples.

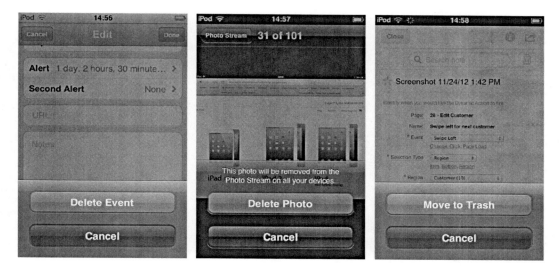

Figure 4-24. *Native iOS delete confirmation dialog*

So, if we want our APEX application to act as native as possible, how can we achieve a similar functionality? Again, as with the custom sorting on the Customer List, the SimpleDialog2 jQuery Mobile plug-in can help us. Chapter 3 explains how to incorporate this plug-in.

 Tip When you need JavaScript and CSS files in multiple pages, you can define the inclusion on every page. But you can also define the inclusion on the Global Page—and conditionally load it only on certain pages or in the Page template.

Once you make sure that the SimpleDialog2 plug-in is loaded on the Edit Customer form, change the definition of the Delete button. Set the Action to "Defined by Dynamic Action" and create a Dynamic Action that fires on a click of the Delete button. The action itself is a piece of JavaScript (see Listing 4-10). This shows another use of the SimpleDialog2 plug-in with the "button mode". The most important line is the one that contains the apex.gPageContext$ variable. Due to the implementation of the plug-in, we have to reset that variable (which contains the reference to the actual page in the DOM) to the correct value.

Listing 4-10. A New Delete Confirmation Dialog

```
$('body').simpledialog2({
    mode        : "button",
    transition  : "slideup",
    width       : "98%",
    left        : "0px",
    top         : "65%",
```

```
    buttons : {
      'Delete Customer': {
        click : function () {
                apex.gPageContext$ = apex.jQuery.mobile.activePage;
                apex.submit("DELETE");
        },
        icon  : false,
        id    : "Delete",
        theme : "a"
      },
      'Cancel': {
        click: function () {
          this.close();
          apex.gPageContext$ = apex.jQuery.mobile.activePage;
        },
        icon  : false,
        theme : "a"
      }
    }
  });
```

We only need two additional lines of CSS to make our example look good (see Listing 4-11).

Listing 4-11. CSS Tweaks to Color the Delete Button Red

```
/* Delete Dialog Tweaks
*/
div.ui-simpledialog-controls a
{
  margin : 1em;
}
a#Delete
{
  background: -webkit-linear-gradient(top, #DC7679 0%,#DC7679 49%, #CD2A27 50%, #C92A29 100%);
}
```

This CSS provides a vendor-specific color setting only for webkit browsers. When you use a different one, like Firefox, you have to add another line for that browser. When you run the Edit Customer form again and click the Delete button, you should see something very similar to Figure 4-25. You can style the background of the button region to make it look even more native, but that's up to you.

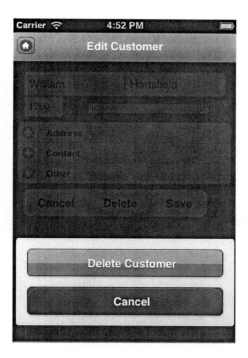

Figure 4-25. *Enhanced delete confirmation dialog*

Changing the Process Success Message

What has been said for the delete confirmation dialog also applies to the process success message. When you save an update on the Customers form, an ugly "Action Processed." message appears at the top of the Customer List, somewhat hidden behind the search bar (see Figure 4-26).

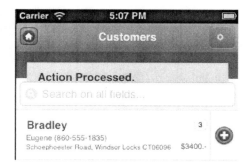

Figure 4-26. *The "Action Processed." message*

When we want to get rid of that, we can just clear the Process Success Message property in the Process Row page process or untick the "Include process success message" property in the Branch. But then we lose all the feedback to our users. So, what can we do to present nice-looking feedback?

The first thing you need is a tiny image that you want to show. Once you've found one that you like, upload it as an Application image via Shared Components. Then navigate to the Templates section of Shared Components and select the Page Type template of the theme you are using (default Theme 50 - jQuery Mobile Smartphone). Enter the Template Editor of the page and navigate down to the Subtemplate section. There you find the Success Message property. Copy the HTML code in Listing 4-12 and paste it into that area.

Listing 4-12. The New Success Message

```
<div id="tick" class="ui-popup-container ui-popup-active"
 style="position:absolute; top: 25%; left: 40%; z-index: 999; width:30%;
        text-align:center;  max-width:150px">
  <div data-role="popup" data-transition="fade" data-theme="a" data-position-to="window"
       data-shadow="true" data-corners="true" class="ui-popup ui-body-a
       ui-overlay-shadow ui-corner-all" style="padding:10%">
    <img style="width:auto;height:auto;" src="#APP_IMAGES#tick.png">
    <p>Saved</p>
  </div>
</div>
<script>
$('#tick').delay(1000).fadeOut(1000);
</script>
```

This piece of HTML will show an image, `tick.png` in the example, just above the center of the screen. After one second, the image will fade away. It should look like the screenshot shown in Figure 4-27. One of the main advantages is that this solution doesn't clutter the page like the old default solution does. It just shows a temporary notification that slowly fades away.

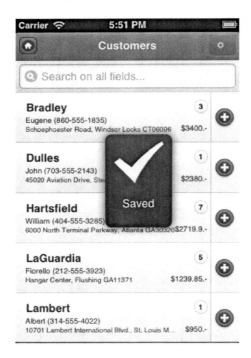

Figure 4-27. The new Success Message

Finishing the Forms

We need a few more steps to finish up our forms. Add a Plus icon in the Customer List to add a new order for the customer. If you haven't done so yet, set the Split Button Target on that list to the following (assuming page 29 is your Edit or Add Order page):

```
f?p=&APP_ID.:29:&APP_SESSION.::&DEBUG.:29:P29_CUSTOMER_ID:&CUSTOMER_ID.
```

You might want to rearrange the items on that page to get a layout similar to the one shown in Figure 4-28, where we set the "Default value" property of the ORDER_TIMESTAMP item to TO_CHAR(SYSDATE, 'YYYY-MM-DD'). You have to use that particular format mask because the HTML5 date picker expects the date value in that format. The HTML5 date input element will also always return the date with that format mask if the page is submitted. When clicking the Create An Order button, the page should branch back to itself. Also, set the HTML Form Element Attributes property of the ORDER_TOTAL item to disabled to prevent user input.

Figure 4-28. *Add Order form*

Next, add another List View region to that form (named Products), as a subregion to the Order region, which will show the order items of the current order by using the following SQL statement:

```
select product_name, unit_price, quantity, order_item_id, order_id
from demo_order_items o
    join demo_product_info p on p.product_id = o.product_id
where order_id = :P29_ORDER_ID
```

This region should have a condition with a Condition Type set to "Value of Item/Column in Expression 1 is NOT NULL" and Expression 1 to "P29_ORDER_ID", so that it will only show up when an order is created. To more easily apply styling, define a Static ID orderItems. In the Advanced section of the Region Attributes, change the "No Data Found" message to <p>You can now add products to this order<p>. You now need to define a button to navigate to the Order Items page to actually enter an Order Item record. Of course, there are many ways to do this. One of them is to define the button by specifying a link in the Region Footer of the Products region:

```
<a href="f?p=&APP_ID.:24:&SESSION.::&DEBUG.:24:P24_ORDER_ID:&P29_ORDER_ID."
   data-role       = "button"
   data-rel        = "dialog"
   data-mini       = "true"
   data-transition = "pop"
   data-theme      = "e" >
   Add a Product to this Order
</a>
```

This link is autoenhanced by jQuery Mobile as a yellow button. Clicking it shows the Order Items page (page 24) as a popup.

After applying the CSS snippet in Listing 4-13, you'll get a result like the one shown in Figure 4-29 when you press the Create An Order button.

Listing 4-13. CSS for Add Order Form

```
/* Reposition the Products/Order Items List View
*/
#orderItems_jqm_list_view
{
  margin : 0px;
}

/* Change the looks of the "No Data Found" message
*/
li.apex-no-data-found
{
  background-image : none;
  color            : white;
  background-color : #3B5998;
  text-shadow      : none;
  text-align       : center;
}
```

Figure 4-29. *Add Order form after creating an order*

Now we need to finish the Order Items page (page 24). Again, some formatting similar to the Add Order form is needed. You probably want to default the UNIT_PRICE item using a Dynamic Action to set that value using the List Price of the selected Product. Similar to the Add Order form, the Cancel button is created using an anchor in the Region Footer:

```
<a href="&HOST_URL.f?p=&APP_ID.:29:&SESSION.::&DEBUG.::P29_ORDER_ID:&P24_ORDER_ID."
    data-role      = "button"
    data-mini      = "true"
    data-direction = "reverse" >
    Cancel
</a>
```

The data-direction="reverse" attribute will result in a transition opposite of the one that was used for this page. The page could look like the one you see in Figure 4-30. Here you can also see the native Select List in action, which is used when there are 10 items or less in the list of values.

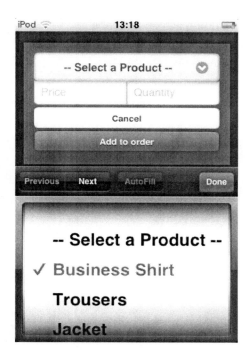

Figure 4-30. *Form to add an order item*

After submit, the page should branch back to the Add Order page and show the added order item in the Products region, as seen in Figure 4-31. You can style that List View as you learned in the previous chapter.

Figure 4-31. *The added order item*

If you're up for more exercises, you can add the following additional requirements:

- Add a button on the Add Order form to select and show a previously entered order.

- Add a button on the Edit Customer form to initially show the form in read-only mode, and make it editable after pressing that button—with a nice flip animation.

- From the Products List View, change the Plus button to an Info button, and show a report of all orders for that product.

- Anything else you can imagine.

Wrap Up

In this chapter, you learned a lot about creating forms for an APEX mobile application. You now know how to style forms to get exactly the look and feel needed by using CSS snippets and a flexible grid layout. You saw the HTML5 input types, like date pickers and number fields, as well as the jQuery Mobile input types such as collapsible content, toggles, and so forth. You even added some cool features like navigation using the swipe gestures, as well as a delete confirmation and a nice delete confirmation dialog. You also added navigation from one form to another.

In the next chapter, you will dive into navigation more deeply and will continue to enhance the application at hand.

CHAPTER 5

▧ ▧ ▧

Displaying Calendars and Charts

Until now, you learned how to handle the most common region types and items: lists, forms, and buttons. But wait, there is more! The region types that you might be familiar with on your desktop, like calendars and charts, do have a mobile version. In this chapter, we will learn how to create these types of regions and examine the differences between the desktop and the mobile versions. We will also look at other charting engines to extend the graphical possibilities of APEX. Finally, we will create a RESTful web service and use it as a data provider for one of our charts.

Calendars

Before we can start creating a calendar, we need some useful data to show. The idea is to build on top of the existing APEX Demo you are already familiar with, a very small customer relationship module. With just one additional table, demo_contacts, we are ready to go. So run the script in Listing 5-1 before continuing in either the SQL Workshop or in your favorite SQL IDE. (Keep in mind that you can download Listing 5-1 and other scripts for this book from the book's catalog page on the Apress.com web site).

Listing 5-1. SQL Script to Create a demo_contacts Table Containing Data

```
drop table demo_contacts
/
create table demo_contacts
  (
    id          number not null,
    user_name   varchar2(50) not null,
    customer_id number,
    start_date  timestamp(6) with local time zone ,
    end_date    timestamp(6) with local time zone ,
    report      varchar2(4000) ,
    done        varchar2(1) default 'N' not null ,
    constraint demo_contacts_done check (done in ('Y','N' )) ,
    constraint demo_contacts_pk primary key (id) ,
    constraint demo_contacts_customers_fk foreign key (customer_id) references demo_customers
(customer_id) on
  delete cascade enable
  )
/
create index demo_contacts_customer_ix on demo_contacts
  (customer_id
  )
/
```

```
-- Generate 30 random contact moments with customers
begin
  for i in 1..30 loop
    insert into demo_contacts
    ( id
    , user_name
    , customer_id
    , start_date
    , end_date
    , done
    , report
    )
    ( select i
      ,         NVL(:APP_USER, USER)
      ,         round(dbms_random.value(1,7)) -- Pick any of the 7 Customers
      ,         contact_date
      ,         contact_date
                + round(dbms_random.value(1,5))/48  -- Appointment lasts between .5 and 2.5 hours
      ,         case when trunc(contact_date) < trunc(sysdate)
                then 'Y'
                else 'N'
                end -- Contacts in the past are "Done"
      ,         case when trunc(contact_date) < trunc(sysdate)
                then  dbms_random.string('l', 50)
                end -- Generate random 50 character string
      from
      ( select trunc( sysdate
                    + dbms_random.value(-30,+30)
                    )                             -- A date between 30 days before/after now
               + round(dbms_random.value(7,18))/24 -- Any hour between 7AM and 6PM
               as contact_date
        from    dual
      )
    );
  end loop;
end;
/
```

Now that we've got the database structure and the data, start the APEX Create Page wizard and select the
Calendar Type page. Because we will combine data from more than one table, choose the SQL Calendar on the next
screen. On the Source page, you need to enter an SQL query with (at least) a primary key and a date column. Based on
the table you just created, use the SQL statement in Listing 5-2.

Listing 5-2. SQL Statement for the Calendar Definition

```
select id
,       user_name
,       ctt.customer_id
,       cust_first_name||' '||cust_last_name as cust_name
,       rtrim(cust_street_address1||' '|| cust_street_address2) as cust_street_address
,       cust_city||'  '||cust_state||cust_postal_code as cust_city_address
,       start_date
,       end_date
```

```
,       done
,       report
from demo_contacts ctt
  join demo_customers cust on ctt.customer_id = cust.customer_id
```

On the Calendar Attributes page, pick the START_DATE as the Date Column. You can leave the Display Column as it is, as we will change that in a minute to something more meaningful. Set the Date Format to "Date and Time" and select ID as the Primary Key Column. At Link Details, set the Link Target to "Create new edit page" and enter **DEMO_CONTACTS** as the Table, **START_DATE** as the Date Column, and include all columns in the shuttle at the bottom of the page. Proceed through the wizard and run the page. You'll see something similar to Figure 5-1.

Figure 5-1. *A calendar in monthly view*

By just going through these few steps, we get a lot in return: not only the monthly view, but also a weekly view (as shown in Figure 5-2), a daily view, and a list view of the same data. A couple navigation buttons to move to the previous or next month, week, or day are included as well.

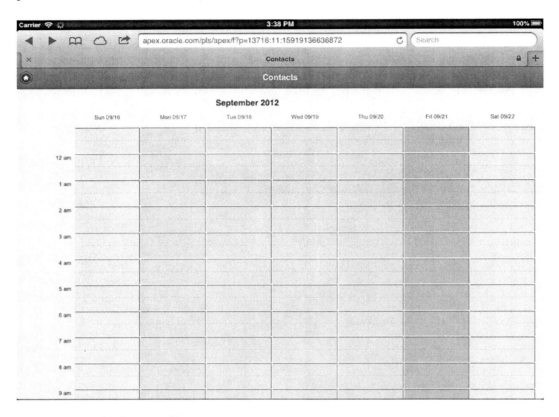

Figure 5-2. *A calendar in weekly view*

And if that was not enough, some swiping gestures are also implemented: swipe left or right for the previous or next month, week, or day. Tapping and holding a date will open an empty edit screen. Even rotating the device has an effect: the page switches from monthly to weekly view, and back—although this functionality may act differently on different devices.

When you click one of the dates with a blue dot, detailed information is shown at the bottom of the calendar. This detailed information contains the column you chose as the Display Column. The time portion of the Date Column is shown on the right side. You can enhance the looks and usability of this function by editing the Calendar page: switch to the Calendar Attributes of the Calendar Region, set the Display Type to "Custom", and the Column Format to the HTML shown in Listing 5-3.

Listing 5-3. HTML for Custom Column Format

```
<span class="ui-li-desc">
  <span style="font-weight:bold">
    #CUST_NAME#
  </span>
  <br/>
  #CUST_STREET_ADDRESS#
```

```
<br/>
#CUST_CITY_ADDRESS#
</span>
```

Reopening the monthly page and clicking one of the dates with a blue dot reveals better-looking and more informative information, as shown in Figure 5-3. This new format now also shows up in the weekly, daily, and list views.

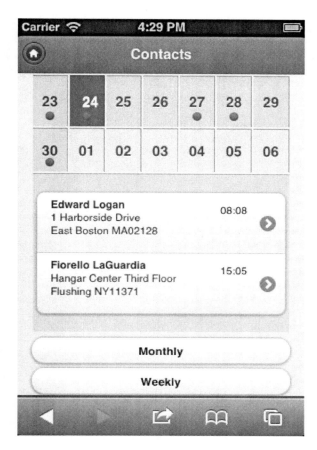

Figure 5-3. *Result of custom column formatting*

This custom column formatting applies not only to the monthly view, but is visible in the other views as well. You can define what should happen when a user clicks one of the list items you see in Figure 5-3. Usually, a transition to a detail or edit page will be expected, but apart from navigating to another page, you can call a JavaScript function—or fire up a Dynamic Action if you need it. The same link is implemented in all calendar views—sometimes as a list item, sometimes as a link on the page. When you switch to another view, you'll notice the different implementation styles.

Apart from the link on your data column, you can also define a Day link. This is implemented as a link on the day number in the calendar. For instance, this could be used for quickly adding a new record, where you default to the date you just clicked.

The last region of the Calendar Attributes is to implement drag-and-drop functionality. Because this functionality is not implemented for mobile devices, everything you enter there is ignored. In a future release, this region might even be hidden in pages designed for mobile user interfaces.

If you need more than the four views that you've already seen, there is a fifth alternative: the Custom Calendar. You can find it when you edit the Calendar template. The Calendar template is actually a set of templates, one for each view. And just like any other template, you can change it to your liking. The most extensive one is the Custom Calendar. It is meant to show a calendar between two dates (or times): Pxx_CALENDAR_DATE, which is defaulted to sysdate, and Pxx_CALENDAR_END_DATE, defaulted to sysdate + 3. So depending on the number of days between those two values, different parts of that template are used. When there are more than seven days between Pxx_CALENDAR_DATE and Pxx_CALENDAR_END_DATE, the "regular" template regions are used, resulting in a monthly type of view display. The "alternate" templates are used for a weekly type of view when the number of days is seven or less.

Within the template, you can use a lot substitution strings, many of which are mentioned in the region on the right side. But there are more, such as #START_MONTH# ,#START_MM#, #START_DD#, #START_YY#, #START_YYYY#, #START_DS#, #START_DL#, and their corresponding END values as well.

You can show this calendar view by defining a button that does a Redirect to URL with the URL Target set to `javascript:apex.widget.calendar.ajax_calendar('C','same'); void(0);`. The first parameter of that call defines the type of calendar you want to show. So apart from the "C" for Custom, accepted values are "M" for Month, "W" for Week, "D" for Daily, and "A" for List View.

Because a calendar is basically just as much an HTML document as any APEX page, you can tweak the looks by applying your own CSS settings. What is necessary to mimic the looks of the native iOS Calendar application you see in Figure 5-4?

Figure 5-4. *The native iOS Calendar application*

Let's forget the (rather cool) feature of scrolling the scheduled event behind the calendar—and concentrate on the other things. Move the Create button to the header of the page and show it as an icon. Then hide the Week button (because you can just rotate the device to get the week view), and switch the template of the Calendar Buttons region to Footer Toolbar (fixed). Now move the Previous and Next buttons to the calendar region and show them as icons. Finally, apply the CSS in Listing 5-4 to the page.

Listing 5-4. CSS for a More Native iOS Look

```
@media only screen and (max-device-width: 480px) {
.m-NonDay
{
  color              : #919EAC;
}
.apex-calendar-has-data
{
  background-size    : 25%;
  background-position : 49% 90%;
}
.m-Calendar
{
  font-size          : 130%;
  position           : relative;
  top                : -35px;
  border-spacing     : 1px;
}
.m-Calendar tr>td:first-child
{
  border-width       : 1px 1px 0px 1px;
}
.m-Calendar tr:last-child>td
{
  height             : 0px !important;
  border-left-style  : none;
  border-right-style : none;
  background-color   : #EEE;
}
.m-Calendar td
{
  padding            : 0px !important;
  height             : 40px !important;
}
div.ui-content
{
  padding-top        : 5px;
  padding-left       : 0px;
  padding-right      : 0px;
}
div#footer td:first-child div
{
margin-left          : 10px;
}
}
```

The first line of the CSS, `@media only screen and (max-device-width: 480px)`, is called a *media query*. It means that the CSS between the curly brackets is only applied to devices with a smaller screen width (not in print mode, for instance) up to 480 pixels. The "only" keyword is used to hide the style sheet for an older browser. We also could have used simply `@media (max-device-width: 480px)`. Media queries are a fundament of *responsive web design*, an approach to provide an optimal viewing experience across a wide range of devices.

After applying the CSS in Listing 5-4, you should see something that is close to Figure 5-5. Of course, you can pick other icons for the previous and next functionality and change the background colors, but I'll leave that exercise up to you.

Figure 5-5. *Month view in a more native iOS look*

When you want to change the look of an event's details at the bottom of the page, you can either edit the Data Display Format of the Monthly Calendar template or override the CSS. When that is not sufficient, you can also replace the call to `apex.widget.calendar.getDayData()` in the Monthly Calendar template to a call to your own JavaScript function. That JavaScript function should return an HTML snippet that contains the data you want to show. With some effort, you can actually accomplish almost anything.

We are lacking a view at the moment. A view shows the duration of an event, just like Outlook or Google Calendar does. It would be very useful in a daily or weekly view, because as it is now, you can't see how long an appointment is scheduled. This is a feature that will probably be added in a future release of APEX. Right now, the only solution that comes close to it is adding the duration or the end time to the Custom Display Format.

Charts

In APEX 4.2, the charting engine is upgraded from Anychart 5.1 to Anychart 6.0. Next to the familiar Flash charts, SVG is used to render HTML5 charts. Identical to desktop applications, you'll define charts for mobile applications. But when you create a new page with a chart, you see only the HTML5 chart options, as shown in Figure 5-6.

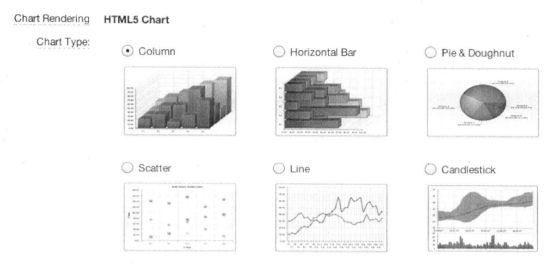

Figure 5-6. *The mobile HTML5 chart options*

With further inspection, you'll discover that the 3D column charts, the gauges, and the Gantt charts are not available for mobile applications. So instead of the 26 charts for a desktop application, you can only choose from 14 different charting options for mobile. However, after creating a chart, you can switch the Chart Rendering option to Flash Chart and the Chart Type to a 3D Column, and it will show 3D Flash when you run the page on a desktop browser. And when running that page with Flash on mobile, it automatically falls down to a corresponding HTML5 chart!

As an example, create a new mobile page with a Sales per Product chart by picking a 2D column chart and entering the SQL statement you find in Listing 5-5.

Listing 5-5. SQL Statement for Sales per Product Chart

```
select null                        as link,
       p.product_name              as product,
       SUM(i.quantity * i.unit_price) as sales
from   demo_product_info p
left outer join demo_order_items i on i.product_id = p.product_id
group by p.product_name
order by 3 desc nulls last
```

In order to render a chart on a non-retina iPhone, you have to set the Chart width and height to something like 300 × 400. Use all screen estate by setting the top and left margins to negative values: –50 and –30. Reduce the space for the x axis by setting the X-Axis Label Rotation to 70 degrees. Running the page on a small iOS device will display the chart, as seen in Figure 5-7.

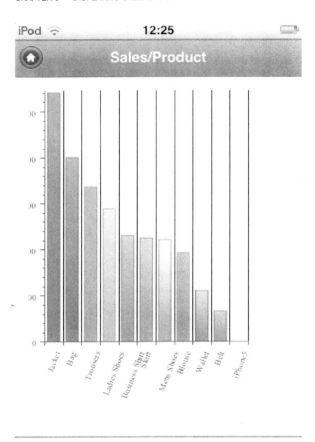

Figure 5-7. *Sales per Product HTML5 chart*

When you run the same page on a device with larger screen estate, such as a retina iPhone, iPad, or a tablet, the chart is also rendered as a 300 × 400-pixel image in the upper-left corner of the screen. To create a chart that uses the full screen estate, you need to set the height and width of the chart in percentages instead of pixels, because pixels result in a different layout on different devices. Alas, that isn't currently possible. As a workaround, we can set—or change—the width and height of the chart after the page is loaded. To accomplish this, set the Static ID of the chart region to a value such as "myChart". Next, define a Dynamic Action that runs on Page Load and executes the snippet of JavaScript you see in Listing 5-6. This code sets the width and height of the SVG element in the div with the "myChart" id to 90% instead of the fixed 300 × 400 pixels.

Listing 5-6. Change Chart Size on Page Load

```
$("div#myChart svg")
    .attr("width" , "90%")
    .attr("height", "90%");
```

Another—easier—way of scaling charts is implemented in APEX version 4.2.1: When you clear out the values for Chart Width and Chart Height (although it looks these values are required, they are not) the chart is automatically scaled to the size of your device. Even when you rotate the device, the chart is scaled correctly.

Other Options

As APEX is an open framework, any other JavaScript or HTML5 graphical solution can be added to your application. Some are very easy to embed, others will require more work. In this section, we will cover some of the most useful solutions.

Google Maps

Embedding a map is one of the most common features of a mobile application. Among all the map options, Google Maps is probably the most popular. You have to be careful when implementing a Google Map, however, because in an increasing number of cases, you need to buy an expensive license. Check the current requirements at https://developers.google.com/maps. If Google Maps is too expensive, it is worthwhile to check out OpenStreetMap (www.openstreetmap.org), which has similar features and is free to use.

For our example, we will create a simple static map using the Google Static Maps API. The only thing we need to do to display a static map, which has no interaction whatsoever, is create a page that contains an IMG tag, which has the src attribute set to a specific constructed URL. You can find all the options on the previously mentioned Google web page. First, check whether your database user is allowed to make a connection to the outside world; there might be limitations from firewalls or access control listing (ACL) settings. Overcoming this issue is beyond the scope of this book, but there are many good resources online that can help you out.

In order to serve all possible device widths and heights, first create an HTML region with no template on the Global Page for the jQuery Mobile Smartphone interface. Create two hidden fields in that region: **P0_DEVICE_WIDTH** and **P0_DEVICE_HEIGHT**, with Value Protected set to No. Next, create a Dynamic Action that fires on Page Load and executes the JavaScript snippet you find in Listing 5-7.

Listing 5-7. Setting the Device Width and Height

```
$s('P0_DEVICE_WIDTH' , Math.round( .9 * window.innerWidth  ));
$s('P0_DEVICE_HEIGHT', Math.round( .8 * window.innerHeight ));
```

Now create a new SQL report page, where we will show the locations of our customers on the map. Use the SQL statement shown in Listing 5-8.

Listing 5-8. SQL Statement for the Google Map with the Customer Locations

```
select '<img src="http://maps.googleapis.com/maps/api/staticmap?'        ||
       'size=&P0_DEVICE_WIDTH.x&P0_DEVICE_HEIGHT.&maptype=roadmap'        ||
       listagg('&markers=color:blue|label:'||substr(cust_last_name,1,1) ||'|'||
               replace(cust_street_address1 ||
                      ','||cust_city||'+'  ||
                      cust_state||cust_postal_code
                      ,' ','+')
              ,'|') within group (order by cust_state)                   ||
       '&sensor=false" />'
       as "Address"
from demo_customers
```

Note the HTML substitution strings &P0_DEVICE_WIDTH. and &P0_DEVICE_HEIGHT. in the SQL statement. When the statement is executed, these will be replaced with the values calculated on the Global Page. The analytical LISTAGG function is used to create one long string of all the customer addresses. All the formatting is done according to the Google Map Static API descriptions, including the use of the "|" separator and the escaping of blanks. Set the Display As property of the Address column to Standard Report Column; otherwise, you will just see a piece of HTML.

Running this on a small device shows you a nice overview of all the customer locations, as shown in Figure 5-8.

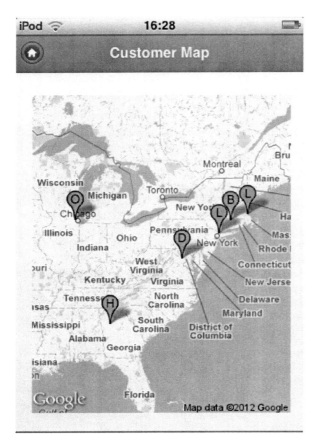

Figure 5-8. *Static Google Map with customer locations*

When you run the same page on a device with larger screen estate, you'll immediately notice that the map is not displayed full screen. This is one of the limitations of the free Map API: it is limited to 640 × 640 pixels. More complex examples of Google Maps will be discussed in Chapter 9.

Highcharts

Another option for creating HTML5 charts is Highcharts (www.highcharts.com). Be aware, depending on the type of application you are building, you might need to buy a license. Highcharts offers a very impressive API for customizing the look and feel of your charts. For easy of use in an APEX environment, you can also buy the NFCharts APEX Plugin from APEX Evangelists.

Using that plug-in and the same SQL statement that we used in the Sales per Product chart, we can get a Highcharts example (see Figure 5-9) up and running in just a few minutes. Highcharts handles the scaling of the charts very well, so no additional effort is required to render a chart on different devices.

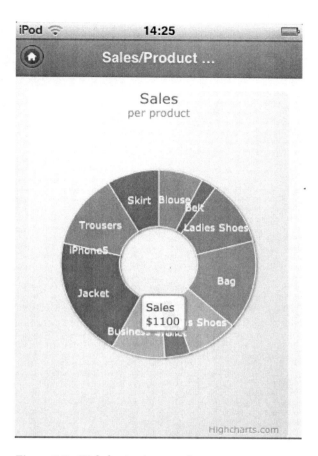

Figure 5-9. Highcharts pie example

Although the previous example might not be very exciting, you can create something similar using the native APEX chart options. You can also create charts with multiple series and an auto refresh. This gives you the opportunity to create an interactive real-time chart, as seen in Figure 5-10.

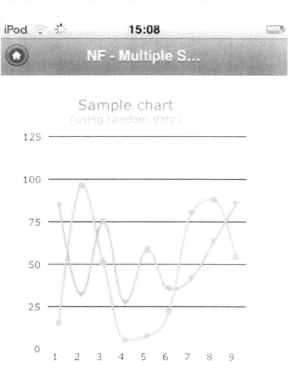

Figure 5-10. *Multiple series, real time—Highcharts example*

Flotcharts

Flotcharts (www.flotcharts.org) is another external charting library that runs very well on mobile devices. Its advantage over Highcharts is that it is free of cost. The disadvantage is that there is no APEX plug-in available yet, so we need to do all the coding ourselves. As with many other charting libraries, such as Sencha Touch Charts, a Flotcharts chart can be fed with JSON data. In this example, we will use the RESTful services that come with APEX 4.2 and are supported by the APEX Listener 2.0 to generate the JSON data and feed the result into the chart. As you can see in the Flotcharts documentation, it expects the JSON data in a fixed layout. So the challenge is to create a JSON string that works with Flotcharts.

First, create a new RESTful services module and fill in the Name, URI Prefix, and URI Template fields, as shown in Figure 5-11. Define a GET method as a Resource Handler and set the Source Type to PL/SQL. We might be able to use just a query, but then we have to do more coding on the JavaScript side. And because I assume you are more comfortable using PL/SQL, let's do the heavy lifting on that side.

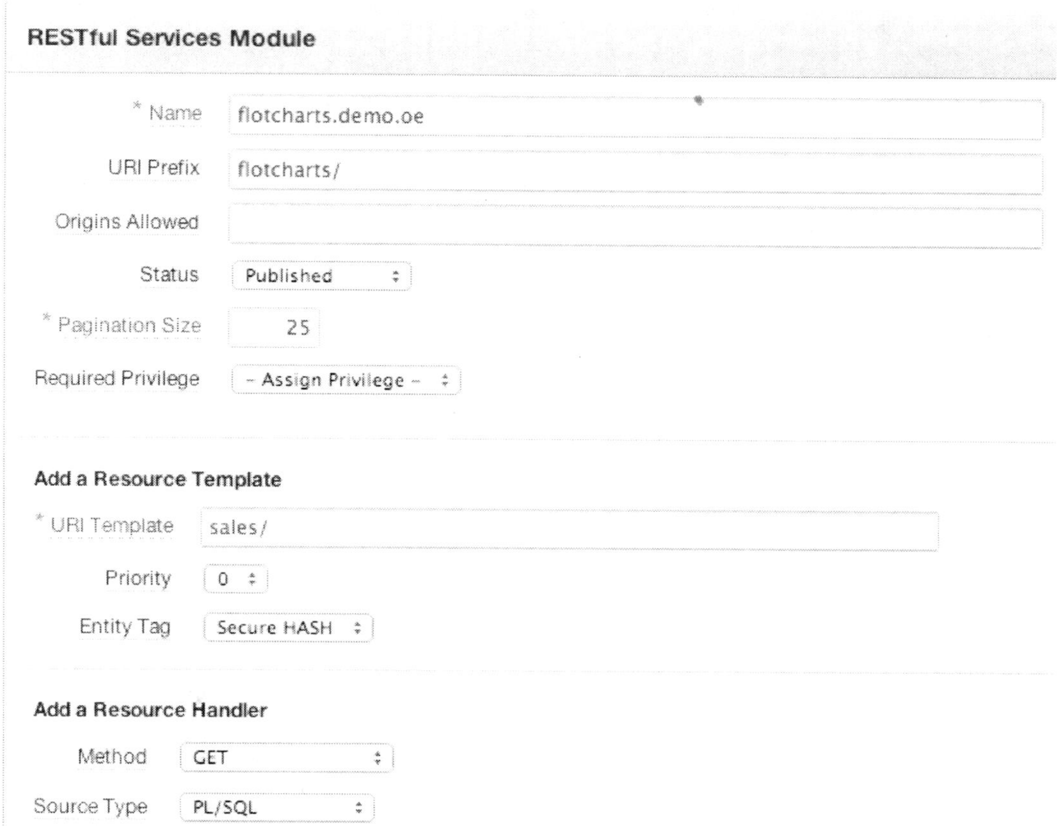

RESTful Services Module

* Name	flotcharts.demo.oe
URI Prefix	flotcharts/
Origins Allowed	
Status	Published ⬍
* Pagination Size	25
Required Privilege	– Assign Privilege – ⬍

Add a Resource Template

* URI Template	sales/
Priority	0 ⬍
Entity Tag	Secure HASH ⬍

Add a Resource Handler

Method	GET ⬍
Source Type	PL/SQL ⬍

Figure 5-11. *RESTful web service definition*

You can copy the PL/SQL that we need for a correct JSON string from Listing 5-9. After saving the RESTful web service definition, you have to change the Requires Secure Access property of the Resource Handler to No. Save that change and press the Test button. When it all works out, you'll get a URL, such as `http://apex.oracle.com/pls/apex/wsdemo/flotcharts/sales/`, and the resulting JSON string. Copy the URL, because we will need it when we call the web service using an Ajax request.

Listing 5-9. PL/SQL Source of the RESTful web service

```
declare
 cursor productsales is
  select p.product_name    as label,
         p.product_id||','||SUM(i.quantity * i.unit_price) as data,
         count(*) over () total
  from    demo_product_info p
  left outer join demo_order_items i on i.product_id = p.product_id
  group by p.product_name, p.product_id
  order by p.product_id;
begin
  sys.htp.prn('[');
```

```
  for r in productsales loop
    sys.htp.prn('{"label":"'||r.label||'","data":[['||r.data||']]}');
    if productsales%rowcount < r.total
    then sys.htp.prn(',');
    end if;
  end loop;
  sys.htp.prn(']');
end;
```

The "wsdemo" part of the URL is configurable via Administration ➤ Manage Service ➤ Set Workspace Preferences. In the SQL Workshop region, you can change the Path Prefix to something else (see Figure 5-12). The default value is the short name of the workspace.

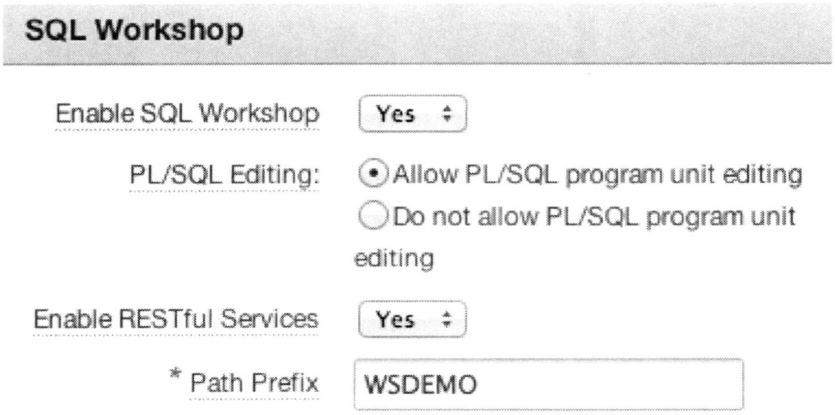

Figure 5-12. *Setting the path prefix of the RESTful web service*

Back to the application side, first download the Flotchart JavaScript library and upload it to the APEX Static Files or your web server. Then, create a new HTML page with an HTML region. The Region Source is just a placeholder for the Flotchart, so enter `<div id="placeholder"></div>` there. Next, edit the page and include the Flotchart JavaScript library by entering `#APP_IMAGES#jquery.flot.js` in the File URL's region when you uploaded the library as a static application file, or use another correct reference to the location of that library. In Execute When Page Loads, we use the JavaScript code from Listing 5-10 to get the JSON data and plot the chart. Note that you need to change the URL in the Ajax call to a URL that points to your own RESTful web service. You can see the result when running the page in Figure 5-13.

Listing 5-10. JavaScript Code for Calling the RESTful Web Service and Plotting the Flotchart

```
// Set Width and Height of the chart to full screen
$("#placeholder")
    .css("width" , Math.round( .9 * window.innerWidth )+"px")
    .css("height", Math.round( .8 * window.innerHeight )+"px")
    ;

// Set the Flotchat options
var options = {
    bars   : { show: true },
```

```
    points : { show: false },
    xaxis  : { ticks:[[]] }
};

// Callback function : plot the chart using the JSON result string
function onDataReceived( data ){
    apex.jQuery.plot( $("#placeholder"), data, options);
}
// Call our RESTful webservice
apex.jQuery.ajax({
    url      : '/pls/apex/wsdemo/flotcharts/sales/',
    method   : 'GET',
    dataType : 'json',
    success  : onDataReceived
});
```

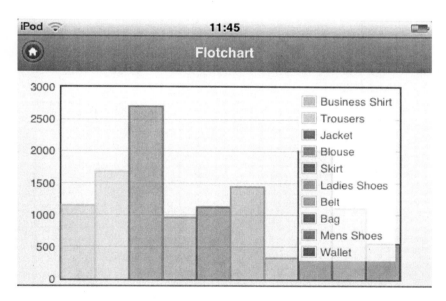

***Figure 5-13.** A Flotchart using a RESTful web service*

Wrap Up

In this chapter, we learned about a region type other than the regular lists, reports, or forms. We saw the Calendar Region type with all its templates, and learned how to tweak and tune the looks to our liking. We discussed the APEX native charts, as well as other external charting engines like Google Maps, Highcharts, and Flotcharts. We even learned how to define a RESTful web service and how to use this web service as a data provider for a chart.

CHAPTER 6

Implementing a Navigation Standard

You have created lists, forms, and other region types. It is about time to provide users a decent way to access these pages. In this chapter, you will start with creating an icon for your mobile device to access the application. Next, you will build a springboard menu to offer initial navigation in the application. After that, you will define quick-link icons at the bottom of the screen. And last but not least, you will build a Facebook-style slide menu.

Let's start by defining an icon on the home screen of the device and showing a splash screen.

Getting More Native

To get a more native feel when we run our web application—one that runs inside a browser, we can define a link to our application on the home screen of the device. The exact way to do that differs per device, but usually it is hidden under the Bookmark feature.

Of course, we don't want a link using a random screenshot of one of the pages, but one using our own icon. We can accomplish that by defining the following between the head tags of the Page template used for the mobile application:

```
<link rel="apple-touch-icon" href="#APP_IMAGES#Directory.png" />
```

The href attribute should point to the icon you want to show. Despite the name, Android also has apple-touch-icon support. For older Android versions (1.5 and 1.6), you need to use the keyword apple-touch-icon-precomposed instead of apple-touch-icon. And if that doesn't work on your Android device, you can use the following:

```
<link rel="shortcut icon" href="#APP_IMAGES#Directory.png" />
```

iOS adds its own styling to the icon: rounded corners, a polished shine, and a drop shadow. When you feel your icon is better-looking without these autoenhancements, use the keyword apple-touch-icon-precomposed instead. After adding the icon to our home screen and defining the title, our home screen now looks similar to Figure 6-1.

Figure 6-1. *Home screen with our own icon*

When you want to support different devices with different icon sizes and you are not too happy with the automatic scaling the device does, you need to use the `sizes` keyword in the link definition. So the code will be something like:

```
<link rel="apple-touch-icon"                      href="#APP_IMAGES#Directory.png" />
<link rel="apple-touch-icon" sizes="72x72"    href="#APP_IMAGES#Directory-72x72.png" />
<link rel="apple-touch-icon" sizes="144x144" href="#APP_IMAGES#Directory-144x144.png" />
```

A device like the Retina iPad and iPhone will use a 144 × 144 icon size. An iPad 1 and 2 will use the 72 × 72 icon. Any other device will use the original 57 × 57. There is much on the Internet about the use of icons, such as how to design a good icon or how to create resizable images. Apple's developer documentation is a good place to start (http://goo.gl/pn9VQ).

The main advantage of using a link on the home screen is to get rid of the standard browser header and footer bars. So you get more screen estate and your web application looks very native.

With a similar directive, you can also add a launch image that shows during startup:

```
<link rel="apple-touch-startup-image" href="#APP_IMAGES#Directory.png" />
```

Take note that this file needs to exactly match the device's size, so you need a couple of sizes—from 320 × 480 for the iPhone/iPod up to 1536 × 2008 for an iPad Retina. The image should be a `.png` file. Also, this only works if `apple-mobile-web-app-capable` is set to "Yes", which is in the default in your Page template. So when you start your application from the home screen, you'll see a picture like the one shown in Figure 6-2 (the one that you uploaded is likely better) and for a longer or shorter period—depending on the time it takes to show the login screen. Alas, at the moment, this only works on Apple devices, but not others, like Android.

Figure 6-2. *An application splash screen showing a launch image*

Creating Your Own Springboard

Typically, a *springboard* is what is referenced as the home screen of a mobile device in order to access all installed applications. But you can create your own springboard to provide access to the different functions within that application. A springboard is usually made up of images that link to certain pages. You can enhance those images by showing certain alerts. And that is exactly what we are going to do right now!

Setting Up Your Springboard

On page 1, the home screen of the application, you might have defined some buttons to access the functionality you've already built. You can either delete those buttons and start from scratch or modify them. But before doing so, find some nice-looking icons that represent the functionality you want to access with these icons. To address the region containing the icons easily in CSS, set the Static ID to "navigation".

Let's start with the Page Item button that links to the Customer List page. If you don't have that item, you can create one now that redirects to the Customer List page. Change the Style of that item to "Image" and the Image to the uploaded image, as shown in Figure 6-3.

Figure 6-3. *Defining an image on the springboard*

Simply repeat those steps for all the images you want to show. We will do the sizing of the images using CSS a little later, but squaring the images at a 100-pixel width and height usually shows up rather nicely.

Apart from the image, we also need a small piece of text that shows just below the image. This is especially useful when the meaning of the picture isn't 100% evident to all users. In this example, we also embed the image and the text within a container to manipulate the looks more easily.

So define a pre- and post-element setting, as shown in Figure 6-4.

Figure 6-4. *Adding text to the image*

Using the Grid Layout settings, you can now specify the number of icons that you want to show on a row and the icon that you want to show in a particular spot. We only have to apply some CSS code to get the look we want. See Listing 6-1 for an example of that CSS.

Listing 6-1. CSS for the Springboard

```
/* Set general look
*/
div#navigation
{
 text-align  : center;
 color       : white;
 text-shadow : none;
 padding-left : 20px;
}

/* Set the size of the divs containing the springboard items
*/
div.container
{
 width     : 75px;
 height    : 75px;
 padding   : 10px;
}
```

```
/* Reduce image size to 57px
*/
div#navigation img
{
 width      : 57px;
}

/* Move icon Text a little upwards and use a smaller font
*/
p.iconText
{
 font-size : 11px;
 position  : relative;
 top       : -15px;
}
```

Running the home page should give you a page that looks similar to the one shown in Figure 6-5, but it's entirely dependent on the images that you used.

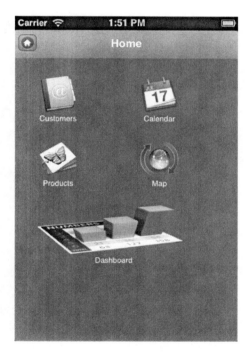

Figure 6-5. *Our new springboard*

In this example, you see that the Dashboard item stretches over both columns. This is done by overriding the standard sizing specified in the CSS, in the Attributes property of the image. In this case, that property is set to `style="width:300%; height:100%;"`.

Enhancing the Springboard

The springboard is already pretty nice, but we could add additional information to the icons. You can use a technique similar to when you are notified on the iOS springboard about a new e-mail or a new message.

Let's assume that we want to show the number of customers, the number of appointments, and the number of products in the same way that we see the number of unread messages on the iOS home screen. This might not be the best use case for this feature, and once you know how to do it, you'll probably find a better one.

First, add a new Hidden item for every counter and give it a value using an SQL statement. Figure 6-6 shows an example of the counter for customers.

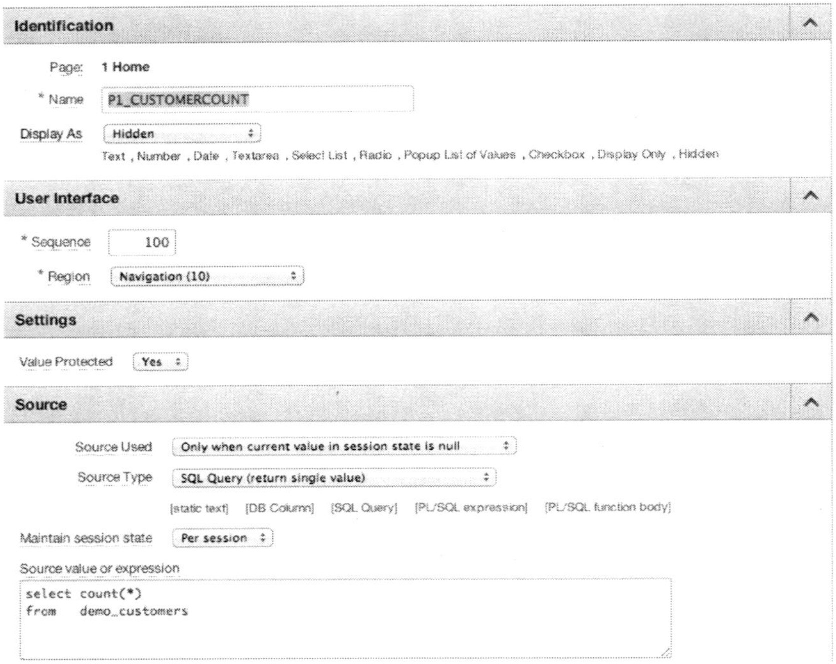

Figure 6-6. *Defining the counter for customers*

Next, create a Dynamic Action that fires on Page Load and executes the snippet of JavaScript that you see in Listing 6-2.

Listing 6-2. JavaScript for Adding a Counter to an Image

```
$('a#P1_CUSTOMERLIST').append('<div class="badge">'+$v('P1_CUSTOMERCOUNT')+'</div>');
$('a#P1_CALENDAR').append('<div class="badge">'+$v('P1_CONTACTCOUNT')+'</div>');
$('a#P1_PRODUCTLIST').append('<div class="badge">'+$v('P1_PRODUCTCOUNT')+'</div>');
$('div.badge').parent().next('.iconText').css('top','-40px');
```

This code adds a div with a badge class to the image that is used as a link (P1_CUSTOMERLIST is the name of the upper-left item on the springboard) and adds the value of the hidden counter item to that div. This is repeated for all three counters. The last line "fixes" the position of the label after the badge is applied.

Next, we have to define how our badge looks. So add the lines you see in Listing 6-3 to the CSS of the page. You might need to tweak the settings a little to match your images or device resolution.

Listing 6-3. CSS for the Badges

```
/* No underline on links
*/
a
{
  text-decoration : none;
}

/* Define looks of the badge
*/
div.badge
{
 color         : white;
 font-size     : 11px;
 position      : relative;
 top           : -70px;
 left          : 50px;
 border        : 2px solid white;
 border-radius : 11px;
 width         : 20px;
 height        : 20px;
 line-height   : 20px;
 box-shadow    : 0px 1px 2px #000;
 background    : red;
}
```

Running the page gives the result shown in Figure 6-7. It almost looks like a native iOS springboard. We've managed to accomplish this with just the standard APEX features and some (maybe less standard) CSS code.

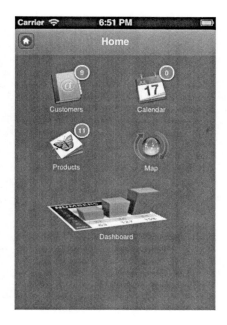

Figure 6-7. *Springboard with badges*

The type and look of the images that you are using for this springboard will have an effect on the user experience. For instance, compare the colorful icons in the example in Figure 6-7 with the minimalistic, two-color icons in Figure 6-8. Each design pattern has its own distinctive look, so it's very important to use an icon set that matches the goal of your application.

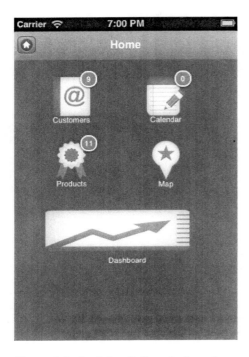

Figure 6-8. *A minimalistic springboard*

Creating a Tab Navigation

In the current application, we have to navigate to the home screen to switch from one function to another—for instance, when switching from Customers to Products. Because we should try to minimize user clicks, we can offer tab-style navigation on the page. This style of navigation is usually offered at the bottom of the page.

In APEX, the easiest way to define tabs is to use lists and list items. So to define our tabs, we define a list (via Shared Components). In this list, define a list item for every page that you want to give our users direct access to. It is enough to only define the List Entry Label, an image (pick one of the standard jQuery Mobile icon names, like "home" or "star") and the Target page.

Because we want to show these tabs on almost every page, define a new List region on page 0—the Global Page. Select Footer Toolbar (Fixed) as the Region template, so that the tab navigation is always visible. And set the Display Point to "Page Template Region Position 8", which is at the bottom of the page. Set the List template to "Navigation Bar". This template relieves us from most of the hard work because it is created exactly for making tab navigation on the page. And to make it easier to write the correct CSS, set a Static ID. All the settings are shown in Figure 6-9.

Identification

Page   0 Global Page - jQuery Mobile Smartphone

* Title   Footer Tabs   ☐ exclude title from translation

Type   LIST: Footer Tab   ▾

Source

* List Template   Navigation Bar ▾

Name: Footer Tab

Sequence	Text	Target
10	Home	f?p=&APP_ID.:1:&SESSIO
20	Customers	f?p=&APP_ID.:27:&SESSI
30	Products	f?p=&APP_ID.:13:&SESSI
40	Agenda	f?p=&APP_ID.:16:&SESSI

User Interface

* Sequence   120

Parent Region   – Select a Parent – ▾

Display Point   Page Template Region Position 8 ▾

[Body] [Pos.1] [Pos.2] [Pos.3] [Pos.4] [Pos.5] [Pos.6] [Pos.7] [Pos.8]

Template   Footer Toolbar (Fixed)   ▾

Item Display Position   Below Content ▾

Grid Layout

Start New Grid   No ▾

Start New Row   Yes ▾

Column   Automatic ▾

Column Attributes

Attributes

Static ID   footer-tabs

Region CSS Classes

Figure 6-9. *Definition of the tab navigation*

When you now run the page, you'll see the tab navigation at the bottom. Alas, it just shows text and the standard icons, but you might want to show your own icons. Therefore, the CSS you find in Listing 6-4 comes to the rescue. Because this CSS is for the Global Page, the best place to put it is in the Inline property of your Page template. It will be available on all pages, just like the tabs.

Listing 6-4. Defining Icons on the Navigation Tab

```
/* Define the icon sizes and locations - assuming your tab navigation region has the Static ID set
to "footer-tabs"
*/
#footer-tabs .ui-btn .ui-icon
```

```
{
 width                  : 30px !important;
 height                 : 30px !important;
 margin-left            : -15px !important;
 margin-top             : -3px !important;
 box-shadow             : none !important;
 -moz-box-shadow        : none !important;
 -webkit-box-shadow     : none !important;
 -webkit-border-radius  : none !important;
 border-radius          : none !important;
 background-size        : 22px 22px !important;
}

/* Define a light and smaller font size on the tabs
*/
#footer-tabs .ui-btn .ui-btn-text
{
 font-size   : 11px;
 font-weight : lighter;
}

/* Define the icons for the tabs - upload your own favourite icons first
*/
#footer-tabs .ui-block-a .ui-icon
{
background : url(#APP_IMAGES#hospital.png) 50% 50% no-repeat;
}

#footer-tabs .ui-block-b .ui-icon
{
 background : url(#APP_IMAGES#address_book.png) 50% 50% no-repeat;
}

#footer-tabs .ui-block-c .ui-icon
{
 background : url(#APP_IMAGES#prize_winner.png) 50% 50% no-repeat;
}

#footer-tabs .ui-block-d .ui-icon{
    background: url(#APP_IMAGES#edit_notes.png) 50% 50% no-repeat;
}
```

■ **Tip**   In the preceding example, the images are served from the APEX images repository. Although this is quite handy when deploying applications with all images, CSS files, and so forth, it is not preferable for a production environment. You should serve these kind of images from the application server so that they can be cached. Also, use images that are about the size you need for the goal; in this case, around 22 × 22 pixels. This also reduces bandwidth and increases speed.

Running this page produces the result shown in Figure 6-10. Just as you are used to with regular (desktop) tabs, you can easily spot which tab belongs to the current page. The current tab is also automatically disabled.

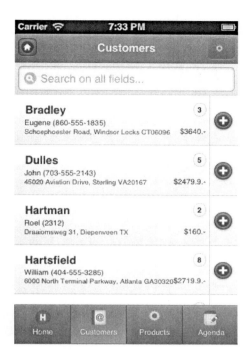

Figure 6-10. *Tab navigation in action*

Before finishing this section, you might want to prevent this tab navigation from showing up on the login page (101) and the home page (1). You can do that by setting the condition of the Footer Tabs Region in the Global Page to "Current Page is NOT in Expression 1 (comma delimited list of pages)" and Expression 1 to "101,1".

Remove HTML-Style Buttons

When you navigate to the Edit Customer page of your applications, you immediately notice the Cancel, Delete, and Save buttons (see Figure 6-11).

Figure 6-11. *HTML-style buttons*

These buttons might work and look perfect on a real web application, but they don't look that good on a native-styled application. You will have hard time finding buttons like that in any native application! Another advantage is that more screen estate is made available to display actual content.

The easiest one to remove is the Cancel button. The user can simply navigate away from the page using the tab navigation (or the menu that we will create in the next section), so it is superfluous.

Next, move the Save button to the header. Create another Region button in the Header region on page 0. Find a nice image (such as a floppy disk) that is often used to represent a Save option. Figure 6-12 shows the settings of this button.

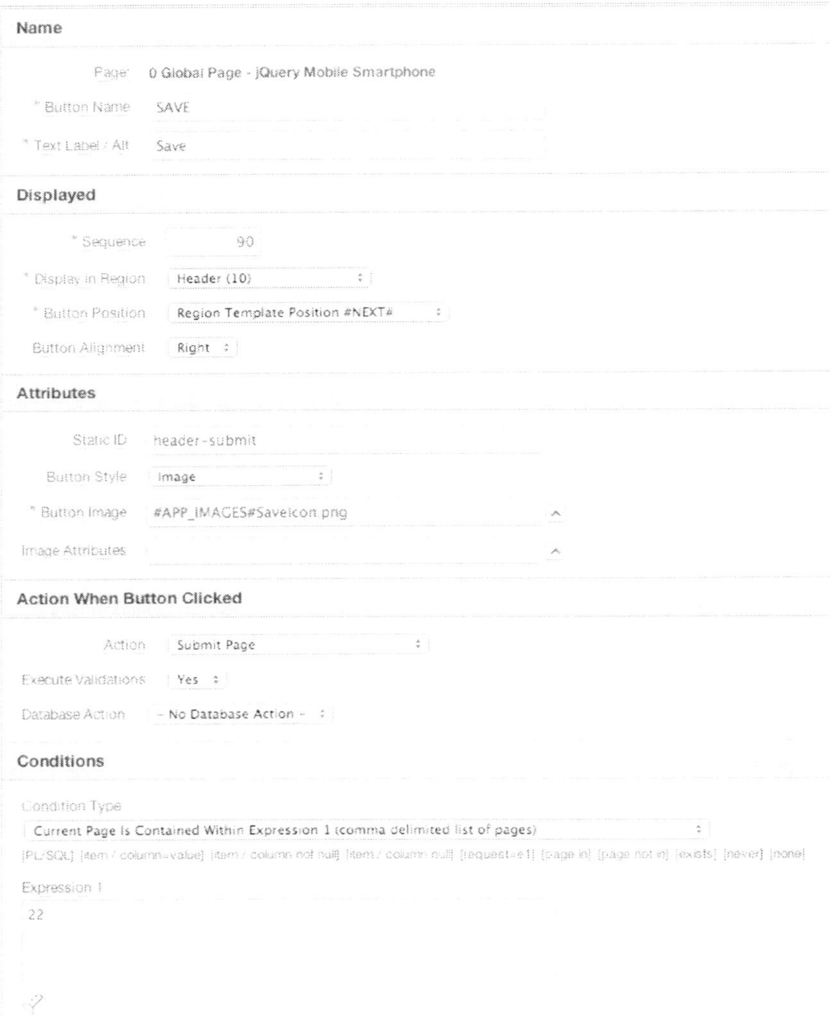

Name

Page:	0 Global Page - jQuery Mobile Smartphone
* Button Name	SAVE
* Text Label / Alt	Save

Displayed

* Sequence	90
* Display in Region	Header (10)
* Button Position	Region Template Position #NEXT#
Button Alignment	Right

Attributes

Static ID	header-submit
Button Style	Image
* Button Image	#APP_IMAGES#SaveIcon.png
Image Attributes	

Action When Button Clicked

Action	Submit Page
Execute Validations	Yes
Database Action	– No Database Action –

Conditions

Condition Type

Current Page Is Contained Within Expression 1 (comma delimited list of pages)

[PL/SQL] [item / column=value] [item / column not null] [item / column null] [request=e1] [page in] [page not in] [exists] [never] [none]

Expression 1

22

Figure 6-12. *Save button settings*

You can follow a similar approach for the Delete button. But before you can delete that button from your page, you have to change the When Button Pressed condition of the Reset Page process to "No Button Condition" (otherwise, you'll get an error telling you the button is still in use). Instead of that When Button Pressed condition, set the Condition Type to "Request = Expression 1" and Expression 1 to "DELETE". This means the process will (still) fire when the request is DELETE.

Next, create another button in the Header region of page 0. Set the Static ID of the Header region to "header" and the Static ID of the button to "header-delete" so that you can fix the positioning using the CSS in Listing 6-5. You can set the Button Position to "Region Template Position #NEXT#" to place it on the right side of the header text. Use an obvious image, such as a trashcan, for this button.

Listing 6-5. CSS for the Buttons in the Header Region on Page 0

```
div#header span.ui-btn-inner
{
 padding : 0px 6px 0px 6px;
}


a#header-delete
{
 right : 50px;
}


div#header img
{
  width  : 27px;
  height : 27px;
}
```

Clicking the button should fire a snippet of JavaScript you've seen before—using the SimpleDialog2 plug-in, as in Listing 6-6. Of course, the simpledialog2 JavaScript source file should be included on the page. You can do that by setting the File URLs property of the page definition to #WORKSPACE_IMAGES#jquery.mobile.simpledialog2.min.js.

Listing 6-6. Calling the simpledialog2 on Page 0

```
$('body').simpledialog2({
    mode        : "button",
    transition  : "slideup",
    width       : "98%",
    left        : "0px",
    top         : "55%",
    buttons : {
      'Delete': {
        click : function () {
                apex.gPageContext$ = apex.jQuery.mobile.activePage;
                apex.submit("DELETE");
        },
        icon  : false,
        id    : "Delete",
        theme : "a"
      },
      'Cancel': {
        click: function () {
```

```
        this.close();
        apex.gPageContext$ = apex.jQuery.mobile.activePage;
      },
      icon  : false,
      theme : "a"
    }
  }
});
```

Clicking the Delete button in the Edit Customer page results in a page like the one shown in Figure 6-13.

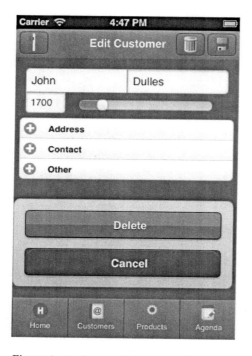

Figure 6-13. *Page with Delete and Save icons*

Creating a Slide Menu

Some of the native applications have a menu that slides in from the left of the screen when you either press a button or swipe to the right. The Facebook application is one of them, as shown in Figure 6-14.

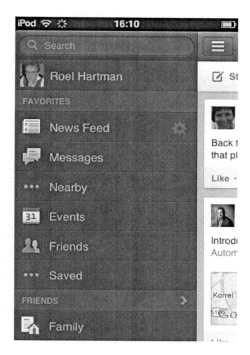

Figure 6-14. *Facebook's slide menu*

Wouldn't it be nice to implement something like that in your Mobile APEX application? It is possible, although not completely obvious how to do it. We need to download a jQuery Mobile slide menu plug-in from http://github.com/tegansnyder/JQuery-Mobile-Slide-Menu.

■ **Note** Because functionality similar to what this plug-in provides is planned for jQuery Mobile 1.3 and thus might be included in future APEX releases, check the documentation to find out whether you should use jQuery Mobile functionality.

The downloaded .zip file contains a demo and other files that you need. Upload the following files to your server:

- jqm.slidemenu.css
- jqm.slidemenu.js
- jquery.animate-enhanced.min.js

But before actually uploading them, you need to apply a tiny fix to the jqm.slidemenu.js file. When you don't apply the fix, the menu works fine on a desktop browser, but it does not work well on a mobile device. This is because a variable that had been instantiated earlier is cleared when this function is called.

Add the following line as the first code in the slidemenu function declaration (approximately line 40 in the file):

```
// Re-instantiate. On device it's empty again
if (sm.length==0){ sm = $('.slidemenu'); }
```

Next, define the contents of your menu. For this goal, a list is the way to go. Lists can be found on the Shared Components in the Navigation section. You can either define a static list by simply specifying the menu structure and the items targeting a specific page, or you can create a dynamic one based on your own tables, or you can use an APEX view like apex_application_pages as the source.

The slide menu plug-in expects the HTML output in a specific format, like the one in Listing 6-7.

Listing 6-7. HTML Output for the Slide Menu Plug-in

```
<div id="slidemenu">
  <ul>
    <li><a href="f?p=106:1:6062154931999::NO:::">Home</a></li>
  </ul>
  <h3>List Views</h3>
  <ul>
    <li><a href="some link">Customers</a></li>
    <li><a href="some link>Products</a></li>
  </ul>
  <h3>Dashboard</h3>
  <ul>
    <li><a href="some link">Sales/Product</a></li>
    <li><a href="some link">Pie Chart</a></li>
  </ul>
</div>
```

We have to define a specific template for our slide menu. Create a new template of type "List" from scratch. Give it a name—like "SlideMenu". We will use this template in our mobile application, so you should select the corresponding theme for the template. The theme class doesn't really matter; just pick one that is custom. Next, fill in all the properties, as follows.

- List template before rows:

  ```
  <link rel="stylesheet" href="#WORKSPACE_IMAGES#jqm.slidemenu.css" />
  <script src="#WORKSPACE_IMAGES#jquery.animate-enhanced.min.js"></script>
  <script src="#WORKSPACE_IMAGES#jqm.slidemenu.js"></script>
  <div id="slidemenu">
  ```

- List template (current and noncurrent):

  ```
  <ul><li><a href="#LINK#">#TEXT#</a></li></ul>
  ```

- List template (current and noncurrent) with sublist items:

  ```
  <h3>#TEXT#</h3>
  ```

- Sublist template before rows:

  ```
  <ul>
  ```

- Sublist templates (all of them):

  ```
  <li><a href="#LINK#">#TEXT#</a></li>
  ```

- Sublist template after rows:

  ```
  </ul>
  ```

- List template after rows:

  ```
  </div>
  ```

The final step is to incorporate the list in your application. Therefore, add a List region to page 0 so that it will be available on all pages. This List region should use the Plain template because we don't need any additional code in this region. And, of course, you should use the newly created template as the List Template value. The Display Point of the region should be set to "After Header". You probably want to exclude page 101 (login), so add a condition for that exclusion. In fact, due to the Ajax loading of the APEX pages, you can also set the condition to include only the region on page 1 (home). Every subsequent page will be added to the DOM, so this region will stay in the DOM. Using that condition, you'll avoid unnecessary loading of content. See Chapter 8 for more information on Ajax and page loading.

When you run your application, your slide menu will be available on all pages and it can be activated using a swipe gesture. To indicate that there is a menu available, it might be useful to include a button in the header of the page. Figure 6-15 shows the definition. Note the Image Attributes setting. It does the magic of opening the slide menu for you, so you don't actually need to define a Dynamic Action to do it yourself.

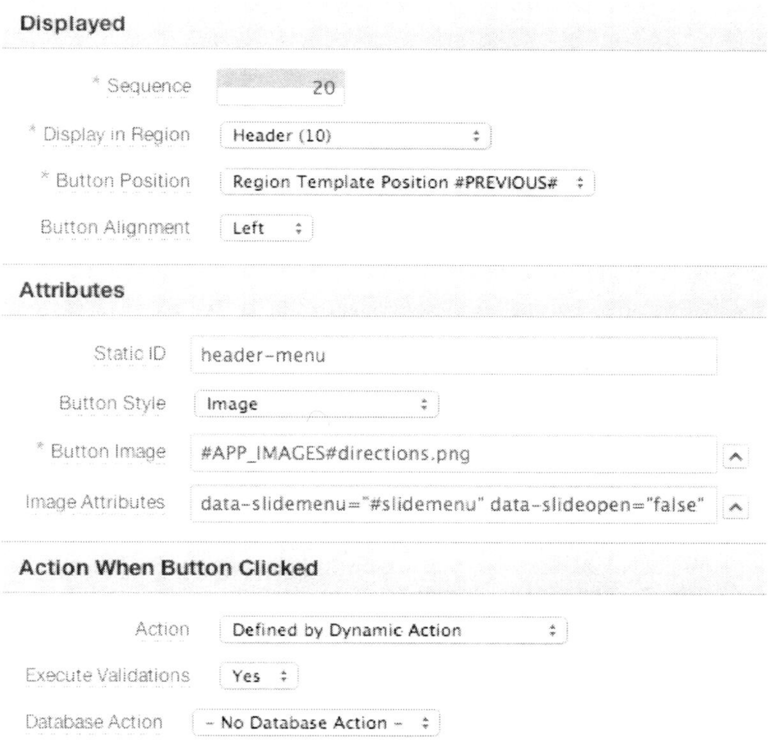

Displayed

* Sequence	20
* Display in Region	Header (10)
* Button Position	Region Template Position #PREVIOUS#
Button Alignment	Left

Attributes

Static ID	header-menu
Button Style	Image
* Button Image	#APP_IMAGES#directions.png
Image Attributes	data-slidemenu="#slidemenu" data-slideopen="false"

Action When Button Clicked

Action	Defined by Dynamic Action
Execute Validations	Yes
Database Action	– No Database Action –

Figure 6-15. *Button definition that activates the slide menu*

Pressing the button or using a slide gesture now opens the slide menu (see Figure 6-16). Note that the actual page is moved to the right, so it is not an overlay of the page. When the menu is too wide, you can change the width values in the `jqm.slidemenu.js` file. In this example, a value of 150 pixels is used, instead of the standard of 250 pixels.

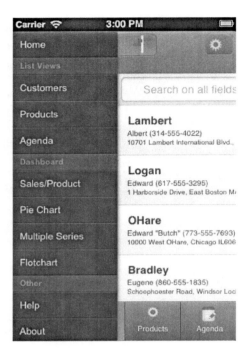

Figure 6-16. *The slide menu in action*

When you notice the button that opens the slide menu is elongated to the left, you can add `style="margin-left:0px !important;"` to the Image Attribute property of the button.

Wrap Up

In this chapter, you learned how to spice up your APEX web application with the use of buttons. Most buttons should be defined in the header bar (including the menu and the Save and Delete buttons) or in the footer bar (such as tabbed navigation). Apart from those buttons, it's important that the home page of your application make a good first impression. You have to define a good-looking springboard on that page. And maybe the best of all, the slide menu—as an appreciated feature of native applications—can be created within a mobile APEX application!

CHAPTER 7

▓ ▓ ▓

Theming Your Mobile Application

Your application already looks pretty good. But we had to use quite a lot of CSS code to get that far. Luckily, using ThemeRoller, there is an easier way to do a lot of the styling of your application. This chapter introduces ThemeRoller and shows you how to use it to get the look and feel you want for your application. You will also look into the possibilities of creating your own images and icons using CSS sprites.

Using ThemeRoller

All the styling implemented in your application so far was handcrafted CSS. Piece by piece and step by step, you enhanced your application with fonts, colors, and button settings to your liking. But there is another way to do a lot of the styling—apart from manually changing the contents of the jQuery Mobile CSS file. This other way is called ThemeRoller Mobile.

ThemeRoller is a tool to create custom-designed themes for your jQuery Mobile application. You can create up to 26 "swatches," A to Z, each with its own color scheme. Each swatch sets the colors, textures, and font settings for the primary elements: a toolbar, the content block, and buttons. Buttons have three interaction states: normal, hover, and pressed. And, as you have seen in the previous chapters, you can use any combination of swatches in your application. So the possibilities are endless.

Getting Started

You can find ThemeRoller when you browse to `http://jquerymobile.com/` and click the Themes tab, as shown in Figure 7-1 (or you can go directly to `http://jquerymobile.com/themeroller`).

Figure 7-1. *Location of the ThemeRoller tool*

Clicking the Themes tab opens the tool (after viewing a short splash screen). When the application is loaded, you'll see a screen like the one shown in Figure 7-2.

Figure 7-2. *The ThemeRoller screen*

On the top of the screen is the color bar. You can change the lightness and saturation of colors through the color bar. When you see a color that you like, you can simply drag and drop the color onto the element that you want.

On the left side of the screen is the Inspector panel. In that panel, you can see and change theme level settings as well as settings per swatch.

In the middle of the screen are the different swatches. Initially, three swatches are defined: a, b, and c. By default, they are all exactly the same. You can add a new swatch by either clicking the Add Swatch . . . link in the right block or by clicking the + tab in the Inspector panel.

To get started based on the default situation of your APEX application, click the Import button at the top of the screen. In the next popup, click the Import Default Theme link in the upper-right corner (see Figure 7-3). The default jQuery Mobile Theme CSS is then loaded into that popup. Now click the Import button in the lower-right corner to load that definition into ThemeRoller.

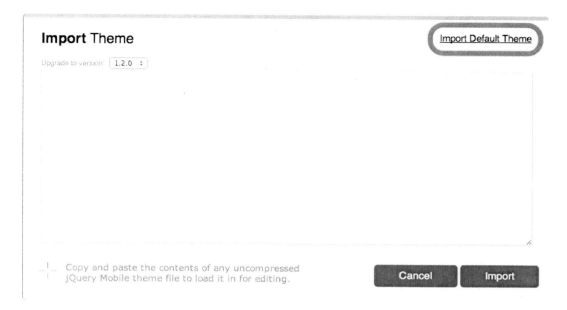

Figure 7-3. *Import the default theme CSS*

The ThemeRoller page is now loaded with the five jQuery Mobile default swatches that you already know from previous theming exercises. In Figure 7-4, you can see at a glance the effect of a swatch setting for every component type.

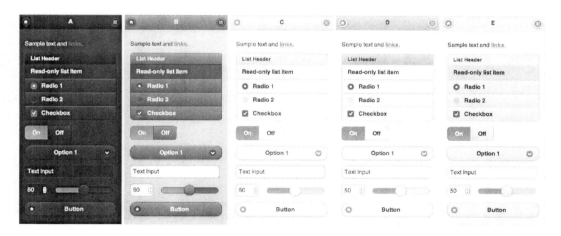

Figure 7-4. *Five swatches at a glance*

Modifying the Default Theme

For each theme, you can select every component, change the settings—and immediately see the effect.

> ■ **Tip** Switch the Inspector on. The Inspector panel will automatically synchronize with the component you select, making it easier to make changes in the right spot.

From the color bar above the swatches (see Figure 7-2), you can drag and drop any color to any component and also spot the effect. For ease of use, you can use one of the many *Adobe Kuler swatches*—a predefined scheme of five colors that (should) match nicely together.

Creating Your Own Theme

Once you've played around a bit in ThemeRoller and have a good feeling about what it does, it is time to create your own theme.

Making Global Swatch Changes

Let's start with making some changes to settings under the Global tab, so that these changes are applied to all swatches. The first thing you can change in this tab is the Font Family of your application. You can provide multiple fonts; the first one that is available on the device will be used. In order to get a similar look on all devices, your font specification should contain a set of similar looking fonts. So, you can set it to Trebuchet MS, Arial, Helvetica, sans-serif.

The Active State is the setting for a currently selected element, like the On in the On/Off switch or a selected option in a select list. You can set the text color as well as the background for these types of items. You can even define gradients for the background with just a few clicks; see Figure 7-5 for an example.

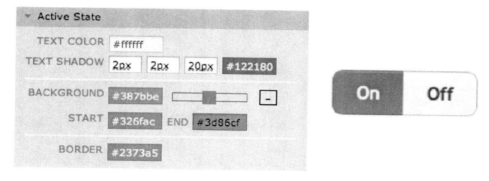

Figure 7-5. Settings for a gradient Active State button

In this example, the text color is set to white (#ffffff). The text shadow creates a slightly darker shadow effect under the text. The background is defined as a gradient that gives a nice fading color from a dark blue to a light blue. With the slider, you can set the start and end colors, where the background color acts as the middle value. But you can also set the start and end color values yourself. For instance, you can create really awful buttons by picking a red color as the start value and green as the end.

The greatest aspect of this tool is that, in the end, it creates CSS for every browser—as you can see in Listing 7-1 from the preceding example. Imagine that you have to code it all by yourself (and this is just one CSS class of many!).

Listing 7-1. The Generated CSS for the Active State Button

```
/* Active class used as the "on" state across all themes
--------------------------------------------------------------------------------------------
--------*/
.ui-btn-active {
        border: 1px solid #2373a5 /*{global-active-border}*/;
        background: #387bbe /*{global-active-background-color}*/;
        font-weight: bold;
        color: #ffffff /*{global-active-color}*/;
        cursor: pointer;
        text-shadow: 2px /*{global-active-shadow-x}*/ 2px /*{global-active-shadow-y}*/ 20px
/*{global-active-shadow-radius}*/ #122180 /*{global-active-shadow-color}*/;
        text-decoration: none;
        background-image: -webkit-gradient(linear, left top, left bottom, from( #326fac
/*{global-active-background-start}*/), to( #3d86cf /*{global-active-background-end}*/));
/* Saf4+, Chrome */
        background-image: -webkit-linear-gradient( #326fac /*{global-active-background-start}*/,
#3d86cf /*{global-active-background-end}*/); /* Chrome 10+, Saf5.1+ */
        background-image:    -moz-linear-gradient( #326fac /*{global-active-background-start}*/,
#3d86cf /*{global-active-background-end}*/); /* FF3.6 */
        background-image:     -ms-linear-gradient( #326fac /*{global-active-background-start}*/,
#3d86cf /*{global-active-background-end}*/); /* IE10 */
        background-image:      -o-linear-gradient( #326fac /*{global-active-background-start}*/,
#3d86cf /*{global-active-background-end}*/); /* Opera 11.10+ */
        background-image:         linear-gradient( #326fac /*{global-active-background-start}*/,
#3d86cf /*{global-active-background-end}*/);
          font-family: Trebuchet MS, Arial, Helvetica /*{global-font-family}*/;
}
```

The Corner Radii is something we have been playing around with in our own hand-coded CSS. Using this CSS setting, you can change the rounding edges of the regions and buttons. With ThemeRoller, it is very easy: just set both settings to ".4em" to get the look created earlier by hand.

The Icon setting applies to the look of the icons on the buttons, the header bar, select lists, and accordions. You specify whether you want to show the icons with or without a disc behind the image. When you specify a disc, you have more control over the visibility of the icon, regardless of the background color.

In the Box Shadow setting, you define the way boxes are displayed.

See Figure 7-6 for an example of the Global settings. You can go really wild with the color settings and the swatch-specific ones, but more colors don't always (almost never) result in a better-looking application.

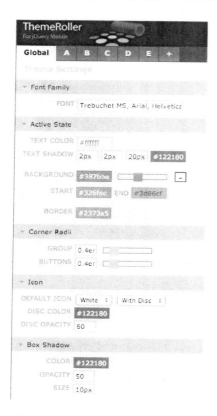

Figure 7-6. *Example of Global settings*

Creating a New Swatch

Proceed by creating a new swatch. Press the + icon in the Inspector panel. For the new F swatch, you have to specify the look of the header and footer, content, and buttons—all with very similar settings—in Active State on the Global tab. Remember, you can drag colors from the color bar onto the objects and change them afterward in the Inspector panel. After some playing around, you'll have a result similar to the one shown in Figure 7-7 (or one that is way better).

Figure 7-7. *The new F swatch*

Adding the Customized Theme to Your Application

So how do you get this new theme in the APEX application? First, you need to download the CSS code from ThemeRoller by clicking the Download button. A popup appears, in which you have to specify a name for your theme, as well as some installation instructions (see Figure 7-8).

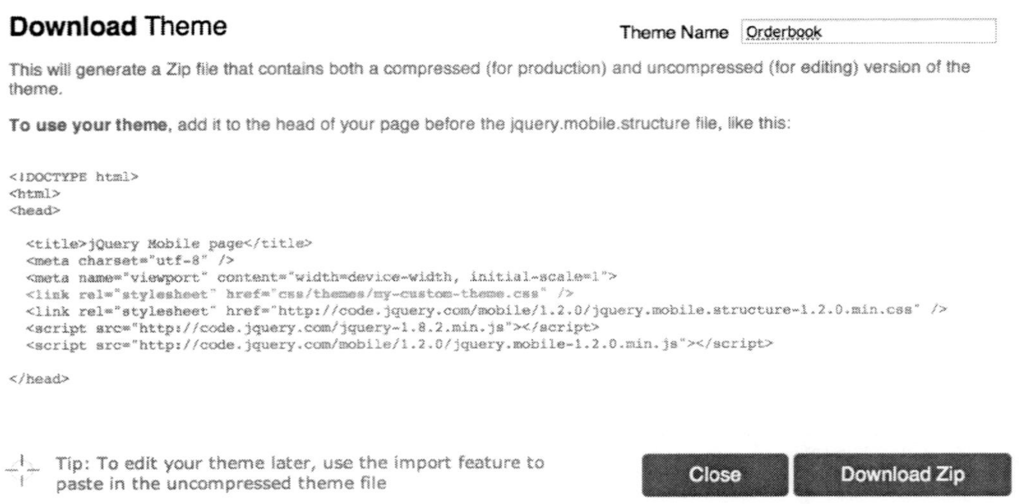

Download Theme

Theme Name   Orderbook

This will generate a Zip file that contains both a compressed (for production) and uncompressed (for editing) version of the theme.

To use your theme, add it to the head of your page before the jquery.mobile.structure file, like this:

```
<!DOCTYPE html>
<html>
<head>

  <title>jQuery Mobile page</title>
  <meta charset="utf-8" />
  <meta name="viewport" content="width=device-width, initial-scale=1">
  <link rel="stylesheet" href="css/themes/my-custom-theme.css" />
  <link rel="stylesheet" href="http://code.jquery.com/mobile/1.2.0/jquery.mobile.structure-1.2.0.min.css" />
  <script src="http://code.jquery.com/jquery-1.8.2.min.js"></script>
  <script src="http://code.jquery.com/mobile/1.2.0/jquery.mobile-1.2.0.min.js"></script>

</head>
```

Tip: To edit your theme later, use the import feature to paste in the uncompressed theme file

Close   Download Zip

Figure 7-8. *Download the new theme*

Now download the .zip file and use it in your APEX application. Because the images are relatively referenced in the CSS, you have to put them in an "images" directory on your web server. You can also upload the image files into the APEX repository and reference these images as follows:

```
.ui-icon-alt {
        background-image: url(#APP_IMAGES#icons-18-black.png);
}
```

In this case, you have to extract the references to the images from the CSS file and put those CSS lines "inline" in the Page template, because substitution strings like #APP_IMAGES# don't work for external files.

The CSS file (minus the image references when you've loaded the images into the repository) should be referenced from your web server or uploaded to the repository.

There are two ways to reference the CSS file in the Page template. The first one is to replace the #APEX_CSS# placeholder with the code provided in Listing 7-2.

Listing 7-2. Replacement of the #APEX_CSS# Placeholder

```
<link rel="stylesheet"
 href="#WORKSPACE_IMAGES#Orderbook.css" />
<link rel="stylesheet"
 href="#IMAGE_PREFIX#libraries/jquery-mobile/1.1.1/jquery.mobile.structure-1.2.0.min.css"
 type="text/css" />
<link rel="stylesheet"
 href="#IMAGE_PREFIX#themes/theme_50/css/4_2.css"
 type="text/css" />
```

When you take this approach, the jquery-mobile-1.2.0.css won't be loaded because it is replaced by the (smaller) jquery.mobile.structure-1.2.0.css and your own theme CSS file. However, you might have to change that reference when APEX ships with a newer version of jQuery Mobile.

The other option is to accept a bit of overhead in loading duplicate resources and content by keeping the #APEX_CSS# as it is and add the reference as a Cascading Style Sheet File URL. If you want to use the minified version of the CSS for regular use, you can use the substitution string #MIN# to include .min in your file URL for a regular page view, and an empty string if the page is viewed in debug mode. So the line in the File URL property would be as follows:

```
#WORKSPACE_IMAGES#Orderbook#MIN#.css
```

When you run your application now, you might notice some changes in the look and feel, but nothing drastic. That's because the application is using theme "c" by default. So you have to change the references to theme "c" to"f" to see the results of the ThemeRoller exercise. Of course, you can also change the "c" theme directly in ThemeRoller, and you won't need to change the references to the themes in the templates. In the previous chapters of this book, you made some CSS changes that overrode the ThemeRoller settings, so you won't see those in effect unless you remove those customizations.

The following is the preferable way of theming your application:

1. Create a functional application with all page types so that you can spot the effect on all sorts of pages.

2. Use ThemeRoller to define a new theme "c" and get the desired look and feel.

3. Customize every page by adding your own handcrafted CSS code.

Changing the Swatch by the User

Quite often in a native mobile application, you can set some kind of preference for the theme of the application. Wouldn't it be nice if we could do that in our mobile web application? And, of course, in a way the application remembers our last setting!

First, you need an additional Settings page, where you can navigate to and from your home page or via the slide-in menu. On that page, create an HTML region, and on that region, a Select List item. Define the Select List as "Static" and set the List of Values definition to the following:

```
STATIC2:Dark Black;a,Bright Blue;b,Light Grey;c,Dark Grey;d,Very Yellow;e
```

(Or use other nice color names that represent your swatches.)

For storing this color selection, you can use the built-in preference feature, so set the Source Type of the Select List to "Preference" and the Source Value to "THEME". That means the source will be read from the APEX user preference named THEME. You might want to set the Default Value to "c" for first-time use.

The Page Action When Value Changed should be set to "Redirect and Set Value" to store the value in Session State and to see the effect immediately. To store the selected value as a preference, you need to add a Before Header PL/SQL Process on the Settings page, which fires when the redirect is issued. Create this PL/SQL Process and set the Session Type to "Set Preference to value of item if item is not null," as shown in Figure 7-9.

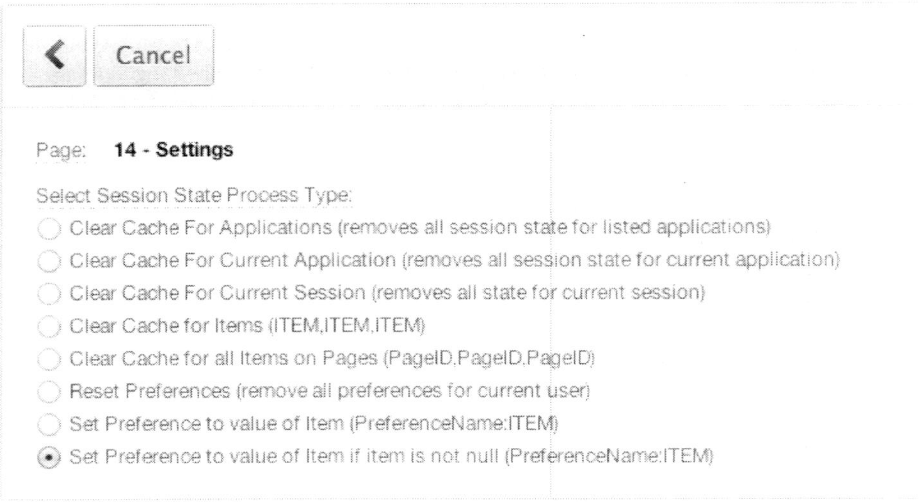

Figure 7-9. *PL/SQL process setting for storing the preference value*

Set the definition of the process to THEME:P14_THEME (see Figure 7-10).

Figure 7-10. *The definition of the Set Preference process*

Now that you've created a preference and the functionality of setting that preference, you want to use that value in the whole application, so you have to create an Application Item named Theme. You can set the Session State Protection of that item to "Restricted". And because you want to store the value of the current Theme preference setting in that item on every page, create an application process that fires "On Load: Before Header" and set the PL/SQL Source to the following:

```
:THEME := apex_util.get_preference('THEME', :APP_USER);
```

So now you've set everything in place to make the final changes to the templates. Therefore, you have to replace all hard-coded references from "c" to the parameterized value "&THEME.". The easiest way to do that is by using the Search Application feature in the upper-right corner, and search for "c" (with the quotes). For instance, in the header of the Page template, you have to change this:

```
<div id="#PAGE_STATIC_ID#" data-role="page" data-apex-page-transition="#PAGE_TRANSITION#"
data-apex-popup-transition="#POPUP_TRANSITION#" data-theme="c" data-url="#REQUESTED_URL#">
```

To this:

```
<div id="#PAGE_STATIC_ID#" data-role="page" data-apex-page-transition="#PAGE_TRANSITION#"
data-apex-popup-transition="#POPUP_TRANSITION#" data-theme="&THEME." data-url="#REQUESTED_URL#">
```

You will find references in templates as well as in your own code. But be aware: there may also be hard-coded references to the other swatches that you want to change!

When you run your application and change the Theme, you can see the effect immediately. And when you log out and log in again—even from another browser or device—you'll see the settings of the last chosen theme.

Creating Your Own Icons

jQuery Mobile comes with a set of standard icons. You can find the same icons set in the ThemeRoller images files. All icons are packed in one file, a CSS sprite, to minimize the download size and the number of files to download when running your application. See Figure 7-11 for part of such a CSS sprite image file.

Figure 7-11. *Part of the ThemeRoller sprite*

In the application, icons are referenced by their background positions, as shown in Listing 7-3.

Listing 7-3. Part of the ThemeRoller CSS referencing icons

```
/* misc */
.ui-icon-check {
        background-position:    -252px 50%;
}
.ui-icon-gear {
        background-position:    -288px 50%;
}
.ui-icon-refresh {
        background-position:    -324px 50%;
}
```

In Listing 7-3, all icons are specified with a 36-pixel width (because 288 – 252 = 36). The height of the image is also 36 pixels. The second value specifies where the vertical middle of the image is located. Although the icons are 36 × 36 pixels, the real size—without the empty space around it—is only 22 × 22 pixels. And to support all kinds of resolution, there is an 18 × 18 version of all icons for low-resolution devices.

When you have a need for other icons, you can shop on the web. There are plenty of web sites that offer icons—free or paid versions. Or you can create your own icons. You don't have to be a full-fledged graphical designer to create (simple) icons! And you don't need expensive tooling like Photoshop either—although it makes your design effort easier.

Let's create an icon to replace the current "ordering" button in the Customer List View. Instead of the current gear image, we want something representing a certain order, like the letters A and Z. As with the standard icon set, we need to create two versions of the image: a high-resolution one and a low-resolution one. Because the high-resolution image is easier to draw, start with that one.

In your favorite image editor, create a new document with a width and a height of 36 pixels and a resolution of 72 dpi. Name this new image ordering-36.png, as shown in Figure 7-12.

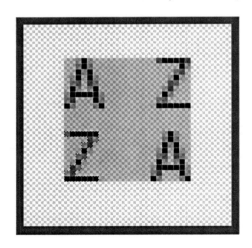

Figure 7-12. Definition of the new high-resolution icon

As with standard icons, we can't use all 36 pixels for our drawing because we need an empty space of 7 pixels on each side. Now it is time to let your creativity flow! Figure 7-13 shows a simple example with the A and Z characters.

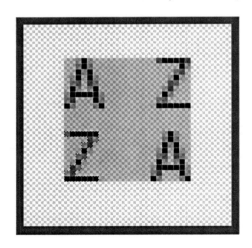

Figure 7-13. Drawing the ordering icon

128

Once you've saved that image as a .png file, create a similar low-resolution version. This ordering-18.png is 18 × 18 pixels in size with a 3-pixel empty area around it. You only have 12 × 12 pixels to draw your image, which makes it quite hard (therefore, you might create different images for different resolutions).

Upload both images to your web server or into the APEX repository. You have to follow the jQuery Mobile standards for the definition of your icon. You've already seen the use of the .ui-icon prefix in previous chapters. Now you will just add one by adding the next line of code to the inline CSS definition of the Page template (#APP_IMAGES# should be replaced by the appropriate reference to a folder on your web server when you've chosen to serve the image from there):

```
.ui-icon-ordering
{
  background-image: url(#APP_IMAGES#ordering-18.png);
}
```

Now you can reference this image in your application by specifying the data-icon attribute using data-icon="ordering" (see Figure 7-14).

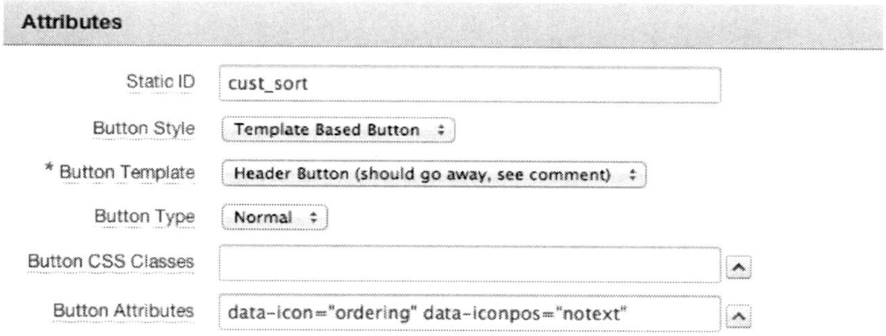

Attributes	
Static ID	cust_sort
Button Style	Template Based Button ⇕
* Button Template	Header Button (should go away, see comment) ⇕
Button Type	Normal ⇕
Button CSS Classes	⌃
Button Attributes	data-icon="ordering" data-iconpos="notext" ⌃

Figure 7-14. *Referencing the custom icon*

The same low-resolution icon is showing up on every device (see Figure 7-15).

Figure 7-15. *The low-resolution icon*

Although this may look good, even on high-resolution devices, you should use the high-resolution version you've created. Therefore, you need to incorporate a media query in the inline CSS definition of the Page template, as shown in Listing 7-4.

Listing 7-4. Using Media Query to Show High-Resolution Icon

```
@media only screen and (-webkit-min-device-pixel-ratio: 1.5),
       only screen and (min--moz-device-pixel-ratio: 1.5),
       only screen and (min-resolution: 240dpi) {

  .ui-icon.ui-icon-ordering
  {
   background-image : url(#APP_IMAGES#ordering-36.png);
   background-size  : 18px 18px;
  }
}
```

Apart from referencing the high-resolution icon, the background-size property is also set. Twice the number of pixels are shown in the exact same space. This results in a sharper image, as you can see in Figure 7-16. In this screenshot, the image is sharper and a slightly different icon is shown.

Figure 7-16. *The high-resolution icon*

Wrap Up

In this chapter, you saw how to create what is really your own. ThemeRoller offers an great, easy quick-start in coloring your application the way you like it. And when you create your own icons, your application will stand out because of its own unique look and feel!

The next chapter dives into Dynamic Actions—particularly those that are special to development for mobile devices.

CHAPTER 8

Working with Dynamic Actions

Throughout this book, you have seen examples that used Dynamic Actions. This chapter goes more in-depth with the topic. The first part of the chapter provides a brief introduction to Dynamic Actions for those that are new to it. The second part of the chapter dives into the changes that were made to the framework with APEX 4.2.

Client-Side Interactivity

JavaScript is the client-side language that brings HTML to life. With JavaScript, it's possible to create rich client-side interactions, overcome many obstacles, and meet just about any front-end development requirement. One of the key reasons to incorporate JavaScript into a web application is to have the application respond to certain conditions and user inputs without submitting the page. You want the page to respond immediately but don't want to incur the cost of sending the current page state to the server. Generally, you only want to submit a page when the user navigates away from the page or executes a specific function such as pressing a button to create, update, or delete data.

You can greatly enhance user satisfaction by having pages intuitively react to the user's input. Some simple examples for input forms include enabling/disabling fields, showing/hiding regions, and validating items immediately. When a user selects from a list, certain related fields and regions may not be required. When a user enters a price into a field, for example, immediately notifying the user that the price is too low or too high is much better than waiting until the user saves the record.

One problem is that you generally must learn JavaScript and perhaps HTML together with Cascading Style Sheets (CSS), and then there is Asynchronous JavaScript and XML (Ajax). That's a lot to learn! This learning curve has always been an impediment that prevented many developers from implementing such functionality. Users love improved interactivity that makes an application more intuitive and responsive, but are turned off if there is too much happening and the pages are "going wild." Another issue is that if you include large amounts of JavaScript code on a page, it adds to the page weight. This can lead to longer page-loading times, especially on slower mobile networks or older phones. Therefore, developers should be judicious in their implementation of client-side interactivity.

Introduction to Dynamic Actions

Dynamic Actions is a framework in APEX that reduces the learning curve and increases productivity by providing a declarative interface to implement rich client-side interactivity. This interface allows developers to stay in the context of APEX components (regions, items, and buttons) rather than their HTML equivalents (div, input, and button elements). At the end of the day, the framework ends up producing JavaScript, and where necessary Ajax, that is generated automatically based on the settings developers have declaratively defined.

The key benefits of utilizing Dynamic Actions rather than writing your own JavaScript and Ajax is that instead of hundreds of lines of code, there are simple declarative statements. Not only is it very quick and easy to define Dynamic Actions, it is just as easy for any developer to maintain or enhance. JavaScript developers have different layout styles and the code can be included in the page definition or collated into JavaScript (.js) files, making it harder to manage. Since the release of Dynamic Actions with APEX 4.0, many JavaScript developers have been stripping out their previous JavaScript code and replacing it with Dynamic Actions.

Dynamic Actions Components

There are three major parts to Dynamic Actions: when, what, and where. The developer first defines the event that triggers "when" actions are performed, and then specifies "what" actions are performed, and finally decides "where" the actions are applied. Here are some common examples:

- The value of a select list changes (when), resulting in the hiding/showing (what), of items, a region, or a button (where)

- The user clicks a button (when) and a PL/SQL process is executed (what) that populates an item (where)

The event portion of a Dynamic Action is referred to as the "when"—defining the triggering incident that is executed by the user. The definition of the when is a combination of an event that is triggered on an APEX component or other element, as well as an optional condition. If a condition is specified, both true and false actions can be defined. If no condition is specified, the Dynamic Action is driven solely by the event and only true actions can be defined against the event.

The action(s) to be performed are referred to as the "what"—defining the actions that will be performed when the event is triggered. You can define any number of actions against each event. Each action can be classified as either a true action or a false action. A true action is executed whenever the event is triggered and there is either no condition specified or the condition evaluates to true. The false action will only be executed if an event condition is specified and it evaluates to false. You can also specify whether each action should Fire On Page Load. Generally, you will want the action to fire when the page loads, which is the default, except in cases such as when user input is required before firing a given action.

Which components are impacted is referred to as the "where"—defining the affected elements of a specific action. For each action defined, you must specify an affected element type and a corresponding value. The type of action specified will determine which affected element types can be selected. For example, you can't enable or disable a region, so this type will not be shown for enable and disable actions.

Creating Some Test Pages

Before going into more detail on the framework, let's create a Dynamic Action so that you can get a feel for how it works. You'll start by creating some new pages for testing in the mobile application you've been working with (or in a new mobile application). These pages can be deleted later when they are no longer needed. Navigate to the application home page and follow these steps:

1. Click Create Page.

2. On the first screen, select Form and click Next.

3. On the Form Type screen, select Form On A Table With List View and click Next.

4. On the List View screen, set both the Page Name and the Region Title to "**Employees**" and click Next.

5. On the Table/View screen, set Table/View Name to "EMP" and click Next.

6. On the List View Page screen, set Display Column to "ENAME" and click Next.

7. On the Form Page screen, set Page Name and Region Title to "**Employee Details**" and click Next.

8. Leave the Primary Key type as Managed By Database (ROWID) and click Next.

9. All the Select Columns should already be on the right side of the shuttle, so just click Next.

10. Given that all the process options for Insert, Update, and Delete are already set to "Yes"—which is what you want, click Next.

11. On the Confirmation page, click Create.

Once created, you should be able to run the List View page to view some employees. Tapping on an employee should take you to the employee details in the form page. You will need to change the Px_<field_name> notation used in the following steps, based on the pages you have just created. For example, if you created page 12 for the EMP Form page, for Px_JOB you would use P12_JOB.

Let's change the Px_JOB item on the form page to display as a select list. Navigate to the Page Definition screen of the form page and complete the following steps:

1. If you use the tree view, double-click the Px_JOB item. If you use the component view, click the Px_JOB item.

2. On the Edit Page Item screen, set Display As to "Select List". Scroll down to the List of Values section and set Display Null Value to "Yes", and set Null Display Value to "**- Select Job -**".

3. Enter the following for the List of Values definition:

```
SELECT DISTINCT job AS display
,        job AS return
FROM emp
WHERE job IS NOT NULL
ORDER BY display
```

4. Click Apply Changes.

Once completed, your new pages should look like those seen in Figure 8-1.

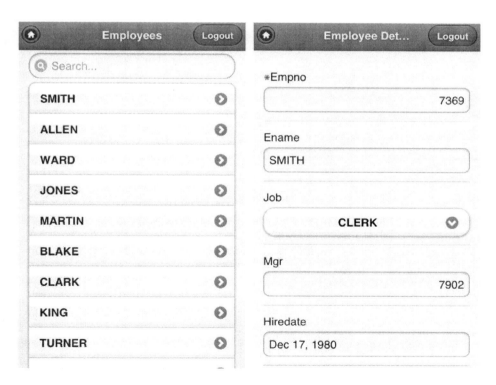

Figure 8-1. *New pages to test Dynamic Actions*

Thinking Through a Dynamic Action

Now that there are some new pages to play with, let's examine a typical requirement and then work through the implementation using a Dynamic Action. Imagine you were handed the following requirement: *Commission can only be entered for salespeople.*

It's often helpful to break the requirement down into the parts of a Dynamic Action: the when, what, and where(s). In this case, you want to modify the Px_COMM item to be enterable only when Px_JOB is "SALESMAN". Therefore, "when" equates to change of Px_JOB with condition of SALESMAN; "what" equates to a true action of "Enable" and false action of "Disable"; "where" equates to Px_COMM for both actions. Thinking along these lines will make implementing requirements using Dynamic Actions much simpler. Note that choosing show/hide true and false actions would also satisfy the given requirement; however, in this case, the enable/disable was deemed more user-friendly.

Note Conditions allow Dynamic Actions to fire both true and false actions rather than just true actions. The JavaScript Expression option offers flexibility when needed.

The Dynamic Action should look like this once you have created it:

- When:
    - Event: Change
    - Selection Type: Item(s)
    - Item(s): Px_JOB
    - Condition: equal to
    - Value: SALESMAN
- True Actions:
    - Action: Enable
    - Item(s): Px_COMM
- False Actions:
    - Action: Disable
    - Item(s): Px_COMM

Dynamic Actions can be used to create client-side rules that prevent users from entering invalid data, such as entering a commission for a person who is not a salesman. However, developers should still develop server-side validations to ensure the data integrity. This can be implemented as APEX validations on the page or integrated into triggers, check constraints, or similar in the underlying table.

Creating a Dynamic Action

With a basic plan in place, you can now move on to creating the Dynamic Action. Navigate to the Page Definition screen of the form page and complete the following steps.

1. If you use the tree view, right-click Dynamic Actions (under Page Rendering at the bottom of the page) and click Create. If you use the component view, click the Create button in the Dynamic Actions region.

At this step in the wizard, you need to provide a name for our Dynamic Action. The authors of this text recommend you choose a name based on when the Dynamic Action will fire rather than on the actions. This practice makes finding and reusing Dynamic Actions easier and prevents the need to rename the Dynamic Action when actions are added, removed, or reordered.

2. On the Identification screen, set Name to "**Job changed (= SALESMAN)**" and then click Next.

Tip Name a Dynamic Action based on the configuration of the "when."

Next, you need to configure when the Dynamic Action should fire. The default triggering event, Change, maps to an event that the browser will invoke when the element's value is changed by the user. That's exactly the event you need for this Dynamic Action, so leave the default. You do need to specify where you want to listen for the change event and configure the condition portion of the when, however.

3. On the When screen, complete the following settings and click Next:

    a. Set Item(s) to "Px_JOB"

    b. Set Condition to "equal to"

    c. Set Value to "**SALESMAN**"

Tip Right-clicking an item in the tree view and selecting Create Dynamic Action will automatically set the selection type to Item(s) and populate the Item(s) value.

In this next step, you will define the actions. When you specify a condition on the event (as you did in the preceding) within the Create Dynamic Action wizard, you can specify both true and false actions within the wizard. There are certain action pairs such as enable/disable, hide/show, and add class/remove class. If you select one of these actions within the wizard, the corresponding false action will be automatically generated for conditional events if you leave the Generate Opposite False Action check box checked (see Figure 8-2). This makes creating the actions in our example very easy because you only need to specify the true action, and then let the wizard create the corresponding false action for us.

4. On the True Action screen, set Action to "Enable" (see Figure 8-2) and then click Next.

The following action will fire when the 'When Condition' is met or when 'No Condition' has been specified.

Page:	12 - Emp
Name:	Job changed (= SALESMAN)
* Action	Enable ▼
	Show, Hide, Enable, Disable, Set Value
Fire On Page Load	☑
Generate Opposite False Action	☑

Figure 8-2. Generate Opposite False Action option for simple actions

In the last step of the wizard, you define the Affected Elements. This is how you specify exactly what elements the actions should work with. In our case, you are simply enabling/disabling the commission. Keep in mind that not all actions will require Affected Elements to be defined.

5. On the Affected Elements screen, set Selection Type to "Item(s)", move Px_COMM in the Items(s) shuttle to the right, and click Create Dynamic Action.

Once your Dynamic Action is created, run the page to test it. When you drill down on an employee from the List View page, you should see that the commission is disabled unless Job is SALESMAN (see Figure 8-3).

Figure 8-3. *Commission field disabled when Job does not equal SALESMAN*

You may notice that when an employee with a job other than SALESMAN is selected from the List View page, the commission field is disabled when the page is rendered. This is due to the other option displayed in Figure 8-2: Fire On Page Load. You should also observe what happens when you change the job selected to and from SALESMAN: the commission field immediately changes as appropriate but the page is not submitted, so you don't lose any other changes made on the page.

Another important thing to point out is that when creating a Dynamic Action, you can add only one true action and optionally one false action. But once the Dynamic Action is created, additional true and false actions can easily be manually added from the Page Definition screen of the page as needed. If multiple true or false actions are defined, their sequence values will determine the order in which the actions are executed.

Declaring a Server Call Example

Our first example only changed the display characteristics of an item. Now let's see how you can retrieve data from the server—again without performing a page submission—using Dynamic Actions. For this example, you want to retrieve the location of and the number of employees in the employee's department.

The first step is to update the department field to use a select list, making it easier for the user to change the department. Navigate to that page, drill into the Px_DEPTNO item, and then complete these steps:

1. If you use the tree view, double-click the Px_DEPTNO item. If you use the component view, click the Px_DEPTNO item.

2. On the Edit Page Item screen, set the Label as "**Department**", set the Display Null Value to "Yes" and set the Null Display Value to "**- Select Department -**."

3. Enter the following for the List of Values definition:

```
SELECT dname AS display
,      deptno AS return
FROM dept
ORDER BY display
```

4. Click Apply Changes.

Now you need to add two items for holding the values returned from the server: Px_LOCATION and Px_DEPT_EMPLOYEES. From the Page Definition screen of the form page, complete the following steps:

1. If you use the tree view, right-click the Edit EMP region (or Items under the Edit EMP region), and then click Create Page Item. If you use the component view, click the Create button in the Items region.

2. On the Item Type screen, set the Item Type to "Display Only."

3. On the Display Position and Name screen, enter the Item Name as "**Px_LOCATION**" and click Next.

4. On the Item Attributes screen, enter the Label as "**Location**" : and click Next.

5. The defaults on the Settings screen are what you want, so click Next.

6. The defaults on the Source screen are also correct, so click Create Item.

7. Next, you create the second item. If you use the tree view, right-click the Edit EMP region (or Items under the Edit EMP region), and then click Create Page Item. If you use the component view, click the Create button in the Items region.

8. On the Item Type screen, set the Item Type to "Display Only."

9. On the Display Position and Name screen, enter the Item Name as "**Px_DEPT_EMPLOYEES**" and click Next.

10. On the Item Attributes screen, enter the Label as "**Department Employees**" : and click Next.

11. The defaults on the Settings screen are correct, so click Next.

12. The defaults on the Source screen are also correct, so click Create Item.

The final step is to create the Dynamic Action for populating the department fields. You want this Dynamic Action to fire whenever the department is changed, so you won't be including a condition. The defaults for the "when" within the Create Dynamic Action wizard are as follows: the Event is "change", the Selection Type is "Item(s)," and the Condition is "No Condition."

1. If you use the tree view, right-click Px_DEPTNO and click Create Dynamic Action. If you use the component view, click the Create button in the Dynamic Actions region.

2. On the Identification screen, set the Name to "**Department change**" and click Next.

3. On the When screen, set Item(s) to "Px_DEPTNO". (Note that this will already be populated if you right-clicked on the item from the tree view.)

4. Click Next.

For this Dynamic Action, you need to use the Set Value action. Once you select an action, the settings change based on your selection. For this action, the first setting, Set Type, will further alter the input fields. The simplest way to retrieve values from the database is to use an SQL Statement. At runtime, this will generate an Ajax call and execute the specified SQL. In order for the Ajax call to utilize a page item, it must be submitted as part of the definition.

5. On the True Action screen, set the Action to "Set Value" and then select SQL Statement as the Set Type.

6. Enter the following for SQL Statement:

```
SELECT d.loc location
,      (select count(*) from emp e
          where e.deptno = d.deptno) dept_employees
FROM dept d
WHERE d.deptno = :Px_DEPTNO
```

7. Set Page Items To Submit as "Px_DEPTNO" and click Next.

Tip   If you are working on page 12, make sure that you replace Px_DEPTNO with P12_DEPTNO in the last two steps; otherwise, this code will not return any data.

This single action will return two values; therefore, you must specify two items to populate. It is very important to ensure that the order of the returned values matches the order of the items selected; otherwise, the wrong values will be returned into the selected items. If you are unsure of the order that you specified in the SQL Statement on the previous step, you can simply show the True Action–Set Value–SQL Statement region, which will display the SQL entered.

8. On the Affected Elements screen, set Selection Type to "Item(s)", move Px_LOCATION and Px_DEPT_EMPLOYEES to the right in the Items(s) shuttle, and click Create Dynamic Action.

When you run the page (see Figure 8-4), you should notice that the location and department employees fields are populated based on the currently selected employee's department. If you change the selected department, the displayed values will also be updated based on the new department.

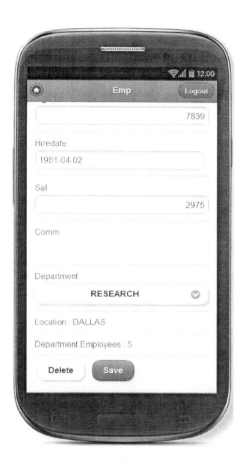

Figure 8-4. *Server call Dynamic Action example*

It is important to understand that the first Dynamic Action that you just defined generated JavaScript to manipulate the display characteristics of the commission field. This second example generated the necessary JavaScript and an Ajax call to the server to populate the location and department employees. These simple examples illustrate the power and ease of using Dynamic Actions. These Dynamic Actions work equally well on desktop and mobile pages. For testing purposes, they also execute whether running the mobile page on a desktop, a mobile emulator, or on a mobile device.

This ends the introduction to Dynamic Actions; however, we recommend you continue familiarizing yourself with the framework. Take time to explore the various events and actions that are available and try to create a few additional Dynamic Actions with these test pages. To see further examples of Dynamic Actions, install the Sample Dynamic Actions application, which is available under the Packaged Applications tab within the Application Builder. Although within the sample application the Dynamic Actions are implemented on desktop pages, the majority can also be implemented on mobile user interface pages.

Changes to Dynamic Actions in APEX 4.2

Many changes were made to the Dynamic Action framework in APEX 4.2. Some of the changes were a result of the newly added support for mobile applications, while others were improvements that could be leveraged in both mobile and desktop user interfaces. In this part of the chapter, you will explore these changes in-depth.

No More Standard vs. Advanced

One of the first changes developers may notice in the Dynamic Action framework is the absence of the standard and advanced options shown in Figure 8-5.

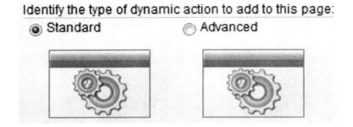

Identify the type of dynamic action to add to this page:

⦿ Standard   ⦾ Advanced

Figure 8-5. *Pre- APEX 4.2 standard vs. advanced option*

These options were created to simplify the creation of some basic Dynamic Actions and they were the first thing one would see when creating a new Dynamic Action. If standard was selected, the event selection would default to the change event and the event selection item would be hidden so that its value couldn't be changed.

In addition, the actions would be limited to hide/show and enable/disable, as seen in Figure 8-6. One of the advantages of the standard Dynamic Actions was that the actions shown had exact opposites, which allowed the framework to create the opposite false action automatically, if needed.

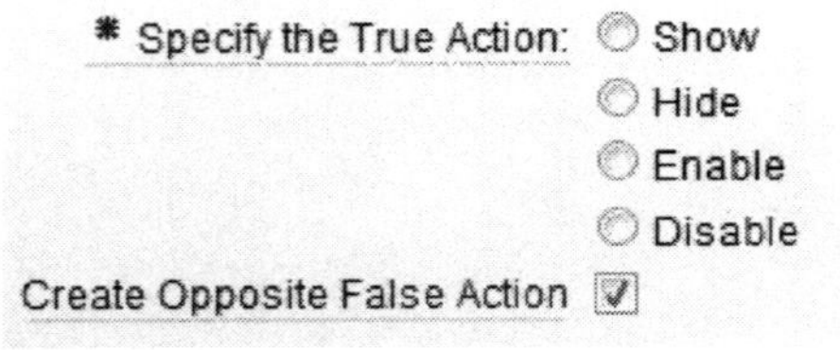

    * Specify the True Action: ⦾ Show

                            ⦾ Hide

                            ⦾ Enable

                            ⦾ Disable

Create Opposite False Action ☑

Figure 8-6. *Limited actions for standard actions pre-APEX 4.2*

At the end of the day, the selection between standard and advanced only changed the wizard used to create the Dynamic Action. Once created, the Dynamic Actions were exactly alike in that one could edit them with all the events and actions available. The problem, however, with the standard or advanced option is that it required developers to remember the event and actions that were associated with standard Dynamic Actions so that they could choose that option when creating a Dynamic Action that fit within the constraints.

In APEX 4.2, the standard or advanced option was removed from the wizard but the advantage of creating the opposite false action was maintained, as seen in Figure 8-7. This simple change in the wizard allowed developers to leverage this ability with any event, rather than only the change event. Additionally, the Generate Opposite False Action option is now available for the Add Class and Remove Class actions as well.

        * Action | Hide   ▼ |

                    Show, Hide, Enable, Disable, Set Value

        Fire On Page Load   ☑

Generate Opposite False Action   ☑

Figure 8-7. *True action step in Create Dynamic Action wizard in APEX 4.2*

■ **Note** A condition must be specified in the "when" portion of a Dynamic Action in order to see the Generate Opposite False Action check box.

New Declarative Events

Prior to APEX 4.2, developers had a total of 23 declarative events to utilize in the Dynamic Action framework. APEX 4.2 introduces 13 new declarative events, bringing the total to 36. All of these new events were added to support mobile development, such as touch events, device rotation, and scrolling through long lists. Here's a list of the new events along with the real event name and a brief description of when the event fires:

- *Orientation Change* (orientationchange): Triggered when the user rotates the mobile device from vertical orientation to horizontal orientation or vice versa.

- *Scroll Start* (scrollstart): Triggered when a scroll begins.

- *Scroll Stop* (scrollstop): Triggered when a scroll ends.

- *Tap* (tap): Triggered when a user quickly taps and releases a target element.

- *Tap and Hold* (taphold): Triggered when a user taps and holds a target element for at least 750 milliseconds.

- *Swipe* (swipe): Triggered when a users drags a finger horizontally more than 30 pixels within 1 second.

- *Swipe Left* (swipeleft): Like swipe, but only triggered when dragging left.

- *Swipe Right* (swiperight): Like swipe, but only triggered when dragging right.

- *Touch Start* (vmousedown): Triggered when either a finger first touches the surface or a mousedown event occurs.

- *Touch End* (vmouseup): Triggered when all fingers stop touching the surface or when a mouseup event occurs.

- *Touch Cancel* (vmousecancel): Triggered when the user cancels the current operation (for example, when pressing the Home button on a phone) or when a mousecancel event occurs.

- *Touch Move* (vmousemove): Triggered when a touch point is moved along the touch surface or when a mousemove event occurs.

- *Virtual Click* (vmouseclick): Triggered when a touchend or a click event occurs. This event is used to overcome problems with click events, which have up to a 500-millsecond delay on most mobile touch browsers, whereas touch events don't have a delay.

APEX automatically filters the events displayed in the event select list according to the user interface (UI) being used. Because the new events are only relevant to mobile applications, they will only be available when using the jQuery Mobile UI. Likewise, there are events that are available in the Desktop UI but not the jQuery Mobile UI. Here's a list of events that won't be available when using the jQuery Mobile UI:

- Double Click

- Mouse Button Press

- Mouse Button Release

- Mouse Enter

- Mouse Leave

- Mouse Move

- Resize

There is a "Show unsupported..." option in the event select list for both UIs, which allows you to see the events that have been hidden; but in general, these should not be used.

As you can see, the majority of the events that are hidden or displayed according to the UI relate to the tool that users use to interact with the application: either a mouse or a finger. When multitouch displays were first introduced, device manufacturers—starting with Apple and the iPhone— had to make sure their touch devices still worked with applications that were built around mouse events. The solution they came up with was to simulate mouse events when touch events occurred.

Mobile-Specific Event Examples

The following examples, while not necessarily representative of the exact functionality you would implement in your applications, serve to highlight how touch events work on a mobile device. One thing to note is that you should always test touch-based Dynamic Actions on a mobile device because they don't necessarily have an equivalent mouse event, and you need to ensure they perform as expected on the intended platform.

Orientation Change Event

The first of the mobile-specific Dynamic Actions you are going to implement is changing the focus to the first item on the page whenever the orientation changes to portrait. From the Page Definition screen of the form page, complete the following steps:

1. If you use the tree view, right-click Dynamic Actions (under Page Rendering at the bottom of the page) and click Create. If you use the component view, click the Create button in the Dynamic Actions region.

2. On the Identification screen, set the Name to "**Orientation Change**" and click Next.

3. On the When screen, complete the following settings and then click Next:

   a. Select Orientation Change as the Event.

   b. Set the Condition to "JavaScript Expression."

   c. Enter "**this.browserEvent.orientation === 'portrait'**" as the Value.

4. On the True Action screen, select Set Focus as the Action, and then click Next.

5. There is no corresponding false action, so just click Next on the False Action (Optional) screen.

6. On the Affected Elements screen, set Selection Type to "Item(s), move Px_ENAME to the right in the Item(s) shuttle, and click Create Dynamic Action.

To test this Dynamic Action, you will have to run your application on a mobile device. Rotating your desktop monitor from landscape to portrait is not particularly easy and it will not fire an event as it does on a mobile device. Log into your application from your mobile browser and navigate to the EMP Form page. Select an item (other than Name) on the page, such as Hiredate. Now rotate your mobile device to change the orientation. If you change from landscape to portrait mode, the focus will move to the Name field. However, if you change from portrait to landscape mode, the focus will stay on the current item.

Swipe-Left and Swipe-Right Events

In Chapter 4, there is a good example of using swipe events to move to the previous or next record (see the "Adding Swiped Navigation" section). Therefore, the next example will utilize swipe events to decrease or increase the salary by 10%, depending on which way the user swipes.

1. If you use the tree view, right-click Dynamic Actions (under Page Rendering at the bottom of the page) and click Create. If you use the component view, click the Create button in the Dynamic Actions region.

2. On the Identification screen, set the Name to "**Salary Swipe Left**" and click Next.

3. On the When screen, complete the following steps and then click Next:

    a. Select Swipe Left as the Event.

    b. Set "Px_SAL" as the Item(s).

    c. Set the Condition to "greater than".

    d. Enter "**100**" as the Value.

4. On the True Action screen, complete the following settings and then click Next:

    a. Select Set Value as the Action.

    b. Uncheck Fire On Page Load.

    c. Select PL/SQL Expression as the Set Type.

    d. Enter "**TRUNC(:Px_SAL * 0.9)**" as the PL/SQL Expression.

    e. Set Page Items to "Submit as Px_SAL".

5. There is no corresponding false action, so click Next on the False Action (Optional) screen.

6. On the Affected Elements screen, select Triggering Element as the Selection Type, and then click Create Dynamic Action.

7. Now for the Swipe Right. If you use the tree view, right click Dynamic Actions (under Page Rendering at the bottom of the page) and click Create. If you use the component view, click the Create button in the Dynamic Actions region.

8. On the Identification screen, set the Name as "**Salary Swipe Right**" and click Next.

9. On the When screen, select "Swipe Right" as the Event, set the Item(s) to "Px_SAL" and click Next.

10. On the True Action screen, complete the following settings and click Next:

    a. Select "Set Value" as the Action.

    b. Uncheck Fire On Page Load.

    c. Select "PL/SQL Expression" as the Set Type.

    d. Enter "**TRUNC(:Px_SAL * 1.1)**" as the PL/SQL Expression.

    e. Set Page Items To Submit as "Px_SAL".

11. There is no corresponding false action, so click Next on the False Action (Optional) screen.

12. On the Affected Elements screen, set the Selection Type to "Triggering Element" and then click Create Dynamic Action.

Now let's run the test application again to see what happens when these Dynamic Actions fire. From the EMP List, select an employee. On the EMP Form page, scroll down the page until the Sal item is visible. Using your finger, swipe to the left and right. Each time you swipe, the value for salary will change—up or down—depending on which way you swipe. Tap on the Sal item so that the user input is displayed, and repeat the swiping from side to side. Notice that regardless of whether the item is selected or not, the swipe actions fire when the appropriate action is performed. Navigate back to the EMP List without pressing Apply Changes.

When you selected the same employee, their salary was the same as it was before you started testing. This is because these events are only changing the value on the client.

Now that you have seen mobile-specific events in action, it is time to delve even deeper into some of the complexities of event handling.

Advanced Dynamic Actions

The following information is included to provide you with a more comprehensive understanding of the advanced capabilities of Dynamic Actions. Should the standard built-in capabilities not meet your requirements, such information will enable you to extend your application's functionality.

Custom JavaScript

The Dynamic Action framework was designed to allow developers to easily extend the built-in capabilities by utilizing the many hooks to incorporate custom JavaScript. JavaScript can be utilized in the event, actions, and affected elements: when, what, and where. In order to build reusable events, developers can build plug-in Dynamic Actions that extend the capabilities of the framework.

Developers who include custom JavaScript code can utilize the this object that provides access to related attributes, including the triggering element, the event object, and more. The specific attributes available in the this object depend on which attribute within Dynamic Actions is selected. The item level help provides information on the attributes.

When writing custom JavaScript code, developers should understand how the apex.gPageContext$ variable is utilized and include it within their code. This variable is important (especially when developing mobile user interface pages) to ensure that the specified jQuery selector has the correct context and only executes on the given page. If this variable is not set, the JavaScript code may execute on other pages with unexpected consequences; for example:

```
jQuery( "<your selector>", apex.gPageContext$ );
```

If the event you need to capture is covered by Dynamic Actions but you need to customize the action performed, you can utilize a standard Dynamic Action event and then specify an action of Execute JavaScript Code. This will allow you to define or call custom JavaScript code for use when the specific action fires for the specified Dynamic Action event. If the JavaScript is specific to one page, it can be defined within the Function and Global Variable Declaration section of the page definition. If this code is required on multiple pages or in multiple applications, it is a good candidate for defining a plug-in Dynamic Action.

Nonstandard Selection Types

When specifying either the When or Affected Element selection types, you can utilize DOM objects or jQuery selectors to provide additional capabilities not found by selecting the more common Item(s), Button, and Region. Using the DOM object, you can specify either the Document Object Model (DOM) object (document,window) or the ID of a DOM object (myElementID). This enables you to customize a Dynamic Action to operate on nonstandard components such as breadcrumbs or navigation bar entries. The jQuery Selector type allows you to specify a jQuery selector string that returns one or more page elements. There is a wide variety of selectors ranging from form selectors (input, text, radio, button, and so forth, which will return all of the elements of that type) to classes (.my_class will return all elements with a class of my_class) and references (#my_id will return the element with an ID of my_id).

As an example of utilizing a jQuery Selector, please install the Sample Dynamic Actions application from the Packaged Application tab within the Application Builder. Once installed, run the application and select the Refresh 2 Dynamic Action. This will take you to page 18: Server Side – Refresh 2, which has a single Dynamic Action DELETE EMP defined.

When a user clicks the Delete icon, you need to fire a Dynamic Action that identifies the specific record, physically deletes the record from the database, and then refreshes the screen. To correctly identify the record, the ID column within the report has a Column Link defined with attributes of id="#ID#" and class="delete".

The DELETE EMP Dynamic Action is a click event with a Selection Type of "jQuery Selector" and a selector of a.delete. The a denotes all anchors or links on the page and the .delete denotes with a class of delete, as specified in the report link. Therefore, when a user clicks on a specific × (Delete icon), the ID of the row selected is available to the actions.

The first action is a simple Confirm action. The next action is Set Value, which uses a Set Type of "JavaScript Expression" with a value of this.triggeringElement.id; to populate a hidden item on the page with the ID of the record on which the Delete icon was clicked. The Execute PL/SQL Code action submits the hidden page item and performs the actual delete from the Oracle table. The Refresh action performs a Partial Page Refresh of the Employees region to show the revised records, and finally a plug-in Dynamic Action of Notification is used to pop up a message that the delete was successful.

Event Scope

Tucked away in the Advanced section of a Dynamic Action definition is a single setting named Event Scope, which determines whether the event is executed only once, for the lifetime of the current page, or until triggering elements are updated by a partial-page refresh (PPR).

The Event Scope setting is not exposed when creating a Dynamic Action but its value, which defaults to Static, can be changed afterward. Prior to APEX 4.2, Event Scope had three values: Bind, Live, and Once. In APEX 4.2, the values available for this option changed to Static, Dynamic, and Once.

The following is a breakdown of the Event Scope options:

- A *Static* event scope binds the event handler to the triggering elements for the lifetime of the current page, but will no longer be bound if the triggering elements are updated via PPR.

- A *Dynamic* event scope binds the event handler to the triggering elements for the lifetime of the current page, including any triggering elements that are re-created via PPR. Specifying Dynamic causes an additional field Static Container (jQuery Selector) to be displayed. Specifying a Static Container can help improve the performance of the way events are handled with a Dynamic Event Scope. This should be an element on the page that itself does not get re-created, but contains the triggering elements that are re-created using PPR. This element reference must be defined as a jQuery selector. For example, if you have a Dynamic Action that does something to the rows of an interactive report region (which is re-created by PPR), this would need an Event Scope of Dynamic in order for the Dynamic Action to still work after the report has been refreshed. And here, the Static Container value could be set to a jQuery selector selecting the region's Static ID value; for example, '#my_region'.

- A *Once* event scope binds the event handler to the triggering elements for a once-only event.

Custom Events

Wherever possible, you should try to utilize the events that are available natively with Dynamic Actions. If the "when" event meets your requirements but the standard actions or selection types are not sufficient, the following detail will assist without your needing to resort to a completely custom event.

While the declarative events available in the Dynamic Action framework include the most common events developers need to work with, they are but a small subset of all the events that could be triggered on a given element.

Some DOM-level events (events defined in the DOM specification) were not included because they are not commonly used or widely supported by browser manufacturers. In addition to DOM level events, there are many custom events that can be triggered by developers manually—something often done in jQuery and APEX plug-ins to provide other developers hooks into how the plug-in works.

Prior to APEX 4.2, the only way to add new events to the Dynamic Action framework was to utilize the plug-in architecture, which was both unintuitive and difficult. Now with APEX 4.2, developers see the custom option displayed in the event select list, as shown in Figure 8-8.

Figure 8-8. *Custom option in the Dynamic Action framework*

For the most part, the Custom option works as one might expect. Upon selecting Custom, a Custom Event input is shown, which allows you to enter any event name you wish (see Figure 8-9).

Figure 8-9. *Custom Event option allows for any event name*

While the new custom event option allows you to create Dynamic Actions for just about any event triggered on any element, there are some exceptions. For example, at the time of this writing, the Dynamic Action framework uses the mobileinit event for pages using the jQuery Mobile Smartphone user interface to initialize Dynamic Actions on the page. However, there are several events that will fire before mobileinit and thus the Dynamic Actions framework cannot be used for these events.

Virtual Click Events

Unfortunately, there are some problems with the way that touch events endeavor to simulate mouse events. The most noticeable issue, which results from the complexities of the multitouch interface, is that the simulated events are dispatched after a brief delay. The amount of time in the delay can vary greatly by OS and browser manufacturer, but averages around 300 milliseconds. For this reason, relying on the click event in mobile applications can contribute to the application feeling sluggish or unresponsive.

The new touch events in APEX, such as Touch Start, are based on a group of virtual mouse events that the jQuery Mobile library introduced to abstract away how the user interacts with the application (the events have real event names that start with a v). These virtual events utilize both mouse and touch events to trigger the virtual event as fast as possible. In addition, they provide normalized coordinate details on the event object.

Figure 8-10 shows a simple application that was created to display information related to events. The event selections (shown collapsed) at the top allows you to select from a number of different mouse, touch, and virtual events, and then interact with the target area with a mouse or a finger.

Figure 8-10. *Event testing application*

After a few seconds have passed without a new event firing, a popup opens to display the events that were triggered, the number of milliseconds it took to fire the event, and the original event that was used to drive the event that was captured. Figure 8-11 shows the results of a simple tap in a mobile browser (iPhone 4S) compared to a simple click in a desktop browser (Firefox 17).

Figure 8-11. *Results from iPhone tap (left) vs. Firefox click (right)*

Notice that in the case of the iPhone, there was nearly a half-second delay before the click event was dispatched. The vclick event, on the other hand, was triggered just after the DOM-level touchend event was dispatched, which is much more desirable. This is one of the main benefits of using the virtual mouse events provided by jQuery Mobile. In APEX, utilizing this event is as easy as selecting the virtual click event over the click event in your mobile applications.

In a perfect world, programmers would be able to use vclick without any potential side effects. But this is not a perfect world, and so the jQuery Mobile documentation advises developers to use vclick with caution due to the delay associated with the simulated click event on mobile browsers. The location where the simulated click event will be triggered is based on the location of the touch events. Imagine a user tapping the Edit button in a list view and a form page transitioning in with a Delete button in the exact same location where the tap event occurred. The simulated click event may actually click the Delete button!

So there you have it: the vclick event is faster but comes with some caveats. Although the other virtual mouse events don't suffer from the same problem, you're not as likely to be using them anyway. If you don't mind the delay associated with the click event and you want to keep things as simple as possible, avoid vclick and use the click event instead. However, if you want to leverage the speed offered by vclick, be sure to mitigate your risks by designing your pages in such a way that a delayed click will not have an adverse effect.

Complete List of Dynamic Action Events

Table 8-1 provides a complete list of the Dynamic Action events available, along with their real event name (if they were introduced in APEX 4.2), and whether they are designed for desktop and/or mobile user interfaces.

Table 8-1. *Declarative Events in APEX 4.2*

APEX Event Name	Real Event Name	4.2	Desktop	Mobile
<u>Browser Events</u>				
Change	change		X	X
Click	click		X	X
Double Click	cblclick		X	
Get Focus	focusin		X	X
Key Down	keydown		X	X
Key Press	keypress		X	X
Key Release	keyup		X	X
Lose Focus	focusout		X	X
Mouse Button Press	mousedown		X	
Mouse Button Release	mouseup		X	
Mouse Enter	mouseenter		X	
Mouse Leave	mouseleave		X	
Mouse Move	mousemove		X	
Orientation Change	orientationchange	X		X
Page Load	ready		X	X
Page Unload	unload		X	X
Resize	resize		X	
Resource Load	load		X	X
Scroll	scroll		X	X
Scroll Start	scrollstart	X		X
Scroll Stop	scrollstop	X		X
Select	select		X	X
Swipe	swipe	X		X
Swipe Left	swipeleft	X		X
Swipe Right	swiperight	X		X
Tap	tap	X		X
Tap and Hold	taphold	X		X
Touch Cancel	vmousecancel	X		X

(*continued*)

Table 8-1. (*continued*)

APEX Event Name	Real Event Name	4.2	Desktop	Mobile
Touch End	vmouseup	X		X
Touch Move	vmousemove	X		X
Touch Start	vmousedown	X		X
Virtual Click	vclick	X		X
Framework Events				
After Refresh	apexafterrefresh		X	X
Before Page Submit	apexbeforepagesubmit		X	X
Before Refresh	apexbeforerefresh		X	X
Component Events				
Change Order [Shuttle]	shuttlechangeorder		X	
Plug-in Components *Event Name [Component Name]*			X	X
Custom Event		X	X	X

Events can be categorized as follows:

- *Browser Events*: Standard browser events.

- *Framework Events*: Events triggered from within the APEX framework.

- *Component Events*: Only available when there is a component, such as a plug-in or native component, within your application that triggers a custom event.

Wrap Up

The power of Dynamic Actions can't be overstated given their extensive capabilities. The ease with which every developer can implement, maintain, and enhance Dynamic Actions, without necessarily needing to learn JavaScript—and possibly Ajax, enables complex client-side interactivity to be incorporated into any APEX application. Improving application usability and making it more intuitive will greatly increase your user satisfaction and should reduce user-training requirements.

CHAPTER 9

Deploying Applications Natively

As more and more people start to access the Internet from their mobile devices, many businesses find that having a mobile app in addition to desktop applications or a web site is necessary to stay connected with their customers or audience.

The mobile landscape can be confusing and sometimes even scary for a business or IT department—it often means a huge investment of time and money. There is a diversity of platforms—iOS, Android, Symbian, and Windows Mobile—and at a certain point, you have to ask yourself if you're going to go native or with a web app. The direction to take your mobile app development is a fundamental decision and there is no right answer; but there are pros and cons to each path, which you will need to evaluate against your specific business needs.

Native, Web, or Hybrid Apps?

Before you move on to the applied sections of this chapter, we provide an overview of the options for developing a mobile app. Essentially, developers can choose from three different application approaches, each with its own set of pros and cons.

Web Apps

A web app, or mobile web site, can be accessed by any mobile device that has a browser. Though browser-based, typically, not all of a device's hardware features can be tapped into. To produce a more engaging and interactive experience, HTML5 and CSS3, in combination with JavaScript frameworks like jQuery Mobile or Sencha Touch, are increasingly used to take advantage of the advanced features offered by these new specifications.

So, what are the pros and cons of web apps?

- Pros:

    - A single codebase that can be accessed by any browser-enabled mobile device.

    - Uses web technologies (HTML/CSS/JavaScript). These are the technologies used for building APEX application interfaces.

    - Performance issues are less of an issue as mobile browsers become faster and their JavaScript engines improve.

    - No app store approval process needed.

    - Updates to the app are made on the server and are instantly available for all platforms and on all devices.

- Cons:

  - Using web technologies means interpreted code (as opposed to compiled code for native apps). Some developers believe that web apps will always be slower than native apps.

  - They don't have full access to all the methods exposed by the device's operating system, which means that you are limited to the APIs made available by the browser. As it stands now, this means no camera, compass, video capture, microphone, user contacts, or file uploading.

  - Requires an Internet connection.

  - They can't be found on the app store.

Native Apps

Native refers to building an app in a device's native programming language. For iOS devices, this means Objective-C, C# for Windows 8 and for Android, it's Java. Native apps are typically fast, reliable, and can access the entire device's hardware (camera, accelerometer, compass, etc.). But it also means that your app is tied to the platform it is built for. An iOS app won't run on an Android device without recoding the entire app to Java.

Let's take a look at the pros and cons of native apps.

- Pros:

  - Better performance (at least for now), smoother animations and transitions, and faster load times.

  - Can be featured and searched for in an app store. App purchase transactions are handled on your behalf.

  - Available offline.

  - Full access to the device's hardware and OS features.

  - Implicit installation of an app to the device's home screen. (On iOS and Android devices, any web app can be added to the home screen, but it's a manual process that the user has to perform).

- Cons:

  - Typically more expensive to build, even for a single platform. Build costs increase significantly for each new platform.

  - Because the codebase needs to be reworked for each OS, the time to build an app for multiple devices can be quite involved.

  - Your app must be accessed through the device's app store, which has two important considerations: your app must go through an approval process, which can be lengthy and arbitrary, and all app updates must go through a new approval process.

Hybrid Apps

A hybrid app is built using web technologies and then wrapped in a platform-specific shell that allows it to be installed just like a native app. Thus, it can be sold/accessed through the device's app store.

PhoneGap is an example of a framework that allows you take a web app and turn it into a native app for iOS, Android, BlackBerry, Windows Phone/8, webOS, Symbian, and more. The hybrid frameworks typically also have APIs that allow you to access the device's hardware and features that are locked out from the browser.

What are the pros and cons of this app type?

- Pros:
  - Allows you to develop on a single codebase offered by web technologies, yet you can still market and distribute your app for each of the major mobile platforms.
  - Provides APIs to access features locked out of the browser, such as the camera, compass, and contacts.
- Cons:
  - Still subject to the store's approval process.
  - No instant updating (this is not entirely relevant for APEX-based hybrid apps).
  - The app's performance is dependent on the device's browser capabilities.

At first glance, you might think that hybrid is the way to go. After all, it seems to offer the best of both worlds—or at least the best compromise between development costs and distribution: a single foundational codebase across multiple platforms. Alas, it's not so simple.

To understand the nature of hybrid apps and how it relates to developing mobile applications with Oracle Application Express, let us first have a look at the architecture and then walk through the details of developing and deploying a hybrid app using PhoneGap in combination with APEX.

PhoneGap Architecture

PhoneGap is an application container technology that allows you to create natively-installed applications for mobile devices using HTML, CSS, and JavaScript. The core engine for PhoneGap is open source and maintained under the Apache Cordova project.

Application User Interface

The user interface for PhoneGap applications is created using HTML, CSS, and JavaScript. The UI layer of a PhoneGap application is a web browser view that takes up 100% of the device width and 100% of the device height. Think of it as a "chromeless" web browser. It renders HTML content, without a toolbar, an address bar, or the window decoration of a regular web browser.

The WebView (see Figure 9-1) used by PhoneGap is the same WebView used by the native operating system. On iOS, for example, it is the Objective-C UIWebView class; it is android.webkit.WebView on Android.

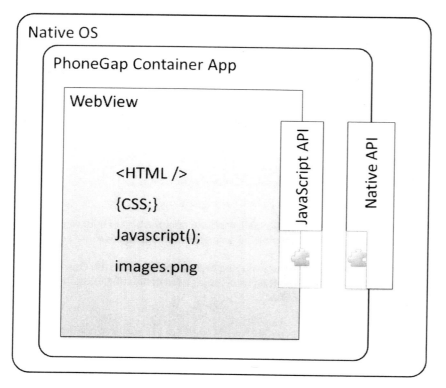

Figure 9-1. *PhoneGap application container and WebView*

The initial application document loaded by the PhoneGap application has a local `file://` URL. This means that if you want to pull in pages from a remote (APEX) server, you will have to refer to them with absolute URLs to that server. Because your document originates from a `file://` URL, loading pages or assets from your remote server is considered a cross-domain request and will be blocked. Your ability to enable cross-domain requests from within a PhoneGap application can be controlled by the whitelist feature, which is discussed in more detail later in this chapter.

The PhoneGap API

PhoneGap provides an application programming interface (API) that enables access to native operating system functionality using JavaScript. You build your application logic using JavaScript, and the PhoneGap API handles communication with the native operating system. This API is divided into two layers: a JavaScript with a standardized method signature across all supported platforms and a native API written in the hosting device's OS language.

API Feature Overview

The matrix in Figure 9-2 shows the device features available through the PhoneGap API (version 2.3.0) on supported operating systems.

	iPhone / iPhone 3G	iPhone 3GS and newer	Android	Blackberry OS 5.x	Blackberry OS 6.0+	WebOS	Windows Phone 7	Symbian	Bada
Accelerometer	✓	✓	✓	✓	✓	✓	✓	✓	✓
Camera	✓	✓	✓	✓	✓	✓	✓	✓	✓
Compass	X	✓	✓	X	X	✓	✓	X	✓
Contacts	✓	✓	✓	✓	✓	X	✓	✓	✓
File	✓	✓	✓	✓	✓	X	✓	X	X
Geolocation	✓	✓	✓	✓	✓	✓	✓	✓	✓
Media	✓	✓	X	X	X	✓	X	X	X
Network	✓	✓	✓	✓	✓	✓	✓	✓	✓
Notification (Alert)	✓	✓	✓	✓	✓	✓	✓	✓	✓
Notification (Sound)	✓	✓	✓	✓	✓	✓	✓	✓	✓
Notification (Vibration)	✓	✓	✓	✓	✓	✓	✓	✓	✓
Storage	✓	✓	✓	✓	✓	✓	✓	✓	X

Figure 9-2. *Supported features*

Not mentioned in Figure 9-2: with release 2.2.0, PhoneGap includes Windows 8 support. Note that applications built with PhoneGap for Windows Phone 8 will only run on Windows Phone 8 devices. If you are looking to target both Windows 7.5 *and* 8 devices, you should use PhoneGap for Windows Phone 7, which implements the same APIs.

Application Packaging and Distribution

PhoneGap applications are developed using HTML, CSS, and JavaScript; however, the final product of a PhoneGap application is a binary application archive that can be distributed through standard application ecosystems.

For iOS applications, the output is an `.ipa` file (iOS application archive); for Android applications, the output is an `.apk` file (Android Package); for Windows Phone, the output is a `.xap` file, and so forth. These are the same application packaging formats used by "native" applications and they can be distributed through the appropriate ecosystems (iTunes Store, Google Play, Amazon Market, BlackBerry App World, Windows Phone Store, etc.).

Configuring an Android Development Environment for Cordova

This section describes how to set up a development environment for Cordova (the open-source core of PhoneGap), and then build and run a sample HTML5 application. We'll cover the following topics:

- Downloading and installing Eclipse Classic
- Downloading and installing Android SDK
- Downloading and installing the ADT plug-in
- Downloading the Cordova/PhoneGap core
- Setting up a project in Eclipse
- Deploying the application

Eclipse is an open-source integrated development environment (IDE) that supports many technologies. Here you will focus on its support of Java, the native language for Android applications. Android is Google's open-source mobile operating system.

In this example, you will use Cordova version 2.1.0. Newer versions of the Cordova distributions should work similarly, but the steps of setting up a project are automated by scripts. To provide greater insight into the relevant components of a Cordova project, you will follow the 2.1.0 installation and setup instructions from the PhoneGap documentation (http://docs.phonegap.com).

Setting Up Eclipse

The first step in setting up your development environment for PhoneGap applications on Android is to download and install the Eclipse IDE.

Android development with PhoneGap can be done in Windows, OS X, or Linux. There are many different installation packages for Eclipse. While PhoneGap may work with other package configurations, the Eclipse Classic package is recommended and already includes the tools that you need to get started with PhoneGap application development.

You need the Java JDK (Java Development Kit), which also includes the JRE (Java Runtime Environment). Install it from www.oracle.com/technetwork/java/javase/downloads/index.html.

Download the Eclipse Classic package for your operating system from the Eclipse project web site (www.eclipse.org/downloads). The Eclipse download will be an archive containing the development environment. Extract the archive to your local hard disk, and once extracted, launch Eclipse by double-clicking the Eclipse application icon. The first time you run Eclipse, you will be prompted to identify a location for your Eclipse workspace. This is where local copies of your projects will live on your file system. Do not create the workspace in a directory path that has spaces in it—that is, not in the default C:\Documents and Settings\... directory presented by default on the initial startup of Eclipse. Instead, it is recommended that your workspace be located at the root of your machine's hard disk; for example, C:\workspace.

Setting Up Android Tools

After you have downloaded and set up Eclipse, you will need to configure your environment to use Google's Android development tools. There are two steps to this process. First, you download and install the Android SDK. Second, you install the ADT plug-in for Eclipse.

The first step in configuring Android tools on your system is to download the appropriate build of the Android SDK for your operating system from the Android SDK web site (http://developer.android.com/sdk) and extract the archive to your local hard drive.

Next, you need to set up the ADT (Android Development Tools) plug-in for Eclipse. ADT extends the capabilities of Eclipse with functionality to easily set up new Android projects, debug your application, and export .apk files for distribution. The ADT plug-in must be installed through the Eclipse Install New Software wizard:

1. Start Eclipse and select Help ➤ Install New Software.

2. Click Add in the top-right corner.

3. In the Add Repository dialog that appears, enter **ADT Plugin** for the Name and the following URL for the Location:

   https://dl-ssl.google.com/android/eclipse/

   (If you have trouble acquiring the plug-in, try using **http** in the Location URL, instead of https; https is preferred for security reasons.)

4. Click OK.

5. In the Available Software dialog, select the check box next to Developer Tools and click Next.

6. In the next window, you'll see a list of the tools to be downloaded. Click Next.

7. Read and accept the license agreements, and then click Finish.

8. If you get a security warning saying that the authenticity or validity of the software can't be established, click OK.

9. When the installation completes, restart Eclipse.

Once Eclipse restarts, you must specify the location of your Android SDK directory. In the Welcome to Android Development window that appears, select Use Existing SDKs, and then browse to and select the location where you unpacked the Android SDK.

With the ADT plug-in installed, you have additional menu options available in Eclipse. Use the Android SDK Manager to download and configure your Android API libraries. To make sure your application is able to run on most devices, you can download and install the latest version of the API. During the setup of a project, you will be asked for the minimum SDK version to be supported. At the time of writing, Android 2.3 (Gingerbread) is running on 50% of all Android devices. Android 4.0 (Ice Cream Sandwich) comes in second place with a 27% share, and the latest Android version (Jelly Bean) has only a 1.8% share. The outdated Android 2.2 (Froyo) still has a 10% market ownership. Up-to-date statistics are on the Google Android Developer web site (http://developer.android.com/about/dashboards/index.html). For this example, version 2.3 of the API package is installed, which will make the app compatible with most of the devices currently in use.

Start the Android SDK Manager from the Window menu, as shown in Figure 9-3.

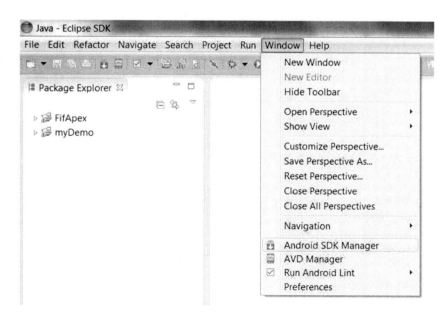

Figure 9-3. *Android SDK Manager in Eclipse*

You are now able to choose and install the API packages (see Figure 9-4). A package contains all the libraries and tools necessary to develop and test your app by using an Android device simulator or by deploying your app to a device connected to your computer.

Figure 9-4. *Android SDK Manager*

Creating the PhoneGap App Project

Creating a simple standard (non-APEX) Android PhoneGap app is relatively straightforward. A wizard guides you through the creation of the Android app project. Enabling PhoneGap for the app is achieved by adding some files to the project and modifying some of the configuration files.

Creating a New Eclipse Project

To create an application, you first have to define a new project in Eclipse.

1. Start the New Project wizard (File ➤ New ➤ Project ...), select Android Application Project, and click Next (see Figure 9-5).

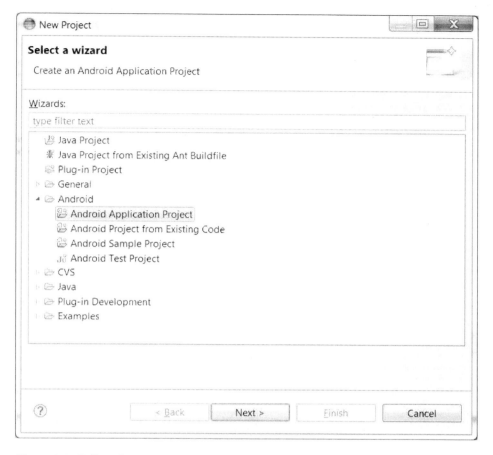

Figure 9-5. Eclipse Create New Project wizard

2. In the next step, you define the properties of your Android app (see Figure 9-6).

Figure 9-6. *Android application properties*

3. Enter an application name for your project. When you publish your app, the Application Name is the name shown in the store and in the application list on the device. The Project Name is only used in Eclipse. The Package Name must be a unique identifier for your application. It will stay the same during the lifetime of your app and across versions. The Package Name, or namespace, is typically the reverse domain name of your organization plus an identifier for your application.

4. The Build SDK is the library used to compile your application. The Minimum Required SDK defines the lowest version of Android that your application will support. A lower API level enables more devices to run your application, but means fewer native features. Just keep the default values.

5. If you want to provide a custom icon for your app, leave the "Create custom launcher icon" box checked. Unchecking it will provide a default icon for your app.

6. Click Next.

7. If you choose to create a custom icon, you will enter the Configure Launcher Icon dialog (Figure 9-7). You can define an icon from a predefined clipart sample or select your own image file. The image is automatically scaled to different sizes for usage on the device's launch pages and the Google Play store. When finished creating the icon, click Next.

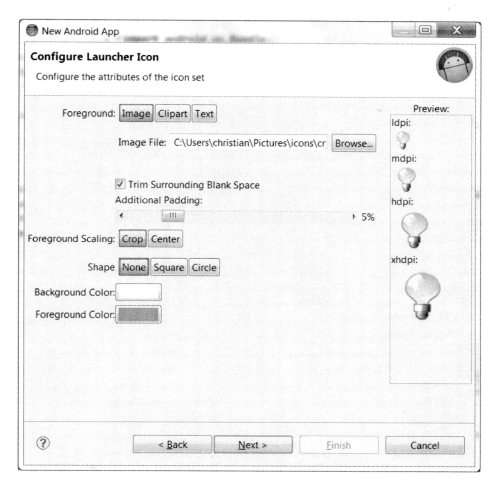

Figure 9-7. Android Launcher Icon dialog

8. Create a Blank Activity (see Figure 9-8) and click Next.

Figure 9-8. *The Create Activity dialog*

9. Accept all defaults in the New Blank Activity dialog (see Figure 9-9) and click Next.

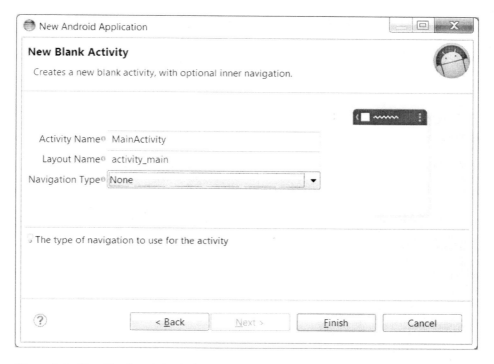

Figure 9-9. *New Blank Activity dialog*

Your application's project is now created and added to the Package Explorer in Eclipse, as shown in Figure 9-10.

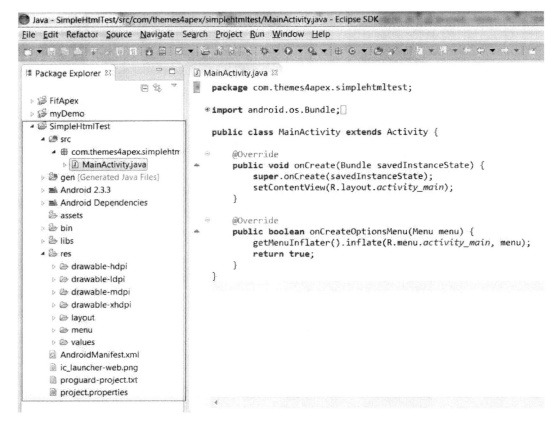

Figure 9-10. The new Android project is added in the Eclipse Package Explorer

Adding PhoneGap to the Android Project

You have to configure the application project for usage with PhoneGap. First, you need to add the PhoneGap libraries.

1. In the root directory of your project, create the following two directories if they do not already exist:

    - /libs

    - assets/www

2. Copy cordova-2.1.0.js from your Cordova download to assets/www (see Figure 9-11).

3. Copy cordova-2.1.0.jar from your Cordova download to /libs.

4. Copy the xml folder from your Cordova download to /res.

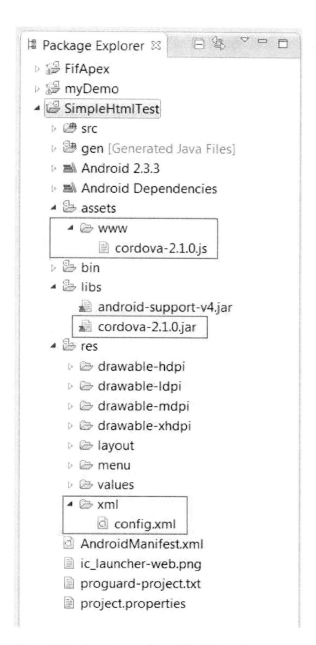

Figure 9-11. *Project tree after adding PhoneGap assets*

The assets/www directory in Figure 9-11 will be used to place all the application's HTML, CSS, and JavaScript files.

5. Verify that cordova-2.1.0.jar is listed in the Build Path of your project. Right-click the /libs folder and go to Build Paths ➤ Configure Build Path.... Then, in the Libraries tab, add cordova-2.1.0.jar to the project (see Figure 9-12). You might need to refresh (F5) the project once again.

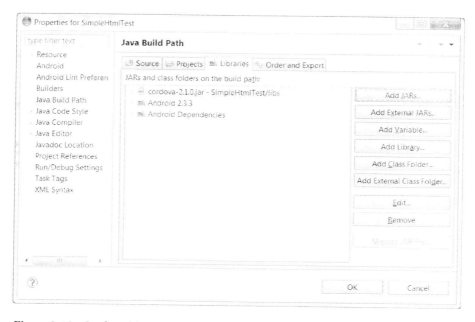

Figure 9-12. *Cordova library added to project's Java Build Path*

Developing a PhoneGap application using HTML means that you have to create HTML files, much like you would build a web site with static HTML files. Instead of invoking some Java code, the native app's main activity has to load an HTML start page in the WebView. Edit your project's main Java file found in the **src** folder in Eclipse (see Figure 9-13).

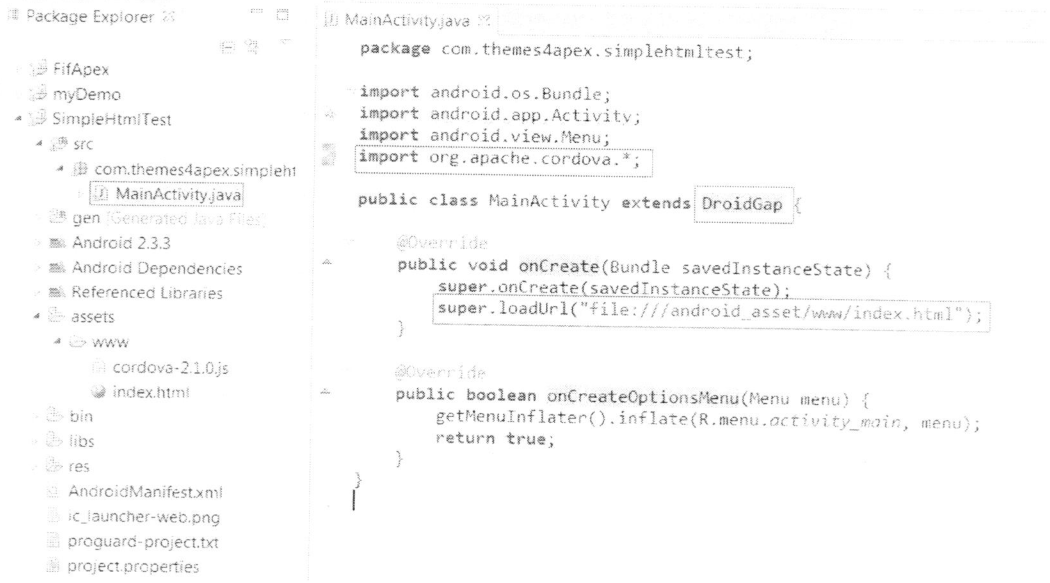

Figure 9-13. *Main activity pointing to local asset (index.html)*

1. Add **import org.apache.cordova.*;** .

2. Change the class's extend from `Activity` to `DroidGap`.

3. Replace the `setContentView()` line with

   super.loadUrl("file:///android_asset/www/index.html");

4. Save the file.

Create a new file named **index.html** in the `assets`/www directory. Open the file in the editor and paste the code from Listing 9-1 (also see Figure 9-14). Then save the index.html file.

Listing 9-1. Basic PhoneGap index.html file

```
<!DOCTYPE HTML>
<html>
<head>
  <title>Cordova</title>
  <script type="text/javascript" charset="utf-8" src="cordova-2.1.0.js"></script>
</head>
<body>
  <h1>Hello World</h1>
</body>
</html>
```

Figure 9-14. *A basic HTML page including PhoneGap library and both local assets*

Configuring the Android App

The next step in the configuration is to modify the `AndroidManifest.xml` file in the root directory of the project. The manifest presents essential information about the application to the Android system—information the system must have before it can run any of the application's code.

1. Right-click `AndroidManifest.xml` and select Open With ➤ Text Editor.

2. Paste the permissions shown in Listing 9-2 between the `<uses-sdk.../>` and `<application.../>` tags.

Listing 9-2. AndroidManifest.xml Granting ALL Device Functionality to App

```
<supports-screens
    android:largeScreens="true"
    android:normalScreens="true"
    android:smallScreens="true"
    android:resizeable="true"
    android:anyDensity="true" />
<uses-permission android:name="android.permission.VIBRATE" />
<uses-permission android:name="android.permission.ACCESS_COARSE_LOCATION" />
<uses-permission android:name="android.permission.ACCESS_FINE_LOCATION" />
<uses-permission android:name="android.permission.ACCESS_LOCATION_EXTRA_COMMANDS" />
<uses-permission android:name="android.permission.READ_PHONE_STATE" />
<uses-permission android:name="android.permission.INTERNET" />
<uses-permission android:name="android.permission.RECEIVE_SMS" />
<uses-permission android:name="android.permission.RECORD_AUDIO" />
<uses-permission android:name="android.permission.MODIFY_AUDIO_SETTINGS" />
<uses-permission android:name="android.permission.READ_CONTACTS" />
<uses-permission android:name="android.permission.WRITE_CONTACTS" />
<uses-permission android:name="android.permission.WRITE_EXTERNAL_STORAGE" />
<uses-permission android:name="android.permission.ACCESS_NETWORK_STATE" />
<uses-permission android:name="android.permission.GET_ACCOUNTS" />
<uses-permission android:name="android.permission.BROADCAST_STICKY" />
```

Note that this is a blanket list of permissions to your application. You should modify this list according to your application's needs before submitting it to Google Play.

3. To support orientation changes, add the following inside the `<activity>` tag:

```
android:configChanges="orientation|keyboardHidden"
```

Your `AndroidManifest.xml` file should now look like Figure 9-15.

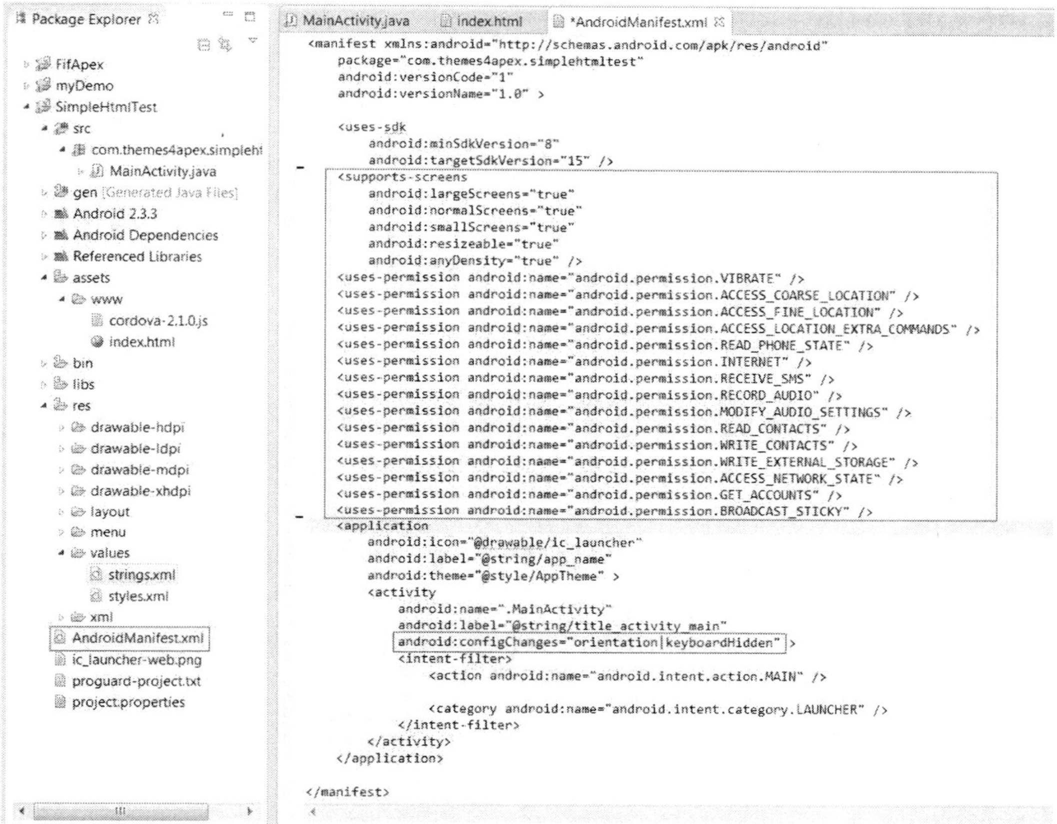

Figure 9-15. *AndroidManifest.xml after preparing it for usage with PhoneGap*

The final configuration step is to change the application name and the title resource. The application name is the text shown with the apps icon on the phone's launch screen. The title appears briefly during startup and initialization of the application. These string resources can be found in the file res/values/strings.xml. Open the file in the text editor and modify the values of the app_name and title_activity_main tags (see Figure 9-16). Save the strings.xml file.

Figure 9-16. *Setting string properties for the app's name and title*

Deploying the App to the Simulator

The "app" is now ready to be run. Before deploying to any device, you can test your application with the simulator—called the Android Virtual Device (AVD), shown in Figure 9-17—that has been installed as part of your Android package.

1. Right-click the project and go to Run As ➤ Android Application.

2. Depending on your configuration, Eclipse will ask you to select an appropriate AVD. If there isn't one, you'll need to create it.

    After starting the emulator (and the Android OS), your application is invoked automatically (see Figure 9-17).

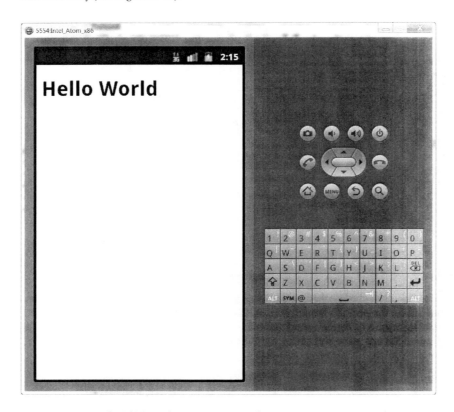

Figure 9-17. *Android Virtual Device running the app*

3. If you close the app and return to the home screen on the emulator, you should find the apps icon installed on it (see Figure 9-18).

Figure 9-18. *Launch icon for app installed on AVD*

Deploying the App to a Device

Because a virtual device does not offer all the functionality of an actual mobile device, working with a real Android device plugged into your system through USB may be preferable. Deploying and running the app is done exactly the same way you would test your app on the simulator. To automatically run your app on your phone or tablet, you have to make sure USB debugging is enabled on your device (Settings ➤ Applications ➤ Development).

The Debug option enables full logging of all activities running on your device. This comes in very handy when testing your app because there is no console comparable to those that desktop browsers offer.

APEX and PhoneGap

The PhoneGap project currently consists of one simple HTML page. The basic idea of PhoneGap is to develop an application using HTML, CSS, and JavaScript, and place all the files and resources into the assets/www folder. These files will then be part of the packaged app and deployed on the device with the app. Oracle Application Express applications are generated dynamically on a server. How do you get your web app into the PhoneGap package? The answer is: you don't.

In the following example, a standard mobile APEX 4.2 application was created on apex.oracle.com. It contains a single page and accepts all the defaults.

In Eclipse, instead of referencing the local index.html, it points to the APEX web application. To do this, the MainActivity.java file in the project was modified and the URL in the super.loadUrl function call was changed, as shown in Figure 9-19.

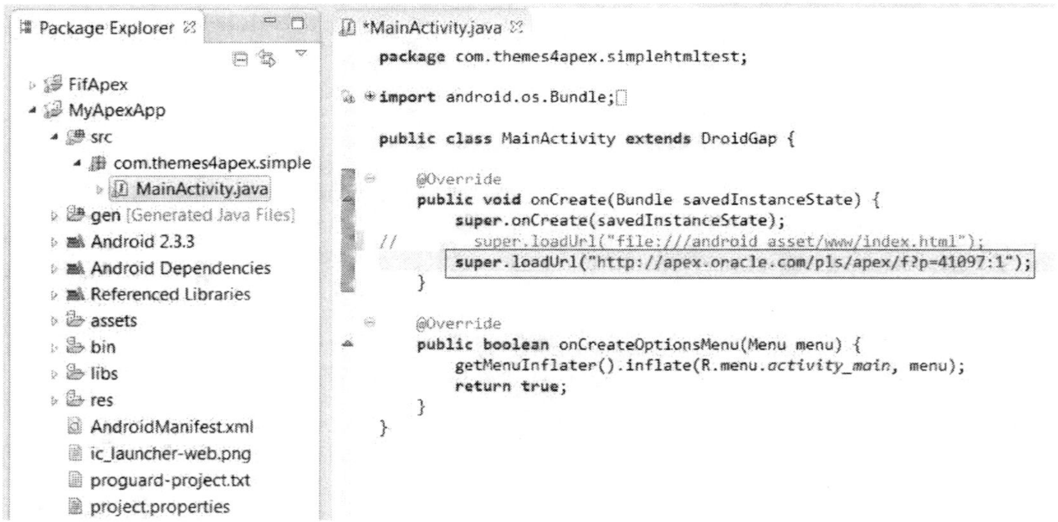

Figure 9-19. *Pointing the main activity directly to an APEX application*

The MainActivity.java file was then saved.

Because PhoneGap expects all resources to be references to local resources (file:///), access to outside domains are blocked by default. Before you're able to access the application from the PhoneGap WebView, you have to allow access to the domain of the web server hosting the APEX application. This mechanism is called *whitelisting*.

Whitelisting

Domain whitelisting in Apache Cordova is a security model that controls access to outside domains. The default security policy is to block all network access. As application developers, we can declare access to specific network domains and subdomains. Currently, every development platform has its own whitelisting implementation that differs in syntax and level of support.

Syntax

Whitelisting uses the `<access>` element described in W3C specification on Widget Access Request Policy (`www.w3.org/TR/widgets-access/`). In the Widget Access specification, the `<access>` element is used to declare access to specific network domains. Zero or more access elements can be placed in the configuration document, as follows:

- Access to yourserver.com*: `http://yourserver.com`

- Access to secure yourserver.com*: `https://yourserver.com`

- Access to apex.yourserver.com*: `http://apex.yourserver.com`

- Access to all subdomains on yourserver.com*: `http://*.yourserver.com`

- Access to all domains: *

On platforms like Android, access to subdomains can be declared by using an attribute (`subdomains="true"`).

Configuration

The whitelisting rules for Android are found in the `res/xml/config.xml` project file and declared with the element `<access origin="..." />` (see Figure 9-20). Android has full support for the whitelisting syntax.

Figure 9-20. A whitelist entry to allow access to an APEX application hosted on `apex.oracle.com`

Having added your domain here, you would save the `config.xml` and redeploy the app to your device.

Actually, this should be the last modification made to the app in the Eclipse project and it does not have to redeploy again. Depending on your experience with PhoneGap, however, you might have to experiment with the configuration a bit. Once you are familiar with it, you should have a template. For now, you can concentrate on developing your web app in Application Express.

Using the PhoneGap API in APEX Pages

At this point, the app deployed to the device is nothing more than a chromeless browser that has a custom icon. But applications built with PhoneGap are not like normal mobile web applications. PhoneGap applications are able to interact with mobile device hardware such as the accelerometer or GPS, which are typically unavailable to normal web applications. The APEX application, when running in the PhoneGap WebView, has access to the PhoneGap API.

Cross-Platform Page Template

One of the attractive ideas behind using PhoneGap and HTML combined with CSS and JavaScript is being able to target multiple platforms with one code base. The PhoneGap SDK provides an API that is an abstraction layer, giving the developer access to hardware and platform-specific features. As PhoneGap abstracts the native mobile platform, the same code can be used on multiple mobile platforms, making your application available to a wider audience.

Because you are not using the local resources, you will have to include the PhoneGap library in your APEX application. Unfortunately, due to the fact that each platform has its own cordova.js file, you can't simply include one version of it and expect it to work on every platform. For instance, this won't work:

```
<script type="application/javascript" src="#IMAGE_PATH#cordova.js">
```

Yes, it works on the platform of the mobile device you're developing for and testing on, but to make it work on another platform, you need the library version for the platform you're targeting.

Of course, there are other ways to solve the problem, but the following approach is really easy and works extremely well.

While loading the page, load the PhoneGap's cordova.js file based on the user agent. This way, the app supports all deployment scenarios, even on PhoneGap Build (described later in this chapter). Include the code in Listing 9-3 in a copy of the APEX application's main-page template header section.

Listing 9-3. Dynamically Including Cordova Library, Depending on OS

```
<script>
(function loadCordova() {

  //Initialize our user agent string to lower case.
  var uagent = navigator.userAgent.toLowerCase();

  if (uagent.search("android") > -1) {
    document.write('<script type="text/javascript" ' +
                   'src="#WORKSPACE_IMAGES#cordova.android.js">' +
                   '<//script>');
  } else if (uagent.search("iphone") > -1) {
    document.write('<script type="text/javascript" ' +
                   'src="#WORKSPACE_IMAGES#cordova.ios.js">' +
                   '<//script>');
  }

})();
</script>
```

This function is executed immediately (not waiting for the document.ready event) and generates a script tag. The Cordova library corresponding to the client's OS is also loaded. In this example, you're only testing for Android and iOS, but you can easily extend the script for other platforms as well. The JavaScript library files itself. It's uploaded into your workspace as static files (Shared Components ➤ Static Files), as shown in Figure 9-21.

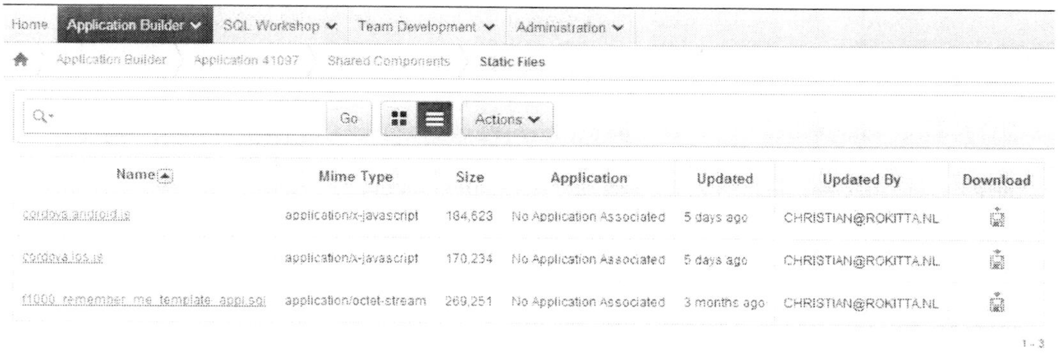

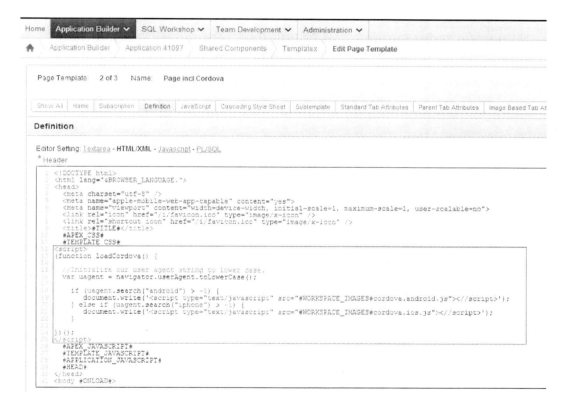

Figure 9-21. *Cordova JavaScript libraries as a static file in an APEX application*

Your page template's header section should now look like Figure 9-22.

Figure 9-22. *An APEX mobile page template with the PhoneGap library*

Make sure that you place the script before the #APEX_JAVASCRIPT# placeholder. The #APEX_JAVASCRIPT# substitution string will be replaced with the jQuery and jQuery Mobile script tags. We found that if the libraries are loaded in a different order—that is, the PhoneGap library after the jQuery libraries—we experienced problems with the initialization of the frameworks. Both frameworks—PhoneGap and jQuery Mobile—are adding events to initialize objects and trigger functions to alter layout and style.

During development with PhoneGap and jQuery Mobile in APEX, we also experienced problems with the jQM method of loading pages by means of Ajax calls, especially when submitting pages with apex.submit(), the standard APEX call used to invoke processing. When jQM loads a page with Ajax, not all of the DOM documents events are triggered because jQM only replaces the DIVs marked with the data-role="page" attribute. To enforce normal APEX behavior, disable the jQM Ajax mechanism by setting some jQuery variables on the document.ready event. Add the following script to the template's JavaScript, Function and Global Variable Declaration section:

```
$(document).ready(function() {
                $.mobile.ajaxEnabled = false;
                $.mobile.hashListeningEnabled = false;
                $.mobile.pushStateEnabled = false;
});
```

By setting ajaxEnabled = false, URL hash listening will also be disabled, and URLs will load as ordinary HTTP requests. jQuery Mobile recommends disabling the pushState feature for installed apps because there are edge cases where this feature can cause unexpected navigation behavior, and because URLs aren't visible in a WebView, it's not worth keeping this active in these situations.

With the modified template in place, you can start using the PhoneGap API in the APEX application. The example application contains a single page, which just happens to be enough for the following example. Your actual application may have multiple pages. Remember to be alert when using two-page templates in your application—the original standard template and the copy that includes the PhoneGap libraries and initialization. The Cordova library may not be initialized or loaded at all when navigating from a non-PhoneGap-enabled page to a PhoneGap-enabled page and using the jQM Ajax page load.

Device Camera Example

One of the most desired native functionalities for mobile applications is the ability to access the device's camera. PhoneGap features an API to capture images from the smartphone's camera. This example is based on the HTML example found in the PhoneGap API online documentation (http://docs.phonegap.com/en/2.1.0/cordova_camera_camera.md.html).

Using a Cordova-Enabled Page Template

You will have to change the APEX application's page template attribute to one that includes the PhoneGap library (see Figure 9-23).

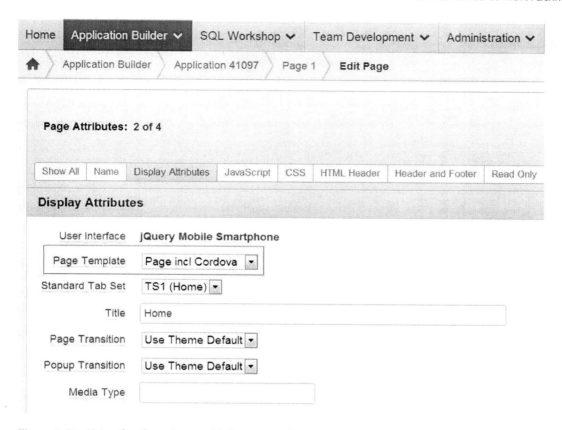

Figure 9-23. *Using the PhoneGap-enabled page template*

Creating a Region

When creating the application, the wizard creates an empty page. Add an HTML region to the page, with code in the region source intended to show the image you'll capture with the camera on your page (see Figure 9-24). Note that in this example, the image placeholder is initially hidden, but an ID for identification is provided.

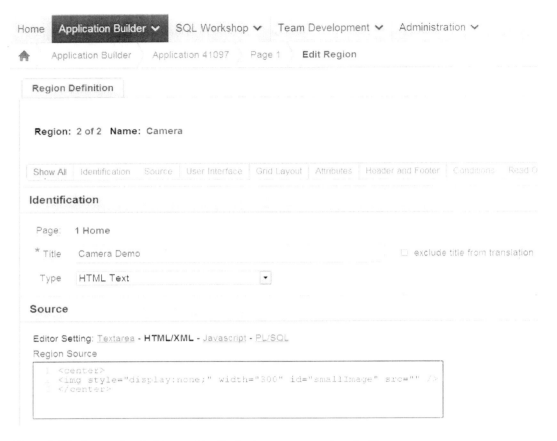

Figure 9-24. *Image placeholder used to display image once captured with camera*

Optionally, you can choose a region template. Just for the looks, the jQuery template Region (With Title Bar) is used in the example.

Adding JavaScript PhoneGap API Calls to the Page

The JavaScript code for calling the PhoneGap API will be added to the page's JavaScript ➤ Function and Global Variable Declaration section.

Let's start with some global variable declarations. Those are needed to hold the API response and to temporarily store the image data.

```
var pictureSource;   // picture source
var destinationType; // sets the format of returned value
var staticImg = '';  // temporary store the image data for upload
```

Trigger the initialization of the camera response objects with the PhoneGap deviceready event by adding an event listener to the page. Before invoking any PhoneGap calls, you should always check whether the PhoneGap library is properly initialized and connected to the Java API and the device.

```
// Wait for Cordova to connect with the device
//
document.addEventListener("deviceready", onDeviceReady, onFail);

// Cordova is ready to be used!
//
function onDeviceReady() {
    pictureSource = navigator.camera.PictureSourceType;
    destinationType = navigator.camera.DestinationType;
    console.log('Device ready!');
}
```

The next function contains the actual call to the PhoneGap API: camera.getPicture. The getPicture function opens the device's default camera application (if parameter Camera.sourceType = Camera.PictureSourceType. CAMERA, which is the default). Changing the sourceType to PHOTOLIBRARY or SAVEDPHOTOALBUM would invoke a photo chooser dialog, from which a photo from the device's album can be selected. Once the photo is taken, the camera application closes and control is returned to your page. The return value will be sent to the cameraSuccess function in one of the following formats, depending on the camera options that you specify:

- A string containing the Base64-encoded photo image (default).

- A string representing the image file's location on local storage.

In this example, you want the Base64-encoded image data and a downscaled version of the picture (quality=50%). This function will be called by the Dynamic Action of a button on a page created later.

```
// A button will call this function
//
function capturePhoto() {
    // Take picture using device camera and retrieve image as base64-encoded string
    navigator.camera.getPicture(onPhotoDataSuccess, onFail, {
        quality: 50,
        destinationType: destinationType.DATA_URL
    });
}
```

The next function is executed once getPicture returns successfully, passing the Base64 image data to it. The image data can be injected into the SRC attribute of the image placeholder tag (by prefixing it with "data:image/jpg;base64,") placed into the HTML region on the page. Also, copy the image data to the global variable staticImg. You will use this variable later when uploading the image to the Oracle database.

```
// Called when a photo is successfully retrieved
//
function onPhotoDataSuccess(imageData) {
    // Uncomment to view the base64 encoded image data
    // console.log(imageData);

    // Unhide image element
    //
    $("#smallImage").css("display", "block");
```

```
    // Show the captured photo
    //
    $("#smallImage").attr("src", "data:image/jpg;base64," + imageData);

    // Copy image data
    staticImg = imageData;
}
```

The onFail function will be called instead of the onPhotoDataSuccess whenever an error occurs during the camera API call.

```
// Called if something bad happens.
//

function onFail(message) {
    alert('Failed because: ' + message);
    console.log('Failed because: ' + message);
}
```

Creating a Button to Invoke Image Capture

To invoke the capturePhoto function from the APEX page, create a button, invoking a Dynamic Action when clicked (see Figure 9-25).

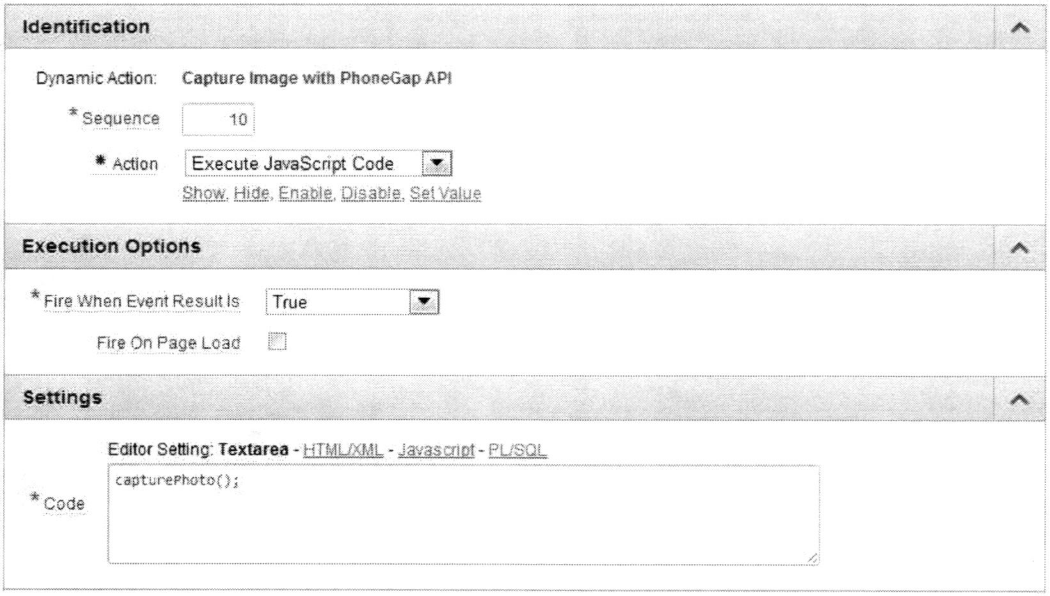

Figure 9-25. The attributes of a Dynamic Action on a button to invoke the device camera

Make sure that you disable the Fire On Page Load option.

With the button in place, you can test-run this application. Remember, you do not have to redeploy a new version of the app; all development is now done on the APEX server and all changes are immediately available to the app.

Also remember that if you want to monitor or debug your application, keep your device connected to your PC and keep Eclipse open. You can write debug output by using the `console.log` command in your JavaScript code.

Uploading the Image to the Oracle Database

The PhoneGap camera API returned the image data as Base64-encoded string. In order to upload this string to the database, you cannot just submit the data as a normal form text field. The string simply might exceed the 32K limit that APEX can handle in form submits. As a workaround, use the Ajax method described by Carl Backstrom (http://carlback.blogspot.nl/2008/04/new-stuff-4-over-head-with-clob.html).

Let's create an `apex.ajax.clob` object that only takes one parameter when initialized, which is a pointer to a function to call when the Ajax request `readyState` changes. Once the `apex.ajax.clob` object is created, you just call the `_set` method passing a string; in this example, the Base64 image string:

```
clob_ob._set(staticImg);
```

This will automatically create a collection in your session named CLOB_CONTENT and populate the CLOB001 column. Once uploaded, you can use the collection in a page or application level process.

The `p.responseText` on successful population of the CLOB will be SUCCESS. For this demonstration, write the following message to a display-only page item (`P1_RESPONSE`):

```
// Function to upload CLOB data using APEX AJAX API
//
// on Success: CLOB is accessible in the apex_collections view:
// SELECT collection_name, seq_id, clob001 FROM apex_collections
// WHERE collection_name = 'CLOB_CONTENT';
// - Note: The collection name "CLOB_CONTENT" is not modifiable

function clob_set() {
   var clob_ob = new apex.ajax.clob(

   function() {
     var rs = p.readyState
     if (rs == 1 || rs == 2 || rs == 3) {
        $.mobile.showPageLoadingMsg();
     } else if (rs == 4) {
        $s('P1_RESPONSE', p.responseText);
        $.mobile.hidePageLoadingMsg()
     } else {
        return false;
     }
   });
   clob_ob._set(staticImg);
}
```

To invoke the function, create another button, an analog to the Capture button, and use the `clob_set()` function in the JavaScript source of the Dynamic Action (see Figure 9-26).

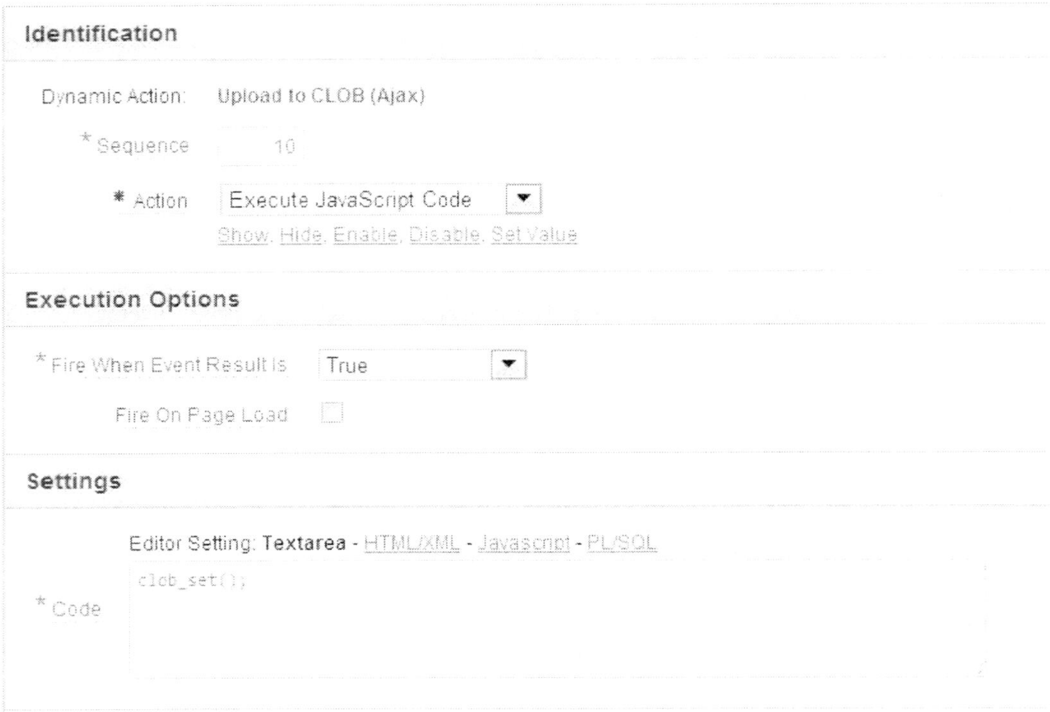

Identification

Dynamic Action: Upload to CLOB (Ajax)

* Sequence   10

* Action | Execute JavaScript Code   ▼ |

Show, Hide, Enable, Disable, Set Value

Execution Options

* Fire When Event Result Is | True   ▼ |

Fire On Page Load   ☐

Settings

Editor Setting: **Textarea** - HTML/XML - Javascript - PL/SQL

* Code

```
clob_set();
```

Figure 9-26. *The attributes of Dynamic Action on a button to (Ajax) upload the image*

The only thing left to do is the actual processing of the CLOB in the collection on page submit by using PL/SQL. The CLOB can be selected from the collection. To convert the CLOB into a binary image file, use the APEX API function apex_web_service.clobbase642blob. Once converted into a BLOB, you can save the image to a table, for example.

```
DECLARE
   l_clob    CLOB;
   l_blob    BLOB;
   l_id      NUMBER;
BEGIN

   -- fetch the image CLOB from the collection
   SELECT clob001
   INTO   l_clob
   FROM   apex_collections
   WHERE  collection_name = 'CLOB_CONTENT';

   l_id     := blob_test_seq.NEXTVAL;

   -- convert base64 CLOB into BLOB image
   l_blob   := apex_web_service.clobbase642blob(l_clob);
```

```
INSERT INTO blob_test(id
                    , blob_content
                    , mime_type
                    , file_name)
VALUES (
          l_id
        , l_blob
        , 'image/jpeg'
        , 'image' || l_id || '.jpg'
        );
END;
```

Figure 9-27a shows the app on an Android phone before capturing an image with the camera and Figure 9-27b shows the phone after uploading the image to the collection.

Figure 9-27. *Android phone (a) before taking a picture and (b) after uploading it successfully*

Using an iFrame to Access the PhoneGap API

The downside of including the PhoneGap JavaScript library in the APEX templates is that these files have to be loaded onto the mobile device (at least once), which can slow down the user experience when accessing the application through a small bandwidth connection. Another problem is that not all APIs seem to work when called from an external page, such as Notifications (vibrate, beep).

An alternative approach to embedding the PhoneGap JavaScript libraries in your APEX page is to embed the APEX application page in an iFrame hosted by the index.html file on the mobile device. The index.html references the cordova.js and contains all the PhoneGap API calls.

The problem is that the iFrame and the PhoneGap app's page run on different domains, and thus they can't see each other. The inner iFrame can't trigger a camera event on the outer frame directly, but it is possible to work around this with cross-document messaging.

Cross-Document Messaging

The main difficulty with accessing the camera from within an iFrame in a PhoneGap application is that the document inside the iFrame (which contains your remote web page) has a different origin than the local web page (which has the PhoneGap shim). Consequently, the remote page can't access navigator.camera. Cross-document messaging makes it possible for them to communicate despite this (see Figure 9-28).

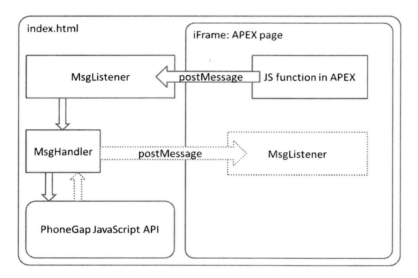

Figure 9-28. *Cross-document messaging schema*

The idea is to send a message from the page, generated by APEX, to the enclosing index.html document. The message listener there will invoke a function that will make the API call. If this call returns data that you want to process in your APEX page, you optionally send back the data using the same messaging mechanism.

Syntax is postMessage(data, targetDomain), described as follows:

- data: The message. According to the specification, it could be any object; but as of now, only strings are supported in major browsers.

- targetDomain: Limits receiving iFrame by the given domain. Can contain *, which doesn't place any restrictions.

Basically, the iFrame document can send messages to the parent (if it's listening) like this:

```
window.parent.postMessage({data: "yourData"}, "file://")
```

Note, the PhoneGap page's domain is identified as "file://", with no other path.

Replace yourdomain.com with the URL for the page that the iFrame is accessing. The iFrame can talk to the parent document (the PhoneGap window that has access to the camera) like this:

```
iframe.parent.postMessage({data: "rad"}, "http://yourdomain.com")
```

Listening for messages is fairly straightforward. In both the PhoneGap file and the remote web page, listen for cross-document messages by attaching an event listener to the window:

```
window.addEventListener("message", function(event) {
  // Check that the message is coming from an expected sender
  // "file://" if you're in the iFrame, or your remote URL for
  // the phonegap file.
  if (event.origin == url) {
    // do something with the message
  }
});
```

Note that the browser guarantees that event.origin contains the real domain, which sent the message. The cross-window messaging security model is two-sided. The sender ensures that the receiving domain is targetDomain. The receiver checks that the message came from the proper event.origin. There is no way for JavaScript hackers to replace it. The messages are passed using the internal browser API. So there is no network communication at all.

The advantage of this approach is that you don't have to include the PhoneGap library in your APEX page template. The library doesn't have to be loaded; it only needs to be initialized once and stays available in the WebView during the entire usage. This is especially handy when you are intending to develop for multiple platforms using Adobe PhoneGap Build, where packages for different platforms are automatically compiled with the corresponding PhoneGap library.

Putting It Together in an APEX Example

In the camera example, you pointed to your APEX application using the super.LoadUrl call in the MainActivity.java of your Eclipse Android project. With this iFrame approach, you need to change this back again and point to the local index.html:

```
package com.themes4apex.simplehtmltest;

import android.os.Bundle;
import android.view.Menu;
import org.apache.cordova.*;

public class MainActivity extends DroidGap {

    @Override
    public void onCreate(Bundle savedInstanceState) {
        super.onCreate(savedInstanceState);
        super.loadUrl("file:///android_asset/www/index.html");
    }

    @Override
    public boolean onCreateOptionsMenu(Menu menu) {
        getMenuInflater().inflate(R.menu.activity_main, menu);
        return true;
    }
}
```

The index.html has to contain the reference to the Cordova JavaScript library, the message listener, and handling JavaScript. In the following example, add a listener function, checking for the events origin and (depending on the data string send) calling a PhoneGap API function. To keep this example simple, let's just check for one "call," the string "vibrate", which will trigger the native vibrate feature of the device. Do not forget to wait for the PhoneGap API to be fully initialized and connected by using the deviceready event:

```html
<!DOCTYPE HTML>
<html>
<head>
<title>My app</title>
<script charset="utf-8" type="text/javascript" src="cordova-2.1.0.js"></script>
<script type="text/javascript">
// Wait for Cordova to load
//
document.addEventListener("deviceready", onDeviceReady, false);

// Cordova is ready
//
function onDeviceReady() {
   // Empty
}

function listener(event) {
   if (event.origin !== "http://apex.oracle.com") return;
   if (event.data == "vibrate") {
      navigator.notification.vibrate(2000);
   }
}

if (window.addEventListener) {
   addEventListener("message", listener, false);
} else {
   attachEvent("onmessage", listener);
}
</script>
<style type='text/css'>
  body,html,iframe {
    margin: 0; padding: 0; border: none; width: 100%; height: 100%;
  }
</style>
</head>
<body>
  <iframe src='http://apex.oracle.com/pls/apex/f?p=41097:2' id='iframe'></iframe>
</body>
</html>
```

The reference to the APEX page is now placed as a value of the SRC attribute of an iFrame tag. The iFrame is styled to take 100% of the WebView's visible space.

In the APEX application, you only need to define the message call, here wrapped into a function and placed in the page's JavaScript section (see Figure 9-29). The first parameter (data) contains the "command" to trigger the "vibrate" handler, and the second parameter (targetDomain) defines the domain of the index.html file in the app container.

Figure 9-29. *JavaScript function to send message to enclosing parent page*

Now you can invoke the function by defining a JavaScript Dynamic Action on a button, for example, or simply an anchor tag in an HTML region source:

```
<a href="#" onclick="vibrate(); return false;">Vibrate</a>
```

Using Adobe PhoneGap Build

In 2011, Adobe Systems acquired Nitrobi Software, the creator of PhoneGap and PhoneGap Build. PhoneGap Build allows you to create cross-platform mobile apps based on HTML, CSS, and JavaScript through a simple web interface (see Figure 9-30). It takes care of all the packaging and compilation, and you get back mobile apps for different platforms in a matter of minutes.

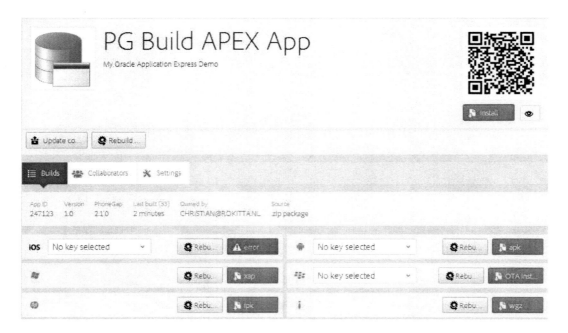

Figure 9-30. *Adobe PhoneGap Build application web dashboard*

To use PhoneGap Build, you need to register an account with Adobe and log in. Adobe offers different plans: one that is free but limited to one private app, and a fee account that allows you to build 25 private apps. Both flavors allow creating an unlimited number of open-source apps, which means that the code (HTML, CSS, JavaScript) for these apps must be pulled from a public GitHub repository.

Preparing Your Application for PhoneGap Build

PhoneGap Build only requires the assets of your application. This is essentially your www directory, which contains your HTML, CSS, image, JavaScript, and other files. The example application did not use the index.html file. There is no access to something corresponding to the Android project's MainActivity, where the APEX application's URL is directly referenced in the super.loadURL method. To ensure the app is redirecting to your application, you have to create a redirect functionality in the index.html or use the iFrame approach discussed earlier. This example simply redirects the WebView to the APEX application using the onLoad event.

```
<!DOCTYPE html>
<html>
  <head>
  <title> Redirect</title>
  </head>
  <body onload="window.location.href='http://apex.oracle.com/pls/apex/f?p=phonegapdemo';">
    </body>
</html>
```

> ■ **Note** Because PhoneGap requires a different JavaScript file for each platform, and using an incompatible `phonegap.js` will result in errors when running your application, the `phonegap.js` library file will be injected into the app during the compile process of PhoneGap Build. So, if you need to reference the local PhoneGap library from the `index.html`—for example, when using the iFrame approach—ensure that the following reference is made in your `index.html`:
>
> ```
> <script src="phonegap.js"></script>
> ```

Configuration Using config.xml

Apps built using Adobe PhoneGap Build can be set up either through a web interface or by using the `config.xml`. The `config.xml` file uses the same syntax and entries as the `config.xml` in your Eclipse project. The difference, however, is that the `config.xml` file has to be placed at the top-level path of the application (the same level as the `index.html` file); otherwise, it will not load correctly.

Compiling Your App

PhoneGap Build gives you two options: you can upload an existing PhoneGap project as a single `index.html` file or as a package zip archive, or link the site to a source control repository that is publicly accessible.

In the APEX application, you have to upload a zip archive that contains the following:

- `index.html` (to redirect to your application or to be used as the parent for your APEX application running in an iFrame)

- Other assets referenced from `index.html`, such as JavaScript or CSS files, images, and so forth

- `config.xml` (defines access to native features and whitelisting rules)

- An app icon image (preferably `.png` format)

After uploading the zip archive, the build process of the apps starts right away. During and after the build process, you are notified about errors that may occur. After the build process has finished, you can download and install the app immediately (by using the QR code shown in the application's main page), depending on which platform you're using:

- **Android**: Ensure your Android device can install `.apk` files from unknown sources (enter Settings ➤ Applications ➤ Enable Unknown Sources).

- **webOS**: You cannot install webOS packages (`.ipk` files) directly from the web; use Palm's palm-install utility for this.

- **Symbian**: Download and open the `.wgz` file on your device. Done!

- **BlackBerry**: Click the OTA install link and follow the instructions on your device. Adobe PhoneGap Build currently only supports BlackBerry OS 5.0 and above.

- **Windows Phone**: You cannot install Windows Phone packages directly from the web; you will need to use Microsoft's tools.

- **Apple iOS**: The process for completing iOS builds is slightly different from other platforms: all iOS builds need to be signed by a developer certificate and a provisioning profile, which is tied to an Apple developer account and the device you wish to test on. You will also need a Mac to configure your certificate and provisioning profile.

Wrap Up

While HTML5 is considered the future of mobile development, it does not yet support all native features. Extending mobile APEX applications with native device features is relatively straightforward using PhoneGap. There are different approaches to choose from, depending on what best suits your app's purpose. Once the PhoneGap WebView package is set up, most of the development is done server-side. Updating and extending your application is much easier than having to distribute an update to the different app stores.

As an APEX developer, you do not have to learn new skills to use PhoneGap, nor do you need to know OS-specific programming languages like Objective-C or Java. And by using Oracle Application Express version 4.2 with the jQuery Mobile framework included, PhoneGap is a great way to extend your application with native device functionality to make your app even more "mobile."

There is only one downside: users might expect a native app and they could be disappointed by the performance of the hybrid app due to network bandwidth, device performance (the WebView has to process multiple frameworks in parallel), or simply because the application does not quite feel like and respond as smoothly as a native app.

CHAPTER 10

Securing Your Mobile Application

You have read about a lot of the features that Oracle Application Express offers in building web applications for mobile devices. Now it is time to use all the knowledge that you've gained and start building your first mobile web application. But first, let's discuss some security considerations that might prevent you from making the wrong decisions.

Considering Security Implications

You are aware that every application that contains sensitive data must be secure. But should a mobile web application be more secure than a desktop web application? And if the answer to that question is "Yes," what are the additional precautions that we need to take?

A desktop web application is typically used in the (relative) safe realm of a company. The application and data are transferred to the desktop over a hard-wired network. But this type of usage is fading as people are increasingly working from other locations, usually their homes. And the home network is either hard-wired or wireless, but not always secured properly. Mobile devices, on the other hand, are used all over the place. Using either a cellular network or the free Wi-Fi at Starbucks—data flies through the air everywhere! This can be a security issue.

Another complication is that although desktops and laptops are stolen every now and then, mobile devices are often lost. Are you sure that no stranger can gain access to your company data when he gets his hands on the phone that he "found" in the train? Although many of these considerations apply to accessing corporate applications from laptops using unsecured (or less secured) networks, there are far more mobile devices out there. And people tend to be less careful with their phones than with their laptops.

So, the clear answer to the question "Should a mobile web application be more secure than a desktop web application?" is a loud "Yes!" What precautions can we take to minimize the risk of our sensitive data ending up in the wrong hands? We will go over a few precautions in the following sections.

Note There are more threats than described in this chapter. Security risks like cross-site scripting and SQL injection are not covered in this book. But this doesn't mean that you don't have to protect yourself against these threats. Because they are not "mobile-specific," it is assumed to be general good practice to take these risks into account.

Applying General Security Settings

APEX offers some security features that are easy to implement. Most of them can be applied by setting a switch. In this section, you will see how to enable the HTTPS protocol, manage timeout settings, and enhance security using encryption of data.

Configuring SSL

Probably the most obvious and easy thing to do is enable HTTPS protocol for your application. Of course, this will only work when SSL is configured on your web server. When you enable HTTPS, all network traffic will be encrypted, and therefore it'll be harder to get to the data that is sent over the air or wire. Be aware that external JavaScript files, like the jQuery Mobile core stored on a CDN, should be accessed using the same protocol.

You can find the SSL setting under Shared Components as a part of your Authentication Scheme definition (see Figure 10-1).

Session Cookie Attributes		^
Cookie Name		
Cookie Path		
Cookie Domain		
Secure	Yes ⬍	

Figure 10-1. *Enabling secure access to your application*

Setting Timeout

What happens when you are using a business application in a public area and you get called away or distracted? Another person can get your device and continue using the application. You can lower this risk by decreasing the time that a user can be idle in the application. When you set that to one minute, for example, a user has to log in again when that minute has passed and he hasn't done anything in the meantime. The risk of someone taking your device, walking away, and using your application within one minute is quite lower than if the person had one hour of time. You can find this setting when you click the Security Attributes link in the Security section of the Shared Components page (see Figure 10-2).

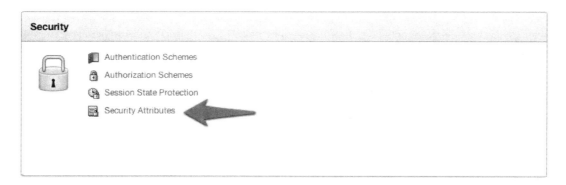

Figure 10-2. *Security Attributes link on the Shared Components page*

Another setting is the maximum session length. This value prevents unlimited use of the application. Any session has a maximum fixed duration, such as ten minutes in the example shown in Figure 10-3.

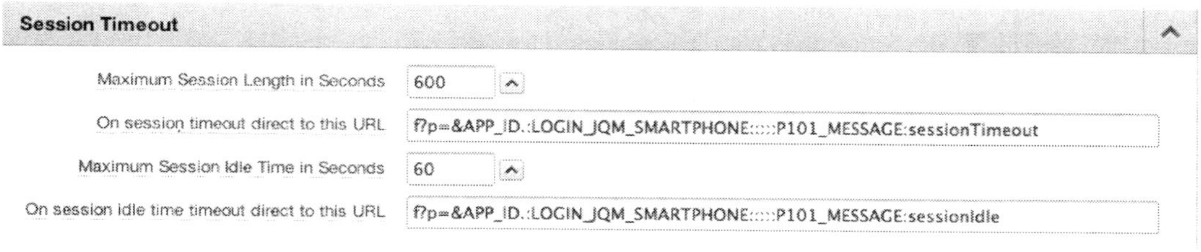

Figure 10-3. *Minimizing session length and idle time*

For both settings, you can specify a URL to redirect to. That can be specific page or the login page, where you show a specific message, depending on the passed value of a parameter. In Figure 10-3, an additional item was created on the login page that is conditionally rendered—depending on the value of P101_MESSAGE. Figure 10-4 shows the definition.

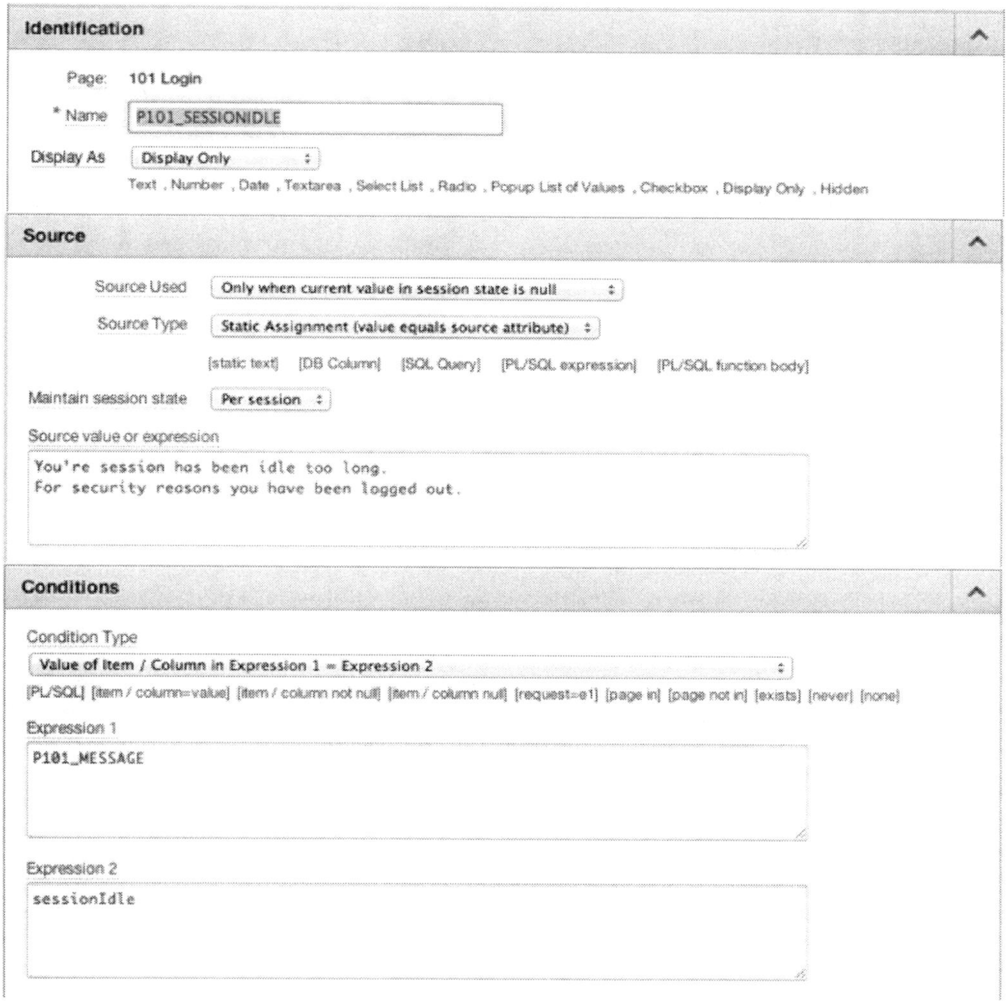

Figure 10-4. *Definition of the item showing the reason for logout*

When you now leave your device on the table for more than a minute and then return to start working again, you'll get redirected to the login screen, which displays a message stating what has happened (see Figure 10-5).

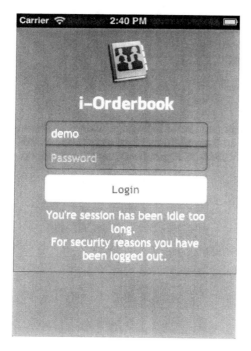

Figure 10-5. *Logged out due to exceeding the maximum idle time*

When you set maximum idle time and session length to be very low, using your application might be more secure, but also more irritating because logging back in every few minutes probably isn't acceptable to the user. There is a thin line between secure and irritating, and you have to figure out where that thin line is, depending on the type of access (short or sustained) and the type of data (very sensitive or less sensitive).

There is another concern. Although the values are acceptable and useful for a mobile device, this might not be the case when you run the same application on a desktop (either using responsive web design or other application pages on a desktop user interface). Usually, desktop sessions tend to last a lot longer, like an eight-hour working day, so it's fine to set the idle time as long as an hour. To overcome the issue of desktop vs. mobile idle time, you have two options. The first is to create two different applications—one for mobile and one for desktop devices—and set the session timeout values differently. Another option is to set the session timeout values to mobile (shorter and more secure) values, and set the values for other devices programmatically using the apex_util.set_session_lifetime_seconds and apex_util.set_session_max_idle_seconds procedures. You can call these page processes using the desktop login screen after logging in. But because you might want to offer the ability to switch between the two user interfaces, you can also call them from an application process that fires on every page. Remember, these procedures will only have an effect when you set the maximum values in the application definition first.

When you use a hybrid approach, as described in the previous chapter, you can set these values more finely. PhoneGap offers a Connection object, so you can detect whether your application is accessed using Ethernet, Wi-Fi, 2G, 3G, or even 4G. And knowing that, you can set the session lifetime or maximum idle time for these different types of connections (assuming some connection types are more secure than others).

Encrypting Data

When you've enabled HTTPS, your network traffic, including data, is encrypted. But data can be stored locally on your device—and that data is not encrypted. So when you use nifty HTML5 features like localStorage or ApplicationCache, you have to be extra careful. You might want to use some kind of encryption for that data. Normally, that data can only be accessed from the same domain that it originally came from, but in the end, it is stored in a file on your device.

The location differs by operating system and browser, but you don't need to know where it is stored. Because the data can only be accessed from the same domain, navigating to the login screen of the application is enough. This brings you into the right domain. Now you can open the console of your browser and type **localStorage**. Figure 10-6 shows that you can now inspect the contents of the object—remember, without logging in!

Figure 10-6. *Accessing localStorage contents*

With the right tools and techniques, someone could easily gain access to data stored in local storage. When you really need to use local storage, keep that stored data to a minimum and never locally store unencrypted sensitive data. You might also consider using sessionStorage instead of localStorage. Of course, that is more secure because the data is deleted when the browser session is closed. Yet that might defeat the whole purpose of using it in the first place.

It is the task of the database administrator to encrypt sensitive data on the server (and backups, as well), but that is way beyond the scope of this book.

Using the APEX Security Features

Just like any desktop application, you can make your Oracle Application Express application as secure or as insecure as you want. If you'd like to learn a lot more about securing your application, I suggest you read *Expert Oracle Application Express Security* (Apress, 2013) by Scott Spendolini. But we will look at the available security features at a high level because, although these features are not specific to mobile applications, they are nevertheless important.

When components of your application shouldn't be accessible to all users, you should use authorization schemes to prevent unauthorized access. You can define these schemes on every SQL and PL/SQL that you can think of (the day of the week, for example) and apply them on every component in your application.

Another major security feature is Session State Protection. When you configure this feature, you see a screen like the one shown in Figure 10-7.

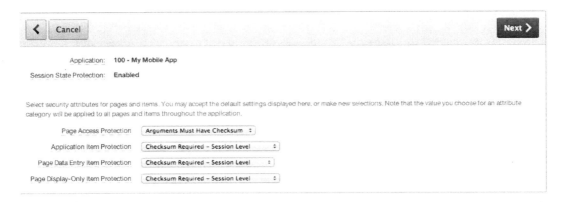

Figure 10-7. *Set Session State Protection*

In Session State Protection, you can set different levels of security for components:

- Page Access Protection can have one of four values.

    - *Unrestricted*: No restrictions are applied; you can request pages with parameters and requests.

    - *Arguments Must Have Checksum*: You can only request a page with parameters or requests when you also provide a checksum. This prevents users from fiddling around with the page numbers or parameters to get unauthorized access.

    - *No Arguments Allowed*: The URL can't be used to assign values to variables; this should all be done in session state.

    - *No URL Access*: This option prevents changes to a URL by an end user, as well as all redirects in your application. Using branches, you can only move from one page to another.

- Application Item Protection can have one of five values.

    - *Unrestricted*: No protection.

    - *Checksum Required*: There are three options here. An item value can be set in a URL, but a checksum is required. This checksum can be specific to the application, user, or session. When you have to construct your own URLs, you should use the apex_util.prepare_url function to construct it, including the checksum. A URL with an Application-level checksum can be used as a public bookmark; a URL with a User-level checksum can be used as a private bookmark; a URL with a Session-level checksum is only valid during the duration of a specific session.

    - *Restricted–May not be set from browser*: You can't submit any changes to this item. It can only be changed using internal processing.

- Page Data Entry Item Protection can have one of four values.

    - *Unrestricted*

    - The same three *Checksum Required* options as Application Item Protection.

▪ **Note** There is no "Restricted" setting for Page Data Entry Item Protection because that would completely block changes to Data Entry Items, and that makes no sense as they are meant for data entry.

- Page Display–Only Item Protection has the same options as Application Item Protection.

You can set all the options as securely as possible, but that will also have an impact on the way you set values, use JavaScript, or move from page to page.

Splitting Applications

In earlier chapters, you learned that you can create two user interfaces within the same application. When you log in, APEX recognizes your device and redirects you to either the mobile version or the desktop version of the login page. Although this is a very nice feature, you have to ask yourself whether the mobile version of your application should have the same level of access and security as your desktop application. As we discussed earlier, mobile applications do imply a higher security risk!

Your mobile application doesn't usually have the same functionality as the desktop version. In most cases, the mobile application is limited in functionality, and therefore has access to less data and can do less with the same data. For instance, many administrative functions do not have a mobile user interface. A lot of data on the mobile application is available on a read-only basis or is not available at all. So a mobile application is smaller and has less functionality, fewer pages, and less data.

A good rule in database management and security is to grant only the rights to any schema that it needs. So the parsing schema used for a mobile application might need a lot fewer grants than its desktop equivalent. With that in mind, it makes sense to create a special mobile schema and use that as the parsing schema for a separate mobile application (see Figure 10-8).

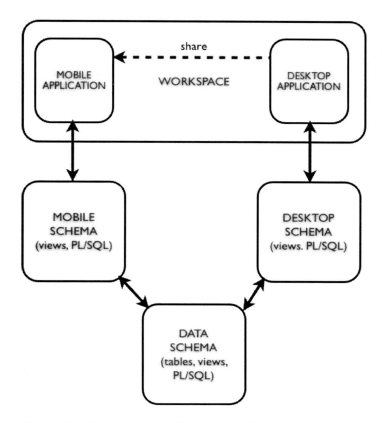

Figure 10-8. *Schema and application dependencies*

Let's walk through the schema in Figure 10-8 from bottom to top. Way at the bottom, you see the *data schema*. This schema owns all the tables (and thus the data) of a certain functional area, like HR. It also holds all the PL/SQL in triggers, procedures, functions, and packages that are necessary for all the processing and business rules.

One level up, there are two separate schemas defined: a "mobile schema" and a "desktop schema". Neither holds any data—unless it is specific to that user interface. They might contain some PL/SQL that is specific to the user interface. The most important thing is that they'll only have grants on the data schema objects that are necessary for running that specific application. So whereas the desktop schema may have rights to select, update, delete, and insert data on the employees table, the mobile schema may need only the rights to select and update certain columns on the employees table. Both the mobile schema and the desktop schema contain mostly read-only views on the data schema tables.

At the upper level, both applications are pictured. In order to share definitions of shareable components, it is wise to keep both applications—the mobile and the desktop—within the same workspace. But each application gets its own parsing scheme!

So what are the advantages of splitting the application into two separate versions? The most important reason is security, of course. If someone, in one way or another, gets access to the mobile schema, the risk of doing any harm is reduced. When the mobile schema has a reduced set of rights, you can protect your company from major data loss!

Another security issue, the session idle time and the session length, can be set differently for mobile and desktop applications, without the need for additional device-checking and PL/SQL calls.

And finally, splitting up the application might ease the maintenance. You can easily solve an issue in the mobile application and roll that forward to test acceptance and production without interfering with the desktop application.

Wrap Up

This chapter discussed the crucial importance of securing your mobile application. We covered the features that APEX offers to make our mobile applications more secure. And apart from these APEX features, you can also opt for an architectural protection by splitting the application into different schemas.

Next Steps

You're now at the end of this book and it's time to use the knowledge you've gained in real life. As always, the best way to get acquainted with a new technology is simply by using it. So find yourself a small part of an existing application that might benefit from "mobilizing." Create your list views, forms, charts, and other page types. But don't start too big. It's better to have a small, well-functioning mobile application than one that does everything—but not very well.

You will certainly enjoy it. Building mobile applications is fun and cool!

Index

M

CPSIA information can be obtained at www.ICGtesting.com
Printed in the USA
LVOW090357170413

329519LV00005B/77/P